THE UNTOLD

SCRATCH AT THE SURFACE AND YOU'LL FIND MOST FAMILIES HAVE A SECRET OR TWO

BARRIE TANKEL

UNTOLD STORIES - NOW TOLD

Cover design by Isabel Holtz

ISBN: 9798842352760

This book is written in memory of my mother, Rachel Tankel, who passed away on 25 August 2018, just six days short of her 100th birthday. I loved the magical moment she whispered, "I'm dying to read your book" with her great sense of humour.

It is dedicated to the memory of Chaim Goluchowski and Wally Wolman, with sincere thanks to them for telling their stories.

And in memory of my beautiful sister, Margaret Hoffmann, who passed away on 1 June 2022.

Lastly, I write this for my daughter Lara,
my son Joel and
my grandchildren – Charlie, Isabel,
Isaac and Levi.

When grandparents boarded ships and fled

with little thought of chapter 1

in some descendant's book,

Their family lives became a mystery.

So,

I must rely

upon memories descendants recalled

and, of course,

significant help from others.

CONTENTS

'There is no greater agony than bearing

an untold story inside you' [1]

—Maya Angelou

AUTHOR'S PREFACE

This book is a gift...

First, to my family, and to the memory of Chaim Goluchowski and Wally Wolman, whose stories were fundamental to its telling.

The biography of Chaim Goluchowski, a Holocaust survivor from 1915–1945, and the diaries of Wally Wolman, Royal Air Force (RAF) pilot in the Second World War, form a major contribution to the writing of *THE UNTOLD*. Their histories would have disappeared without trace, lost for our descendants if not recorded. Their stories matter, and so must be told.

Chaim Goluchowski, my mother's first cousin, had written a secret memoir of his experiences during the Holocaust.

Flight Sergeant Morris Lewis Wolman, my mother's brother, was killed when his plane struck a hill in 1943. His journey through the war is brought alive through his personal diaries.

Other family stories are based on conversations, memories and recently discovered documents.

These voices flowed through private writings that remained secret. Had they not been transcribed in this book, they would have remained forever untold – hence the title of this book.

A brief introduction at the start of each chapter describes the story being told.

My reasons for writing

The envelope dropped through my letterbox in August 2009 – the writer purported to be my grandfather's granddaughter. I had just learned of my secret aunt, Yvonne.

Ken Golish, a stranger, posted his message on Facebook in January 2011 – he suggested that our grandmothers were sisters; we met that September when I learned of his father's memoir.

Wally's diaries were only discovered in my mother's apartment after she died in 2018.

And then, in January 2021, I discovered an older sister, Annette.

These events have combined to become a treasure chest of jewels that deserve to be recorded for my family, which I as a writer now share with you.

> Note: The references for the footnotes are listed at the back of the book.

PROLOGUE

Our mother had died six days short of a century, and despite the delay in funeral arrangements caused by the August Bank Holiday, she still couldn't make the full 100 years before she was buried.

I recollect standing outside the Prayer Hall at Bushey Cemetery when l felt this sudden urge to complete my book. As I stood there, a religious man with a short grey beard, dressed in a black suit, a black hat perched neatly on his head, appeared and beckoned us inside the hall, guiding us to sit on three low stools.

He tore my shirt just above my heart – a religious custom that visually expresses how a heart is torn in sorrow and grief in the face of death.

After the appropriate blessing, Rabbi Lawrence repeated the custom with my two sisters.

My mother's coffin stood proudly in the centre of the room, draped with a long black cloth that hung majestically across its four corners, as friends and family joined us inside the hall. The men gathered to the left of the coffin and women to the right, in accordance with Jewish tradition.

Seeing her in a state of death, I was aware her physical death was so much more than just her spirit leaving her body. It was a dissipation of her love, her speech, her unique dialect and facial expressions, as well as her particular perfumed smell.

Prompted by the rabbi, I read the 'Mourner's Kaddish', a special prayer for the dead that showed my ultimate sign of love and respect.

יִתְגַּדַּל וְיִתְקַדַּשׁ שְׁמֵהּ ר

"Yisga-dahl, v'yis-ka-daash sh'may rah-baw," the Rabbi intoned, "Amen!" The congregation responded in harmony: "Amen."

Uncontrollable tears seeped from my eyes, washing down the side of my cheeks. My throat cracked up with emotion, realising the same heartfelt prayer and probably the tears would be repeated every week for the next 11 months, throughout the entire mourning period.

As I stood with my prayer book in hand, I pondered what my children really knew of our family and our history. Were they too busy growing up to be interested in anything about their ancestors? While I am certainly aware our story does not hold the magic of Churchill or Shakespeare, and that, no doubt, it is similar to the tales other Jewish families tell, it's an important part of our history, and maybe it will answer questions sometime in the future when a younger Barrie, generations down the line, asks, "Mummy, who was I named after?"

Many of my friends have shared their regrets of not having had conversations with their grandparents about their lives in Poland. They said: "We never asked our grandparents about life in Poland, and why they left – or at the very least, asked for their favourite cheesecake recipe or ingredients for those wonderful East European dishes they served at our shared Friday-night dinners."

The drivers that finally pushed me to complete my work were three monumental events: my mother's passing; the discovery of the hidden diaries and letters of my Uncle Wally, recorded during military service in the Royal Air Force; and, of equal importance, the secret memoir of Chaim Goluchowski, my mother's first cousin, whom she never met in person, and which revealed his terribly traumatic suffering in the Nazi occupation of Poland and his eventual escape to freedom.

My mother's passing made me realise the time had come to research and scribe our family history before it, and I, finally evaporate.

So, with papers scattered across my desk, I will now continue my journey of discovery, and tell the stories of our family that, until now, have remained untold.

FAMILY TREES

Tankel Family Tree

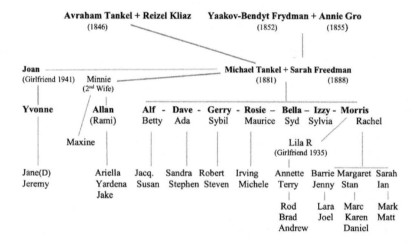

Avraham Tankel + Reizel Kliaz
(1846)

Yaakov-Bendyt Frydman + Annie Gro
(1852)   (1855)

Joan
(Girlfriend 1941)

Minnie
(2nd Wife)

Michael Tankel + Sarah Freedman
(1881)   (1888)

Yvonne

Allan
(Rami)

Alf - Dave - Gerry - Rosie – Bella – Izzy - Morris
Betty Ada Sybil Maurice Syd Sylvia Rachel

Maxine

Lila R
(Girlfriend 1935)

Jane(D)
Jeremy

Ariella
Yardena
Jake

Jacq.
Susan

Sandra
Stephen

Robert
Steven

Irving
Michele

Annette
Terry

Barrie
Jenny

Margaret
Stan

Sarah
Ian

Rod
Brad
Andrew

Lara
Joel

Marc
Karen
Daniel

Mark
Matt

Wolman Family Tree

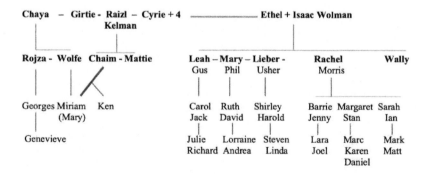

Chaya – Girtie - Raizl – Cyrie + 4 ——————— Ethel + Isaac Wolman
Kelman

Rojza - Wolfe Chaim - Mattie

Leah – Mary – Lieber -
Gus   Phil   Usher

Rachel
Morris

Wally

Georges Miriam Ken
(Mary)

Carol Ruth   Shirley
Jack   David Harold

Barrie Margaret Sarah
Jenny Stan   Ian

Genevieve

Julie   Lorraine Steven
Richard Andrea   Linda

Lara   Marc   Mark
Joel   Karen   Matt
       Daniel

5

Chapter 1

FAMILY SECRETS: 1

Introduction

His first marriage was a well-kept secret until it wasn't.

My father's divorce papers, tucked away on the top shelf of a cupboard in his office were found as I, aged 20, rummaged for the sake of it. Shocked at what I found, and probably naive to think this could never happen in my family, I was afraid of his reaction if I spoke up, and so it remained 'our' secret. But I did wonder if he had other children.

For my entire life I was the eldest child, until in one nanosecond I discovered I wasn't. Annette is my new older sister.

Wednesday, 27 January 2021

The discovery of my new half-sister Annette this evening has detonated my emotions. I'm traumatised. A previously unknown sibling was disclosed through a DNA match.

Joel's wife Hillary chose to use the Ancestry.com DNA testing service as a gift to 'unlock his family story' – a bit of fun intended to relieve the monotony of Covid-19 in December 2020.

Meanwhile, 10,000 miles away from Joel's Bronx home, my 83-year-old half-sister Annette Irvine lives with her husband Terry in the small coastal town of Worrowing Heights, near Jervis Bay, New South Wales, Australia. Raised by her mother, Lila Rodda, and stepfather, Joseph Manly, she grew up not knowing her birth father's identity and had not asked her mother the obvious question, so his name remained a blank space on her birth certificate.

In January 2021, as her ladies' genealogy group decided to explore their chromosomes on Ancestry DNA, they spat into saliva-collection tubes and waited nervously as the laboratory analysed and matched them against millions of others seeking a fit. The test came with a health warning that read: *Some clients may find the test results disturbing.*

Joel is my son

Joel and Annette had received identical Ancestry DNA messages on the 15 January, advising of a possible match – to me, the figure of 93% is far more probable than 'possible'. Annette had learnt she was 50% European Jewish and the rest was Irish. The Jewish DNA came from her father.

Intrigued, Joel popped the message below to her via Ancestry DNA.

My DNA match has shown you as a first cousin. I wonder how this is.

Annette then replied with the following message:

Good morning, Joel. What a surprise to have your message. I only received my DNA results yesterday. I am not sure of the connection either... Is it ok to look at your family tree? Annette Irvine.

Joel asked another question: *What is your father's name?*

To which she replied:
That I guess is the question!
I have all the information on my mother's but father's side is a blank! Mother died back in 1968 so I am unable to find out... So, you are the first.

I must emphasise that I just want to find my possible heritage, for myself, certainly not to open a Pandora's Box for anyone else, or any other family...Annette

The dictionary definition of a Pandora's box is "A present that seems valuable but that in reality is a curse".

Joel was euphoric but, being conscious of the implications, immediately told Lara, his sister. Both were equally concerned about the emotional impact on their family.

Let's have a family Zoom catch-up tomorrow xxx. Joel

Joel had contacted me, serendipitously on Australia Day, Tuesday, 26 January 2021.

Lara's response subtly included an exclamation mark: *Lovely idea! x*

I was delighted, for these family-type chats are infrequent.

At 7:00pm the next day (London time, that's 2:00pm in New York where my children live), the three of us met over Zoom for a chat.

"Dad, I got the results of my DNA test."

I knew of the test, BUT. So often there's a BUT.

"Well," he said, "Ancestry notified me of a 93% DNA relationship with this woman Annette Irvine. She lives in Australia."

The existence of another potential relative in Australia was hardly a surprise, I thought, since Rami, my father's half-brother, had migrated to Melbourne in the 1970s, so she must be his relative.

Then he replied: "No, Dad, it's not them. It's someone different. I asked why she thought we have a 93% connection. It turns out she's..."

I sensed the slight pause in his voice before he continued: "...she's your father's daughter, your sister... well, half-sister. Our aunt."

The saga had begun two weeks earlier, with Joel's email to Annette, appropriately headed 'Revelation'. By now, Annette had established that Morris Tankel, my father, was also her father, and had written the below to say so:

At this point I can understand that this might come as a surprise/shock to you and the Tankel family, as it was to me! I can only hope that Maurice's return to England brought happiness and fulfilment to all the family there.

Annette was delighted she'd discovered her roots and acknowledged that if we were in any way upset, we might not wish to continue, but the reverse was true...

Annette added:

...if you are willing to share information, my email address is...

Did our mother know of Annette? That was another burning question.

I decided that it was unlikely, as had she known something, she would surely have said so during the 48 years following our father's death.

There is, however, a slight doubt that revolves around a comment Rosie, my father's sister, made, which her daughter Michele told me: "You don't know the half of it."

We had previously put that comment down to our grandfather's misspent life, but now, who knows? All the protagonists are gone, so there's no-one left to ask.

Whatever the truth might be, I am horrified that my father procreated then deserted a baby girl, his daughter.

It was now time to tell my two sisters – or rather, my two other sisters, Margaret and Sarah – so at 7:20pm I pressed the Facetime button to contact my youngest sister Sarah first:

She replied: "Can I call you back?"

But I insisted, "Absolutely not, we must speak right now!"

Margaret, the middle child (as she had been before Joel's call), responded immediately from her Johannesburg kitchen, and now, with the three of us face to face, she asked the obvious question: "What's up?"

I hesitated. How do I break the news? But the words just blurted out: "I'm no longer the eldest!"

Quizzical looks were followed by shock and the sheer disbelief in what I had said. Questions fluttered through my mind; few were sensible or answerable in that moment. Sarah, the youngest and most laid-back, was equally affected.

Then her husband Ian piped up: "Not another one?"

(He was referring to Mike, who'd also fathered a daughter, Yvonne, while married to our grandmother, Sarah.)

Margaret's scream of "What!?!?" brought her husband Stan running to join the Zoom call.

Stan then blurted out: "What's happened now?"

Thursday, 28 January 2021

My mind kept buzzing throughout the night, disturbing my sleep as I resurrected memories of an unhappy childhood. Whenever thoughts of my father come to mind, I feel contempt, and this news just intensified my negative feelings.

My father Morris was never the father he should have been, never demonstrative with his family, showing no love and certainly no affection. Maybe he never connected emotionally with Annette, either?

The angry shouting he always displayed after a poor day in the office is the one memory that lingers. Why did he have children? Were we simply a byproduct of our parents' physical relationship, only to become an encumbrance?

"I paid for schooling, meals and clothes," is what I can visualise him saying in response to my questions, the words reverberating loudly in an aggressive voice. But that's surely not the kind of love a child needs or wants to remember.

I think back to the family holidays I never had. My parents spent annual vacations in Nice at Christmas and took summer trips on cruise ships, but I was excluded. Why was I left at home when they took vacations, except of course for the one weekend at Pontins, because Fred Pontin was his friend? One two-day vacation in 17 years does not really count, in my perception.

The positive outcome is that it guided me to share great family vacations with my children and grandchildren. But was my father's dearth of attention the faultline in my own lack of self-confidence?

Questions burdened me throughout the day. Did he know of Annette? Did he actually leave Australia to avoid his responsibilities towards her? What were his emotions during this episode? Did he feel guilty? Or, like my grandfather after him, was it simply all a joke? How did this experience mould his behaviour as a father towards us? Was the existence of Lila or Annette the reason his emotions were detached from us?

Friday, 29 January 2021

It is less than two days since our new sister was revealed, but the news has still not been fully digested. Perhaps I will feel more comfortable once we meet on Zoom.

So far, our recent revelation has only been shared with close Brighton buddies, friends from childhood, as discussions with my siblings continue and we try to reconcile the situation in our minds – so many questions, but no answers.

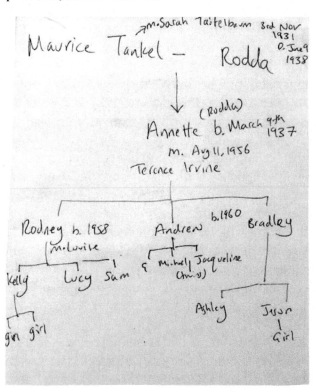

Emails packed with ancestry data flowed between Annette and my family, enabling my daughter Lara to produce an 'Irvine' family tree.

My two children have shown great compassion towards us in this difficult situation, which is so endearing.

Annette's selection of photographs, particularly when she was a child, indicate a strong likeness to the Tankels' physiognomies. She and Margaret actually look like sisters (haha!), and there's a strong resemblance between Lila and my mother; that's not surprising, as people are often attracted to similar-looking partners.

My 30-year-old father may have been a gambler who miscalculated the odds when he and Lila screwed around in the storeroom, having little regard to the repercussions if Lila fell pregnant. But she did.

I do not criticise the affair, for perhaps he had an unhappy marriage, but I am hugely upset that he deserted his child and never retained any contact. He missed the life that followed, the three grandsons born before he died in 1970, all of whom could have been a part of his life had some communication been maintained after he returned to London.

Saturday, 30 January 2021

I have now been told similar tales from others of tracing lost relatives.

For example, a daughter attended her father's funeral, only to discover he had created another family elsewhere, which was somewhat reminiscent of the BBC drama *Mrs Wilson*.

I asked myself, "Who is Annette?' Did he ever see her? Did he support her? How has our father's personality manifested itself in her? How does she 'think' compared to us? What prompted him to leave Australia straight after the divorce? Was he worried about his parents' anger if they discovered the truth about Annette?"

Sunday, 31 January 2021

It's 8:00am. In two hours precisely, we will meet on Zoom. Questions flow through my mind, mostly repeat questions.

What thoughts did he have during his 63-year-short life? Why did he never disclose the truth towards the end of his life, when he was aware that he was terminally ill? Was he still too ashamed?

I'm feeling very nervous ahead of the call.

Family Zoom

The second hand of my watch slowly ticked towards 10.00am in London – that's noon in Johannesburg and 9:00pm in Worrowing Heights, New South Wales, roughly a two-hour drive from the southern tip of Sydney.

I realise I must not forget to record the conversation for my children.

Later, following the call

We've now spoken. Annette, her husband Terry and son Andrew joined the call with Margaret and Sarah. In an odd synchronicity, perhaps, all three girls all wore red blouses.

I am elated. They are delightful, and we felt a strong connection with Annette and Andrew.

What does it mean?

This discovery means something different to each of us.

Margaret, Sarah and I were brought up together, knowing our parents, developing family relationships as we grew. We had a loving mother and an extremely difficult father. Now, suddenly, we have found a new sister.

I recall the day I collected my mother from the hospital after Sarah was born, and the ride home in a taxi. I had no relationship with Sarah then, for she was but a few days old and I was 16, but from that day on, we became emotionally tied.

Annette cannot feel the same connection that we enjoy. She has spent the past 83 years not knowing her father and fantasising about who he might be, with no idea of her siblings. This is an equally new experience for her.

Now that she knows her father's name, she has met her siblings and discovered her Jewish heritage. She goes to church and sings in a choir, whereas we certainly do not have melodic voices! And her son Andrew is blessed with a great deal of hair, which definitely does not derive from a Tankel gene.

The affair

Apparently, the shoe company Clyde Bootery had appointed Morris as the manager of its most important city store branch in Melbourne.

Annette's mother, Lila Rodda, known as Miss Rodda, worked in the store, and the affair started in 1935. Evidently, they soon became 'soul mates'.

Lila Rodda

Annette was told by her mother that the 'owner' of the store chased her around the boardroom table, but after she saw Morris's photograph, she reflected: "I wonder who was chasing whom and who was caught!!! What a handsome man."

The affair lasted until the summer of 1936 and ended with Lila's pregnancy. I can visualise their brief conversation as: "Morris, I've something to tell you. I've missed my period. I might be pregnant."

Annette's birth in a private clinic, in March 1937, was paid for by Morris..

Monday, 1 February 2021

Annette's son Rod sent me a link to my father's divorce papers.

We already knew Morris had gone to Melbourne in late 1928, that he got married to Sarah Taitelbaum in 1931 and divorced in 1938, but the rest was an unpleasant revelation.

Sarah's divorce affidavit is pretty damning about Morris, Lila and the affair, but it remains a one-sided story as we don't have his response.

Despite disliking my father, I cannot reconcile Sarah's descriptions with my own memories, particularly about him getting drunk and having a gambling addiction. He certainly enjoyed alcohol, whisky or gin and tonics every day, but I don't recall him ever being drunk, nor do I believe he had a gambling addiction, despite the fact he was working in a gambling business.

I recognised him as very calculated, and that the commission he earned was more than sufficient for my parents to enjoy a good standard of life, including frequent travel.

In 1938, there was no DNA, no mobile phone or Facetime, and travel between these two distant continents was prohibitive, so at that time there was not even a remote chance this piece of his life would be discovered. DNA testing only became available in 1987, 17 years after he died. I wonder how might he have reacted if a 20-something-year-old Annette had travelled to England in the 1960s in search of her father?

Annette's story

Lila's mother Emma cared for Annette while Lila worked until she married Joseph Manley in 1939. Annette's sister Sandra was born in 1940 and Joseph's sister Millicent helped with the children, often pretending that Annette was her own daughter.

In 1960, Annette discovered that her father's name was not registered on the birth certificate, but it still never occurred to her to ask Lila for his name. The opportunity to learn the truth disappeared after her mother died suddenly in 1968.

Terry and Annette on their wedding day

Annette and Terry were married in 1956. Terry owned a pharmacy and other businesses in Darwin for over 33 years; he then moved around Australia to Canberra, where Annette worked for Aboriginal Hostels in Alice Springs, Adelaide and in Sydney, before they retired together to Worrowing Heights in March 2020.

Their three sons, Rod and the twins Andrew and Brad, were born over the next four years. All were my father's grandchildren, suggesting the gene for twins had passed from our maternal grandmother Sarah, who had lost two sets of twins at birth. My sister Sarah has twin sons, and my cousin Steven fathered twins. Andrew is also the father of twins, so it is evident the twin gene is very strong in our family.

My father's gene for ballroom dancing was passed on to Andrew and Brad, both of whom were teenage dance champions. According to this, it seems there were several powerful genetic codes in my paternal family!

Reflections on Chapter 12

The discovery of my 'new' sister prompted me to reflect on a paragraph I had written some two years earlier (*see page* 263) as a backdrop to this incident:

> *...a quick Google search identified Ariella as a master tailor, living in Melbourne, Australia.*

This made me wonder: Was she an unknown offspring of my father (another surprise?), since he'd lived in Australia for 10 years from 1928?

As Chaucer wrote, *A man may say full sooth [the truth] in game and play,* which is usually interpreted as "many a true word is spoken in jest".

It turns out that the above line, at the time written in jest, is partially factual, since there was indeed an unknown offspring of my father. It has made me wonder how different our lives might have been with the influence of an older sister.

Sheep story

Long-term residents living close to the Murrumbidgee River in New South Wales know that heavy rains can breach the flood plains, so Andrew and Bev built their new home in 1998 on stilts, just in case.

The investment paid off, for in 2012 the heavens opened, the land flooded and their home remained dry as a bone; but still the 300 sheep they owned had to be saved.

This tale, comparable only to the story of Noah in the book of Genesis, was carved out as sheep – heaved into a dingy – were coaxed up carpet-covered stairs to the veranda by Bev gently whispering, "Come on, up you go." The carpet had caringly been laid so sheep couldn't see through the gaps in the steps and get spooked.

The sheep on the veranda (Andrew Irvine: User Gen)

The animals were banned from entering the house and separated from the four rams, obviously, but they enjoyed magnificent views from the veranda until the water subsided, and then back to the fields they went.

Poor Andrew, our nephew, was left to hose down the veranda until it was spotlessly clean.

Postscript

My daughter Lara sent several of my mother's recipes to Annette – 'Rachel's chicken soup' was the first, to be followed by others, all apparently loved by Annette's family.

Annette, welcome to your Jewish roots.

Chapter 2

WHY POLAND?

Introduction

As I began working on this project and read Chaim's memoir of the Holocaust, it made me realise there were many unanswered questions I still had to address in order to put my family's journey in context. For example: Why did the Jews leave Israel and make their homes in Eastern Europe? And why in Poland, particularly?

Discovering the Holocaust

I remember the day I first learned about the Holocaust.

I was age 14 and on my way home from school when I saw this image on a book cover that would haunt me for years. It was a black-and-white photograph of living skeletons in loose, striped clothes peering through a barbed-wire fence. I turned the page and began to learn about the Holocaust.

My parents never mentioned the atrocities members of our family experienced, but then nothing important or newsworthy was ever discussed with us children, so I remained ignorant of the facts. The horrors of the event, being so close to the end of the war and still raw in their minds, may well have been the reason.

I knew our grandparents originally came from Russia, but as a youngster it just never occurred to me to ask why they lived there or why they left, and since I knew nought about the Holocaust, there was little reason to connect the dots between Poland and this abominable persecution of our ancestors.

The word 'holocaust' is derived from the Greek word *holokauston*, a translation of the Hebrew word *olah*, meaning a burnt sacrifice offered wholly to God. This word was chosen from among various others also in circulation because in the Nazi 'final solution' killing programme, the bodies of the victims were consumed whole in crematoria or in open fires.

The 'final solution' of the Holocaust was intended to achieve the genocide of an entire race, as well as other groups not tolerated by the Nazis. Under Adolf Hitler's direction as leader of the Nazi Party, the Holocaust was a planned, systematic extermination and ethnic cleansing of six million European Jews, Roma (Romani-speaking peoples originally from South Asia and widely dispersed across Europe and the Americas), homosexuals and Jehovah Witnesses.

Hitler was the dictator of Germany from 1933 to 1945. This fanatical anti-Semite rose to power as leader of the Nazi Party to become one of the most reviled figures in history as he orchestrated both the Second World War and the Holocaust.

The knowledge that three million of these Jews were murdered in Poland begged the question: Why did so many Jews live there, having originally inhabited the warm Mediterranean climate of the land of Israel?

The answer began in around 66 CE, as explained below.

Migration

Around 45 BCE, Julius Caesar accepted Judaism as a legal religion and allowed Jews to live peacefully. That all changed in 66 CE when the Judeans' rebellion against tax laws led to the first of the Jewish-Roman wars. After they were crushed, the Second Temple was destroyed, and large numbers of Jews were enslaved or murdered.

In 135 CE, Emperor Hadrian defeated the Jewish revolt led by Bar Kokhba. As a result, 600,000 Jews were killed and the land was renamed Syria Palaestina to sever the ties of Jewish peoples from Israel, their historic homeland.

Jewish immigration to Germany began around 320 CE, but during the Crusades, a mass slaughter caused the Jews to flee to Poland.

Following this, various pogroms against Jews continued globally with limited exceptions, notably in India, until 1343, when King Casimir III invited them to live in Poland, and the country became known as a 'paradise for the Jews'. Eventually, 75% of the world's Jewish population lived there.

Further support came when Jews were expelled from Spain in 1492: the Ottoman leader, Sultan Bayezid II, sent ships to fetch them and take them to a safe haven in Turkey.

Fiddler on the Roof

Jewish life around 1905 in Poland is famously depicted in the musical *Fiddler on the Roof*, a story set within the Pale of Settlement – the region of Imperial Russia that became home to my own and many other Jewish families. So, if you are of Jewish heritage, look deep inside the narrative for your ancestors to understand their journeys and why they came to have a Russian or Polish – or other East-European – background.

Catalyst for Migration

The assassination of Czar Alexander II in 1881 triggered hundreds of anti-Jewish events that caused the death of thousands of Jews, and became the catalyst for two million to emigrate over the next 35 years. Many travelled away from Europe, seeking safety in countries such as America, South Africa and the United Kingdom. The men usually travelled first to find the jobs and make a place to call home, then their wives and children followed.

At the outbreak of the Second World War, 10% of all Poles were Jewish – it was home to Europe's largest Jewish population, with a total of 3.5 million Jews. During the Holocaust, three million were murdered, and the remainder mostly left the country. In recent times, the population of Jews still in the country has grown to an estimated 30,000.

Map of the Russian Empire in 1914

(Source: https://nzhistory.govt.nz/media/photo/map-russian-empire1914)

Chapter 3

SECOND WORLD WAR

Introduction

On 3 September 1939, the howling noise of air-raid sirens warned of impending air attacks. With gas masks in hand, Londoners fled to newly opened shelters, and the capital braced itself for German bombers. But this was a false alarm, caused by Allied aircraft being mistakenly identified as the enemy.

Those Londoners who had dismissed the threat of war, expecting it to be averted at the last moment, were stunned into disbelief when Neville Chamberlain's announcement floated across the airwaves. Chamberlain had become Britain's prime minister in 1937.

This so-called 'phoney war', (because little happened in the first eight months) came to an end abruptly as Germany invaded Norway in April 1940.

The 'Evacuate forthwith' order was issued in late August to implement the UK government's plan to move millions of vulnerable people out of London to avoid loss of life akin to that seen as a result of the devastating air attacks on Barcelona and Guernica in Spain and in Shanghai, China.

Why declare war? But first, there was Sudetenland

Originally known as Moravia, the little-known Eastern European country became a part of Austria in the 18th century, and was renamed the 'Province of Sudetenland' after the First World War, when she was annexed to the newly created Czechoslovak Republic. Then, frontiers and borders were redrawn – a situation reluctantly accepted by Sudetenland's largely German population, which became a powerful political force during the 1930s.

Hitler's demand to annex Sudetenland to Germany was rejected, so he threatened to invade unless the Czech government ceded Sudetenland by 2:00pm on 28 September 1938.

Prime Minister Chamberlain told the British nation: "This is a quarrel in a faraway country between people of whom we know nothing.

"Hitler's attitude is unreasonable, and we will not abandon efforts for peace . . .

"Volunteers are still wanted for Air Raid precautions, Fire Brigade Police Services and for Territorial Units, all ready to play their part in defence of this country."

Desperate to avoid a war so soon after the Great War (the First World War, from July 1914 to November 1918), Chamberlain faced a stark choice between war and appeasement until Hitler announced this was his final territorial claim in Europe.

The commitment persuaded Chamberlain and then-French Prime Minister Daladier to agree to Hitler's demands. The 'Munich Agreement' was signed on Hitler's terms, allowing Nazi Germany to annex Sudetenland and (supposedly) prevent war.

Their joint statement read:

We, the German Führer and Chancellor and the British Prime Minister, have had a further meeting today and are agreed in recognising that the question of Anglo-German relations is of the first importance for the two countries and for Europe. We regard the agreement signed last night and the Anglo-German Naval

*Agreement as symbolic of the desire of our two peoples never to go
to war with one another again.*

Congratulated by King George VI, Chamberlain waved the
historic piece of paper from the Royal Balcony with cheering,
jubilant crowds celebrating the expected peace.[2]

Chamberlain further announced: "This settlement achieved is in
my view only the prelude to a larger settlement in which all of
Europe may find peace."

The celebrations were short-lived, however. One year later,
Hitler derided the Treaty as a "scrap of paper" and despatched 1.5
million troops to Poland on 1 September 1939; air attacks were
simultaneously launched in Warsaw, marking the beginning of the
Second World War.

Declaration of War, 1939

Forced to declare war on Germany in order to honour Britain's
guarantee to Poland, Chamberlain addressed the British public: "I
am speaking to you from the Cabinet Room at 10 Downing Street.
"This morning, the British Ambassador in Berlin handed the
German Government a final note stating that unless we heard from
them by 11 o'clock that they were prepared at once to withdraw
their troops from Poland, a state of war will exist between us.

"I have to tell you now that no such undertaking has been
received, and consequently this country is at war with Germany."

My grandparents were horrified. Their Polish family was now
exposed to Nazi racial policies, and they faced the prospect of the
Germans bombing London.

Key events as the war unfolded

Hitler's peace offering the following month was truly spine-chilling,
for it included a 'condition' that he be permitted to solve his 'Jewish
problem'.

The proposal was rejected outright, and the British public soon
learned of German concentration camps and orders for Jews to wear
a 'Star of David' badge.

Dunkirk

Britain was close to defeat when the entire British Army Expeditionary Force was trapped along the Dunkirk beaches from 26 May to 4 June 1940. However, the successful evacuation of 338,000 troops, including 125,000 French troops, through 'Operation Dynamo' – which in part succeeded due to a surprise pause in hostilities by the Germans – was a great boost to British morale. [3]

Winston Churchill, who replaced Neville Chamberlain as UK prime minister in May 1940, addressed the House of Commons on 4 June 1940.

These are the words of this famous speech: "We shall go on to the end, we shall fight in France, we shall fight on the seas and oceans, we shall fight with growing confidence and growing strength in the air. We shall defend our Island, whatever the cost may be, we shall fight on the beaches, we shall fight on the landing grounds, we shall fight in the fields and in the streets, we shall fight in the hills; we shall never surrender."

And again, later that month: "Let us therefore brace ourselves to our duties, and so bear ourselves, that if the British Empire and Commonwealth last for a thousand years, men will still say: 'This was their finest hour'."

Aliens (Movement Restriction) Order, 1940

The threat of dangerous aliens and spies forced the British government to grant emergency powers to screen Germans, Austrians, escaped resistance fighters and survivors from ships sunk by enemy action.

Refugee Jews who escaped Nazi oppression registered as 'enemy aliens', and a special tribunal was set up to decide if they were genuine refugees or Nazi sympathisers/German spies attempting to infiltrate sensitive jobs – or even to carry out terrorist acts.[4] Those found guilty were either interned on the Isle of Man or executed.

In early June, Churchill explained to the House of Commons: "Parliament has given us the powers to put down fifth-column [a group of people in a given country who actively support a wartime enemy of that country by engaging in acts of espionage or sabotage in anticipation of war] activities with a strong hand, and we shall use those powers subject to the supervision and correction of the House, without the slightest hesitation until we are satisfied, and more than satisfied, that this malignancy in our midst has been effectively stamped out."

Immigrants were required to hold Certificates of Registration with the instruction: "You must produce this certificate if required to do so by any Police Officer, Immigration Officer or member of His Majesty's Forces acting in the course of his duty."

Certificates of Registration for our grandparents, Isaac and Hetta [Ethel] Walman [Wolman]

Our grandparents had lived in England for the previous 25 years, so they were not considered suspects.

B'nai B'rith Magazine described the situation in an article on 19 September 2016:

Fuelled by anti-Semitism, hysteria escalated until Winston Churchill issued an order to 'collar the lot', and arrest both the dangerous and the harmless.

Men were taken from homes and offices in police cars, while crowds gathered in the streets to jeer.

There was significant overcrowding at Hutchinson camp, located in the town of Douglas on the Isle of Man, where rations were augmented by locally supplied fish, dairy and produce. Jews became known as 'Yom Kippers' due to their fondness of the Manx catch of 'kippers'.

Interned faculty members of the Hutchinson Camp 'university' included world-renowned scholars who taught outdoor classes in language, law, math and science.

As early as July 1940, complaints from innocent inmates were supported by sympathisers in the UK who realised that these aliens shared their desire to defeat Hitler, and gradually they were offered the opportunity to enlist or work for the war effort.

The Battle of Britain, 1940

Hostilities against Britain commenced in July with German attacks on coastal targets, the English Channel docks in South Wales and ships in the English Channel, followed with attacks on airfields and communications centres. This led to the Battle of Britain and the Blitz.[5]

The Battle of Britain was the first battle in history to be fought exclusively in the air. The Germans believed that if the UK's Royal Air Force (RAF) could be destroyed, their planned invasion could proceed, but if the RAF survived, it would ensure Britain's safety from invasion. Germany needed control of the skies.

Despite facing 1,000 attacks a day, the superiority of the RAF overcame the German Luftwaffe, and by 31 October 1940, the Battle of Britain was won – although 15,000 civilians had died during the process.

Praising the RAF flyers, Churchill said: "Never in the field of human conflict was so much owed by so many to so few." His statement led them to be known ever after as 'the Few'.

The Blitz, 1940

The intense bombing campaign undertaken by Germany against the UK, known as 'The Blitz', began on the afternoon of 7 September when 350 German bombers dropped their 500lb bombs on London, causing devastating damage to buildings throughout the city and killing 430 people on the day now remembered as 'Black Saturday'. The Blitz continued on through to May 1941.

The word 'Blitz' was derived from the German term *Blitzkrieg*, meaning "a fast, intense military attack taking the enemy by surprise to achieve a quick victory".

I'm horrified to think how much our London families suffered through this carnage – something we never discussed at home.

Four months later, the Second Great Fire of London began on 29 December when the Luftwaffe bombed London with 100,000 bombs and 25,000 incendiary devices. Ferocious fires spread throughout the city, including the fire in St Paul's Cathedral dome.

Ballistic missiles

A taste of the German Reprisal V rockets arrived in mid-1944; the first was the V-1 flying bomb, which was followed three months later by the V-2 long-range ballistic missiles.

The V-1 bombs, also known 'doodlebugs' because of the distinct sound they made in flight, were launched towards London as a 'reprisal weapon' in response to the mass Allied bombing of German cities. A horror-struck London public heard a buzzing sound from their jet engines; the eerie hush that followed was the terrifying alarm warning them to seek shelter before detonation.[6]

Germany fired around 10,000 V-1s, killing over 6,000 civilians. By the time the last V-1 landed on Orpington in Kent in late March 1945, the war was nearly over.

The second reprisal weapon was the V-2, the 'Vengeance Weapon 2'. It was the first long-range guided ballistic missile to fly at supersonic speed, and the first to reach the edge of space. These 46-foot-long sticks of dynamite fell onto London buildings and exploded before the sound of missiles could be heard, creating massive pits in the ground.

The first warning of a V-2 rocket attack was its double-crack noise followed by the sound of a heavy body rushing through the air. Its psychological effect was considerable since there was no effective defence.

The Germans failed in their plan to build 2,000 rockets per month as fuel production was dependent on the potato harvest – the launch of one rocket required 30 tonnes of potatoes and food was very scarce.

The man responsible for these monsters was a young German rocket scientist by the name of Wernher von Braun. The Americans were so impressed with his rocket technology that they secreted him away to the USA to work on their space programme at NASA before the Russians could grab him.

End of the war

Hitler committed suicide on 30 April. The date of 8 May 1945 is recognised as the official day the Second World War in Europe came to an end, although several Nazi generals surrendered their armies on various dates from 2–7 May 1945.

News of Germany's surrender quickly reached the rest of the world and joyous crowds gathered to celebrate in the streets, clutching newspapers that declared Victory in Europe (known as 'V-E Day').

Chapter 4

CONNECTED THROUGH FACEBOOK

Introduction

In January 2011, Ken Golish, an amateur genealogist, found the link to his English relatives and posted a message on Facebook in the belief our grandmothers were sisters. His father, Chaim, was in fact my mother's first cousin. When we met, Ken told me of his father's harrowing memoir, which I relay in Chapter 5.

I am grateful to media magnate Mark Zuckerberg and genealogy geek John Sittner for creating Facebook and Ancestry.com for otherwise Ken Golish would not have found me. His Facebook message triggered an amazing journey.

Ken's Facebook message

Re: Wolman

Barrie: I believe your grandmother was Kirszenbaum, the sister of my father's mother Raizl. Their parents were Abraham Leizor.

*I am fairly certain about this, but you will have to look at my
family records, and particularly a letter my aunt, Mattie Blatt, wrote
to her aunt, who I believe was Ethel. I have the letter.*
It was returned to sender in 1946.

This immediately intrigued me, and I was totally hooked.

I knew that Wolman was my mother's maiden name, and that
Ethel Wolman (née Kirszenbaum) was my grandmother. Marfit
Lane was sufficiently similar to Marlpit Lane where she lived, but
London was wrong, for in 1946 Ethel's home was in Old Coulsdon,
Surrey, so the envelope landed back on Mattie's doorstep in Toronto
marked 'Insufficiently Addressed' and 'Return to Sender'.

A letter was the only way to communicate in 1946, but the
address needed to be accurate. Few people had telephones, and
international phone calls were prohibitively expensive.

Ethel died in 1962 and never connected with her nephew,
Chaim Goluchowski, Ken's father.

Chaim was an innocent 14-year-old when his sister Martha (aka
Mattie) left Poland in 1929 and emigrated to Toronto, Canada. By
1945, he was a Holocaust survivor. Every other family member was
murdered by the Nazis, and only Chaim, Mattie and their aunt Ethel
Wolman, my grandmother, remained alive. (Ethel had travelled to
England in 1914.)

The Jewish Agency helped Holocaust survivors to find missing family members and provided addresses to help them reconnect. Chaim wrote to Uncle Ayzik, his father's brother, in America, with a letter as below for Mattie asking that she write to their aunt Ethel in England.

Mattie's letter written in Yiddish

The English translation reads as follows

To my very dear auntie, uncle and children, from me Matti, your sister Raizl's daughter.

This is to let you know that we are all in good health and well. May we receive the same good news from all of you always.

Dear auntie, I am at present in Toronto with my husband and children. I received one letter from my brother [Chaim] in Germany. He is the only one that remains from six brothers and one sister; we both are the only ones left. He has sent me your address and asks me to tell him how you succeeded in finding him.

I've put announcements in the Jewish press looking for you, but I couldn't find you. I was very happy to get your address from my brother and to learn that someone from our family has remained.

Dear auntie, I have become old and grown grey hair from weeping so much from distress and anguish.

I haven't received any letter from my brother. If we get one it is only after it has reached my uncle, my father's brother.

I can tell you that this Uncle Ayzik has offered him to come to America, but he must first wait for his 'quota' opening.

Dear aunt, please, let me know how you all are in health and what is news. Please, tell me everything in your next letter, and then we will let you know more. I have cousins in London and I asked them to find you, but they didn't succeed in finding you.

This is all the news I have. Stay healthy and well from your always-to-be-remembered niece Mattie, her husband and her children Goluchowski, married name of Blatt.

Please answer directly. Good-bye
Mattie, your niece

The forgotten envelope gathered dust in some hidden corner with a pile of other papers over the next 65 years until, in January 2011, Ken found it among his aunt's documents.

Instinctively, he attempted to trace lost family members through the internet using the name 'Ethel Wolman', and eventually found her name linked to a family tree on Ancestry.com.

Ken's Aunt Mattie (centre) wrote to Ethel

Meeting Ken

Confident that Ethel Wolman was his grandmother's sister, Ken checked related names online, until the name 'Barrie Tankel' appeared on Facebook. There is only one Barrie Tankel in the world spelt with an 'ie', and so I received the message from a second cousin I had never known. Six decades after the letter was first posted, Ken finally made the connection.

My visit to Toronto for a wedding later in the year was an opportunity to meet Ken face to face, and since he lives in Windsor, Ontario, about 220 miles west of the city, he made a special trip.

We sat outside a cafe in a local fashionable square discussing family connections in warm September sunshine, where Ken told me of his shock at finding his father's secret memoir, which revealed details of his parents' horrendous experience.

The memoir was discovered in 1996 after his father died. Chaim's life is described from his birth in 1915 to the end of the Second World War. It includes his first recollections of growing up in a happy household. Chaim then told of his experiences of anti-

Semitism, the occupation by the Nazis and his internment in concentration camps.

It would be incorrect to assume his children were suddenly delighted to discover the truth, because there's no such thing as 'delight' in Holocaust families, there's only trauma.

Ken (left) and I in September 2011
The day that we first met in Toronto, Canada

I don't yet know Ken well enough to discuss the impact of his parents' experience on his own life, but studies suggest that Holocaust trauma inevitably impinges on relationships between parents and offspring, and can transmit to future generations.

I wonder if the memoir answered their question about the significance of the number 1498 that was tattooed on his arm – or had the numbers been removed?

Trauma is a central concept in the historiography of the Holocaust. In both the historiographical and the psychoanalytical research on the subject, the Holocaust is perceived not as a finite event that took place in the past, but as one that continues to exist and to affect the families of survivors and the Jewish people.

[An extract from 'Transgenerational Transmission of Holocaust Trauma and its Expressions in Literature' by Dr Bina Nir.][7]

Ken's forensic mind worked overtime. He wanted to be 100% certain that our two grandmothers, Ethel and Raizl, were sisters and not half-sisters with different mothers, so I took a DNA test with the same American lab he had used, Family Tree DNA. The results proved conclusively that our grandmothers were sisters.

So why is this memoir so relevant to us? Because Chaim Goluchowski was my mother's first cousin. She was now frail, in her late 90's and I doubt she had ever known of Chaim. Her memory was failing and it would have been too disturbing for her to hear the content at that age.

For the rest of us, let's acknowledge Chaim's memory. I urge you: inhale every word, breathe in every experience, share every suffering.

Chapter 5

CHAIM GOLUCHOWSKI

Secrets are the stones

That sink the boat

Take them out

Look at them,

Throw them out and float.

—*Lemn Sissay MBE* [8]

Introduction

New stories of the Holocaust are continually coming to light, particularly as we pass the 75th anniversary of the Second World War, which ended in 1945. Survivors and their descendants are now recalling unthinkable and difficult memories. Most of these were tragic circumstances in which people were helpless to fight back, yet a few of them document the heroic deeds of resistance and survival against all the odds.

Each of these stories deserves to be heard, yet for many, the need to stay silent about their experiences is still mandatory. Chaim's story has so far remained untold... until now.

In *The Collective Silence, German Identity and the Legacy of Shame*, a book edited by Barbara Heimannsberg and Christoph J Schmidt, the silence surrounding the Holocaust continues to prevent healing – whether of the victims, the Nazis or the generations that followed.

They wrote:

Psychotherapists explore the ways in which a legacy of shame, guilt and abuse has conspired against families and hidden aspects of German identity. In vivid reflections, parents, grandparents, children and grandchildren, perpetrators, resistors and victims alike break their silence and begin to heal the emotional ruptures caused by the Holocaust.

Stories from families of Holocaust victims, as well as from children of Nazis, reveal how history has been repressed by the silence surrounding the horrors of the Third Reich.

Introducing Chaim

So, too, it was with Chaim Goluchowski, a man who recorded but never shared how he survived the Holocaust. Despite the emotional turmoil it must have caused him to write his story, it was likely cathartic for him to fight through his disturbed memories in graphic detail.

This chapter is adapted from a secret memoir Chaim wrote of his life from his childhood in the small village of Lechow, Poland, through to his capture by the Nazis, and his escape and further internment until Germany surrendered in 1945.

Although Chaim (born 1915) and my mother (born 1918) were first cousins, they never met. My grandmother, Ethel Wolman, emigrated to England in 1914, while her sister, Raizl – Chaim's mother – married Kelman Goluchowski in 1898 and remained in Lechow.

Captured by the Nazis in 1941, Chaim slaved in labour camps for the duration of the war. His memoir, written during the postwar years he lived in Canada, records the horrendous experiences of his incarceration. The contents remained a secret that was never discussed until its discovery after his death in 1996 at the age of 81.

How wrenching it must have been for his adult children as they first discovered the terrible pain and suffering their parents experienced! Was there a volcanic eruption of emotions as they read his private words, which evoked memories of a happy family life in Poland before the atrocities of the war years?

Perhaps it was too distressing even to read. Written in broken English, it is limited to his first-person viewpoint of world events. This chapter and the quotes that follow are extracts from his story.

Perhaps he wrote it because he was striving to exorcise demons. Or maybe it was a last, desperate attempt to divulge this travesty to his children, having spent years protecting them from the truth.

I cannot imagine how Chaim concealed his memoir for all those years, but I can visualise his son Ken arriving with his siblings at their father's apartment to sort through old knick-knacks and family memorabilia; I can hear the light-hearted discussions over who gets the crockery, cutlery or jewellery, and can see them shedding some tears along the way.

Then, after the clothing is bagged up and the books are stacked ready for despatch to the local charity shop, a plain manila envelope is suddenly found on a shelf, as if waiting to be discovered. Ken blows off the dust and draws out 120 pages of foolscap paper full of typed words on pages he had never seen before.

He must have stared in disbelief at the front sheet headed 'No.1' as he digested the first line:

I have been born in the year 1915 in the city so called Lechow.

No.1

I have been born in the year 1915 in the City so called Lechow
Province of Kielce. Poland.I was living with my Mother and father,
brothers,and sisters, Alltogether we were a family of 10. Six brothers
and 2 sisters. The names of my brothers were as follows. Harry,
Joseph, Jacob, Moris, Max, and I myself Chaim. The firs, of my
sisters was Martha the oldest, the joungest sister was Lea. The date
of them were as follows Harry born in 1900, Joseph born in 1904.
Jacob born in 1906, Moris born in 1909. Max born in 1912. I was
born in 1915 . My oldest sister was born in 1898, My youngest
sister born in 1920.In that time we were living all together. Since
1918 my memory,We had a grandmother living together in a small
room she used to give my brother Max and me food to eat at a littte
table to eat in very tiny plate.

First page of Chaim's memoir

*The following stories are taken from Chaim's memoir, with my
words added for background information and context.*

In the beginning

Chaim was born on 15 February 1915, the seventh child of Raizl and
Kelman Goluchowski. His eldest sister Martha (Mattie) was 17, and
the five boys were Harry, 15, Joseph, 11, Jacob, 9, Morris, 6, and
Max, 3. Their youngest sister Leah was born five years later in 1920.

Chaim was three years old when my mother was born in
London.

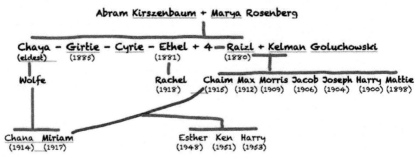

Family tree, based on Chaim's memoir

He wrote:

Since 1918, from my memory, our grandmother Marya lived with us in a small room. She used to give my brother Max and me food to eat in a very tiny plate at a little table.

Their two-bedroom home was a house with a small grocery store run as a family business, located in the village of Lechow (population 1,200). Kelman also owned a mill trading in lumber. The older children helped in the shop while their parents collected supplies from the wholesale merchant 20 miles away, in the town of Kielce, travelling by horse and wagon.

Life was difficult for the family. While Chaim was too young to remember the details as they were happening, he later learned of the harrowing tales of how his family maintained a strong sense of dedication and love for one another, despite the realities of their situation.

He recounted some of them in his memoir:

In that time there was a war between Poland and Russia. My brother Harry was 18 years of age and was drafted into the army, taken to a camp at Czestochowa to train.

I remember when my mother had baked bread for him. In that time, I believe there was no bakery to buy from. It was a depression, we were very poor, and she took a few loaves of that bread and carried it on her back to Czestochowa, 80 miles from Lechow. She had to walk by foot as there was no train. It was very far; I believe it took her a few days to come back.

When she came home, she was sitting and crying. 'Who knows whether he will come home from the war?' My mother was going many times to see Harry until he was sent to the Russian battlefront in the Polish–Russian war. He was captured after a few weeks and taken to Russia as a prisoner of war until the war ended in 1921 and he returned to us. My cousin Mordechi decided not to go to the army, so hid out. When the police came, he climbed inside an oven used to bake bread and was never found by the Nazis.

I have heard that he was killed in London during the Blitz.

Growing up

Chaim's memoir had so many stories to tell of what life was like – like the time young soldiers dressed in blue uniforms came into the family's store. "They're Russian Bolsheviks," his father Kelman said. There was another story about German soldiers who were still friendly towards the Jews during the war between Poland and Russia. The Germans had planned to hang 10 Poles accused of spying, but after Kelman asked, "They can't read or write, so how can they be spies?", the accused were released.

Chaim continued by describing his life as a boy:

As I grew older, my mother sent me and also my brother Max to a Cheder [a private Jewish school teaching Hebrew and religious lessons] to another town, Daleszyce. We stayed with our Aunty Cyrle. They visited every week, winter and summer, even in the biggest frost, to bring food.

One of the daughters got married in 1926. I remember her wedding. It was in wintertime, and it was a very cold winter. My parents also came to the wedding in their horse and cart. In that time my brother Harry came to the wedding, and he got to know one of the other daughters, Ides, and became engaged to her. One year later they got married.

Chaim's other brothers and family members also had major events occur as they struggled to survive and to enjoy their lives.

My brother Joseph enlisted in the army in 1927, and a year later my brother Jacob also started national service.

In 1928, Chaim had been living at home and earning money to help the family. Then Raizl was diagnosed with malignant cancer, and after spending three months in a Warsaw hospital, she returned home, where she died four weeks later.

Chaim's other brothers and family members also had major events occur as they struggled to survive and to enjoy their lives.

Chaim recalled:

There came to us three salesmen who wanted to make a deal to buy lumber for transporting to London, England. One came from England, one from Lodz and one from Kielce. They bought a few thousand logs and we brought them from the forest and put them in a big lot to ship to England. We made nice money at that time, and some was used to pay the hospital their bill for looking after Raizl. We were just lucky because that year was a depression.

Chaim, now 13, returned to live with his Aunty Cyrle, and spent the next year as a tailor's apprentice. The same year, his sister Mattie emigrated to Toronto, Canada; Joseph got married; and his other brother Morris was drafted into the army. Then in 1930, Chaim's father Kelman was remarried to Gurdie, his late wife's sister.

In 1933, Chaim joined his brother Joseph's family in Kielce, a much larger town with more opportunities, and stayed in his home at 34 Bodzentinska Street. Chaim's memoir explained that Joseph introduced him to a builder, Mr Levenreich, and he started to work as a painter's apprentice.

I did not make much money, only about 15 zloty a week. I was eating most of the time at my brother's place, but I had to buy lunch – just one quarter of a loaf of bread was my lunch. My boss never knew what I was eating. I went out to eat in places where nobody saw me, then I came back to work.

A year later, his friend Shapiro got him a painting job for a Mr Gutman, earning 25 zloty a week. He was very happy making more money.

Chaim continued:

I worked with him for one year. One day we were painting a building for a Dr Shats. We had to paint a staircase to make some flowers, but I never had done it, so Mr Gutman hired a special artist, whose name was Mr Mendel Rubenstein, and he was the only one in that particular city. He asked Gutman for a helper and I was willing to help as I wanted to learn more. He was a master of art, but was working by himself, and needed someone to help him all the time, so he asked me if I would like to work for him, and the following week I started and stayed for six months.

Life then carried on back home:

My Aunty Gurdie, my father's second wife, became sick in 1935. She had a stroke, then died five days later. This was a tragedy for all of us. Some of the family I don't remember, none survived except for my cousin Miriam (Mary) who I met for the first time in 1935. [This was probably because it was his first cousin once removed.]

Mary, who was from the town of Chmielnik, had left home and gone to look for work in Kielce. Chaim helped his cousin get a job working for a man named Lewandowski in a grocery store on 36 Bodzentynska Street, next door to where he lived at number 34. After the Second World War broke out, she witnessed Mr and Mrs Lewandowski and their four children being lined up against a wall and shot. Shocked by the experience, she went home to her parents in Chmielnik. She was eventually taken to the labour camp at Skarzysko–Kamienna.

Miriam (Mary), circa 1950

In 1935, Chaim served in the Polish army for 18 months, then returned to work for Mr Rubenstein for a further six months until his brother Morris invited him to join him in the city of Lodz.

In Lodz

Poland's re-emergence as an independent country at the end of the First World War was confirmed by the Treaty of Versailles in 1919. The city grew to become a major European multicultural and industrial centre, and one of the largest cities in Poland.

Kielce was a *shtetl* – a small market town. *Shtetls* were typically occupied by between a few hundred and up to several thousand Jews, and surrounded by countryside. Gentiles usually lived outside the towns. The streets were generally unpaved and the homes were constructed of wood.

Lodz was a *shtot* – a larger city – with 200,000 Jews and full of all the excitement, amenities and work opportunities a city provides. Its population thrived during the 1930s, growing to around 600,000 people. It had a large religious community and was favoured by the arts. Several Jewish artists and writers resided there, including world-renowned pianist Arthur Rubinstein, composer Aleksander

Tansman, and poets Julian Tuwim, Itzhak Katzenelson, David Frischman and Jacob Cohen.

Chaim and Morris lived with the Tempelhofs – a poor but kind family, all of whom played the violin. The young men enjoyed the Tempelhofs' music and strolled the busy streets every night with thousands of others mingling together.

Chaim, likely in 1935, roughly
20 years old

Chaim's two brothers, Morris and Max

Anti-Semitism

(Note: While many Poles were also Jewish, the reference to Poles or Polish below and elsewhere is entirely to non-Jews.)

> *The Polish people started to discriminate against the Jews, but we did not pay much attention until the bloody Germans attacked Poland.*

> *Then came the first trouble. The Polish people could not stand that the Jewish people had all the business. They were saying to one another, "Do not buy from a Jew – buy from your own people. Don't support the Jews, they're our enemies. All Jews should go to Palestine."*

> *My father was still living in Lechow together with Jacob, Lea, and Harry with his wife Ides and their three children, but the Polish people did not now come in very much to their little grocery store. The discrimination was so great that they could hardly make a living.*

Chaim remembered these and other horrible situations in his memoir.

Many Jews began emigrating to Palestine, even though it was still illegal for them to go there. Chana, Mary's sister, married Zeev Ciecierski in 1939. They planned to emigrate after the wedding, but Chana's father, Velvel Pasternak, persuaded Zeev to go ahead and secure a place for his wife to live, and then she would follow.

He arrived safely with a group from a *kibbutz* and survived, but Chana, like the rest of her family, was murdered by the Nazis before she could be reunited with her husband.

[*Kibbutzim* – the plural form of *kibbutz* – were first established early in the 20th century as a Jewish collective community traditionally based on agriculture. This utopian-style community was a combination of socialism and Zionism, and all income was used to run the *kibbutz*. A *kibbutz* member, known as a *kibbutznik*, became an integral part of a unit that was larger than just his own family.][9]

Chana Pasternak and Zeev Ciecierski,
likely after they announced their engagement

The outbreak of the Second World War, 1 September 1939

As Chaim explained in his memoir:

The first day when the German attacked Poland, the Polish government mobilised all people, drafting them to the army. A few bombs were dropped, but the Germans were careful to preserve the factories for their own use.

After the railway tracks were destroyed, Max had to walk the 30 miles to enlist at his training camp at Skarzysko–Kamienna, but he was captured en route by the Gestapo. Jacob never volunteered to fight; he stayed home.

German troops arrived in Lodz on 8 September. This was before Morris and Chaim could enlist, so they just watched as tanks entered the city and prepared to surround it entirely.

Chaim continued:

Many of the younger Jews followed as the Polish army marched towards Warsaw. We decided to join them, and had walked about 30 miles towards a town called Brzeziny when we saw the whole army destroyed by airplanes, as bombs dropped one after the other, fires burning everywhere. We all ran in different directions.

Thousands of Volksdeutschen [people who had German language and culture but were not German citizens; these ones had lived in Lodz since before the war][11] *who had been hiding inside the Wicczyn Forest suddenly appeared, firing their weapons at the Poles and especially on the retreating Jews. We got scared and turned back for Lodz.*

By the time they got home it was dark, and they discovered the Nazis had imposed a blackout. They sat around in silence until the radio was turned on and then listened to the latest news.

Meanwhile, the noise from outside warned that the Germans were continuing to march into Lodz. By morning, the entire city was occupied.

Chaim described the moment when everyone's lives changed:

I was working the same day painting a residence on 22 Piotrkowska Street. When the announcement came on the radio, it was 12 o'clock noon.

The owner gathered all the workmen together and said to us: "My dear friends, do you know what I am going to tell you?"

"No. What?" we asked.
"Just leave the painting. This is not going to be for us anymore. The Germans will kill all the Jews."

He did not make a mistake. I could not believe that this would happen.

I left my work and went home. When I came home, everybody was already in the house. Everybody was shaking. We were worried about what will become of us. First of all, we were not prepared with food. We were all wondering, what are we going to do for a living? How will we live in a situation like that? What could we do?

For us Jews, it was very bad. Everyone was against us Jews – the Poles and the Germans. We could not defend ourselves from those enemies.

Definitions

Nazis: Members of the Nazi Party, a radical far-right movement and political party led by Adolf Hitler. Nazi ideology was racist, nationalist, anti-democratic, violently anti-Semitic and anti-Marxist.

Gestapo: The official secret police of Nazi Germany, created by Hermann Goring in 1933.

Luftwaffe: The official name of the Nazi air force.

SS: (the *Schutzstaffel*, or protection squads) were established as Hitler's personal bodyguard unit.

The SS later became the elite guard of the Nazi Reich and Hitler's executive force, appointed to carry out all security-related duties with no legal restraint. They were involved in numerous atrocities and were later judged to be a criminal organisation at the Nuremberg Trials.

SA: *Sturmabteilung*. This was a paramilitary organisation of the Nazis that was integral to Hitler's rise to power. It violently enforced party norms and influenced elections. It eventually lost power to the SS.

Wehrmacht [armed forces]: The unified armed forces of Nazi Germany during the period from 1935 to 1945.[10]

Chaim knew nothing about war – he could only recall stories his father had told him of fighting for the Russian army in the war against Japan, and about the time he lived in the United States between 1912 and 1914. [My maternal grandparents came to England during these same years.] The declaration of war stopped his plan to return with the family four weeks later.

By morning, street signs were erected that said: "All Jews shall wear a Magen David [the Star of David on white material] badge." The Germans, wanting to identify every single Jew, issued a warning that anyone not wearing this badge would be shot to death.

Poles were employed as 'Jew Hunters' and bribed with the promise of extra rations for every Jew they handed over to the Nazis. Jewish shops were forced to display the Star of David in their windows, and a 5:00pm curfew was imposed on Jews. However, this made little difference as most Jews were too scared to leave their homes during the day, let alone at night.

A blue Star of David on a white armband was worn in parts of Poland.
Different styles were used elsewhere.[12]

All the Jewish bakeries were swiftly confiscated. Ration cards were issued that permitted Jews to buy only minimum amounts of bread, sugar, salt and butter, but never in enough quantities to continue to feed everyone. Chaim recalled arriving just before 4:00am to receive his rations and waiting in the queue, only to be told they were sold out by the time he reached the front. Food shortages were a constant worry, but the Jews were powerless to get more officially

Fortunately, the Germans needed bakers and employed Morris, Chaim's brother, who managed to smuggle bread out of the bakery. Sometimes he even stole a sack of flour, which was enough to feed the whole family for a few weeks.

Chaim added to his memoir:

Meanwhile, the Polish people didn't have food to eat. They went around like crazy looking for food and where to buy it. I remember very well they were coming to our place where I was living to ask where they can buy some food. Most of the time, these were tricks to find out which Jews had something so they could be reported to the Nazis.

Work became increasingly difficult for Jews to find. Chaim had spent so much of his wages on having fun that he had saved very little by the time war broke out.

Needing money, he found a local factory that made candles and soap – scarce essentials that were in high demand. Chaim bought and successfully traded the goods in the street market for a few weeks until the Germans grabbed every business owned by any Jewish person.

Chaim reflected on this:

The last time I came to that factory, the owner said to me, "I am sorry I can't make any more business with you. The factory is not mine anymore."

That was the end. At first, I did not believe him. I thought he was joking. The Germans came in and closed everything.

The few hundred zloty Chaim saved was enough to live on for a while, but not for long. He and Morris bought a load of onions at the market to store and resell over the winter months, but the Germans confiscated the lot in less than a week. Finally, they tried selling tomatoes, but the Germans took those as well.

Chaim recalled:

The Germans looked around for Jewish people to work and grabbed anyone who wore the Magen David badge. We had to cover up the ditches the Poles had dug to protect themselves, so that when the Germans entered, the Germans wouldn't be able to come through. That was one of the stupidest protections from the Poles.

The Poles were helping the Germans as well. They showed them who the Jews were. If they saw one on the street, they had to point him out. They favoured bearded Jews for slaughter.

It was hard to believe that such a thing would happen. The whole world knew what was happening, but not a voice spoke out in our favour. The world lay in silent indifference. We were circumscribed by enemies; we were prisoners awaiting execution.

The Jews thought that after a few weeks, the Germans would relax and not bother them anymore. They were wrong. The longer the Nazis were there, the more Jews they murdered.

18

Certain Jews to superwise others. In The City of Lodz The designated certain Jew was wás named Rumkowski. He was the only one The German spoke to. He in turn gave orders to others in the City. The firsf day they took 20 men to the synagogue; stood them against the wall and shot them one at the time. That was on Wolborska street. After that they burned the synagogue.In the same time they burned down two others. One on the street Aleja Kosciuszkiego, another was the one on Zachodnia street. The third was the one refered to as the Hollandish Synagogue. I lived near the one on Wolborska street when that synagogue was burned down/ I witnessed it by myself. They had done the same thing to ather one. What they did Jews were not allowed to see the brutality. They were evicted from their homes and driven away to portals of death. Jewish cadaves hung throughout the city of Lodz. The Nazis grinned proudly at the spactacles. What could we do without weapons? The Jews were thunder struck with fair, but no one could do a thing about it.

An extract from Chaim's memoir

'Certain Jews' were designated to supervise the other Jews. In Lodz, Chaim Mordechaj Rumkowski was appointed head of the Jewish Council in the ghetto. German authorities spoke only through him, and he passed on orders to other Jews. They became known as "the Jewish Law & Order" service.

Ghettos were developed to forcibly segregate, isolate and control the Jewish population. Polish Jews were mostly concentrated in large towns and cities near railway lines, and no two ghettos were the same.

The first major ghetto was created in Lodz in February 1940. The Nazis' initial plan was to remove all the Jews from Poland and deport them to the island of Madagascar.

In mid-November 1939, the Nazis stood 20 Jews against the front wall of the synagogue on Wolborska Street, then shot them and set fire to the synagogue. Chaim, who lived nearby, witnessed the whole incident. This beautiful, tall synagogue with two women's galleries and 1,500 seats was the building where all official public ceremonies were held.

The synagogue on Wolborska Street
set alight by the Nazis [13]

Two of the other synagogues in the city were also destroyed the same day, one on Aleja Kosciuzkiego Street and the other on Zachodnia Street.

The Nazis grinned proudly at the Jewish cadavers they had hung throughout the city of Lodz. Jews were evicted from their homes and forced to observe the brutality.

As Chaim observed:

What could we do without weapons? The Jews were thunderstruck with fear, but no-one could do a thing about it. We were unable and afraid to defend themselves.

Trying to escape

Chaim left his home many times without wearing his Magen David badge, though he knew he risked his life each time. His main debate with friends was whether to remain in Lodz or look for somewhere that might be safer.

The Nazis continued to transport Jews to concentration camps in the newly created ghetto, but although Chaim was petrified that he would become a victim of a random Nazi killing, he remained in Lodz until the end of 1940.

He planned his escape from Poland, travelling first to Warsaw, from where he intended to cross the border into Russia, ignoring the rumours that people were being sent back. He began to worry, however, when he saw that the Warsaw station was packed with people returning from Russia. "Why have you returned?" he asked a passenger.

"So many are sleeping outside on the ground, there's not enough places to stay and the Russians want all newcomers to join the army," the passenger told him.

Chaim had been taught that the Russian system was one of the best: a praised way of life, they had no discrimination, people worked well together and it was free to attend school. Everyone could have everything under the sun. But he had just discovered that little of this was true.

Devastated to hear that the Russians were refusing entry, he changed his mind and bought a ticket home to see his father, who had been living with his brother Jacob in the town of Lechow, in Kielce Province. But first he would visit Joseph. That was on 31 December 1940.

In his memoir, Chaim recounted his journey:

I went into the train and sat on my seat. Sitting beside me were Polish people travelling home to different destinations. While I was sitting in the train, the Polish people started talking about the Jews. My heart was beating like a machine. The Poles were saying they should kill all the Jews, and not to leave one of them. They said the Jews are all rich and we are poor people. They told each other that at least they would have our houses.
I was very lucky it was dark in the train and they did not recognise that I was a Jew – otherwise, they would have thrown me out of the train. Can anyone imagine how I felt sitting with a bunch of murderers?

Chaim disembarked at the terminal, excited to have arrived, only to discover that he was not in Kielce after all. He would now have to catch another train to take him there.

A porter directed him to the correct station, which was two miles away, and said he must cross a bridge on route.

Chaim's story continued:

When I crossed one little bridge, I had no trouble until I went a little further. There I saw one German guarding the bridge and I had to pass him, but I was afraid he will stop me because I am Jewish and put me in jail. I stopped to think what I should do. Not far from there I saw a young Polish boy standing a little bit further from that German guard. I was afraid of him too, but I took a chance and came closer to him.

I asked him, "Excuse me, my friend. Could you tell me how I can cross that bridge? There is a German guard standing, and I am afraid that he will not let me through."

"I know that," he replied. He did not recognise me as Jewish.

"I know that German guard personally, so I will take you through. Give me five zloty and I will give him that money so he will let you pass."

He told me I should follow him, and that I should not say one thing. He asked me if I have a passport. I said no. He also did not recognise that I am Jewish, because I took off the armband. Finally, I went over the bridge.

I was very happy.

Chaim slipped across to the other side, but lost his bearings in the darkened night sky.

After wandering around in circles, he laid on the grass and fell asleep. There he stayed until he was disturbed by the sound of loud footsteps. Scared it might be a German, he was relieved to find it was a Polish man returning home.

Chaim went on:

"Excuse me, how far is the train station?" I asked the man.

"It is only a mile further. You must hurry, the train leaves in 15 minutes and the next one's not due for another two hours," he answered.

I had also to go through the wicket where a German was checking everybody. He did not have much time to check me, so he let me through, but I did not have my badge on my arm, or else he would have stopped me. I quickly ran into the train and sat down on a seat. I was happy to be inside.

But what happened after I got on the train was that I met same Polish people, who were again sitting near me. Imagine hearing from the Poles the same conversation about the Jews! My heart itself was going like a train.

Finally, it took me about three or four hours until I came to the city of Kielce. If I had not been so afraid, I would have killed them all. Until that time, I had never realised that we Jews were living in Poland with such enemies.

Chaim left the station and walked nervously to Joseph's home since it was dangerous to go out at night without a permit, but he arrived safely at his brother's house.

The knock scared Dora, who thought the Gestapo had come to take her husband. So, when she saw Chaim, she was relieved and hugged him affectionately. It was two years since Joseph had seen his brother, whom they thought was dead.

Next morning, Chaim observed the damage compared to Warsaw. The Luftwaffe bombers had dropped around 600 tonnes of high-explosive bombs in late September 1939, badly damaging the Polish capital. The attack was reputed to be the largest air raid ever seen.

Chaim knew he needed to earn some money. He tracked down his former boss, Mr Gutman, who was still painting at the city hall, only now he was working for the Germans. Mr Gutman employed him immediately.

The Gestapo regularly checked in on their progress, shouting, *"Ver luchter Juden. Arbeit schneller, schneller!"* ("Cursed Jews. Work faster, faster!") and beating them with a whip. Chaim worked for weeks without the mandatory permit until finally Gutman obtained it, but Chaim soon regretted having it when the Nazis took him.

Taken by the Nazis

Chaim documented what happened:

I was unlucky to obtain that permit. One day I went to visit my Aunty Ethel Spivak, who was living in Stolarska Street.

While I was sitting there eating lunch at about 12 o'clock, a Gestapo man came in and he said to me: "Do verfluchter Jude [Damn Jew], come with me."

I did not know what was going on at the time. He took me to a truck outside with other young and fit men. The Nazis were going around the city picking up every Jew they saw on the street.

"Where are we going?" I asked.

"You will find out when you get there," the Gestapo responded sharply.

"Why don't you tell us where we're going?" I asked again.

"We are taking you to work," he replied.

"I am a painter. I'm already working in City Hall. Let me go!" I protested.

"No. I don't believe you are working," he said.

Chaim and the other Jews were taken to the nearby synagogue and pushed inside the main hall, which was filled with two thousand other adults. It was so crowded it was impossible to find a place to sleep.

Their cries for help filled the hall, but no-one dared assist them, for everyone was scared of the Nazis' brutality. Chaim wrote that he was afraid Nazi arsonists would set fire to the synagogue and raze it to the ground, burning them all alive.

A mob of loved ones were gathered on the streets outside. They screamed and begged the Nazis to release their children, but their cries were ignored, and the Nazis batted them away with their enormous guns.

The synagogue was surrounded by hundreds of Gestapo with German Shepherd dogs barking ferociously and held on tight chains.

Early next morning, the front doors were swung back on their hinges and the stale atmosphere inside was replaced by fresh winter air as the prisoners were unceremoniously pushed out. They had been starved of food and water the whole night. Outside on the street, they were surrounded by the Gestapo murderers and their dogs.

Meanwhile, Chaim was still trying to prove he was employed. He wrote:

At 12 o'clock they took us outside and told us to stand in a line of six, and then they made us walk to the train. I was thinking that Mr Gutman might be able to help me because I was working in City Hall on a job, so I believed that the bloody Germans would let me go. However, Mr Gutman did not show up, so he was not any help.

The prisoners were lined up and pushed down the street as distraught loved ones followed closely behind. The carriage doors at the railway station hung open, ready to devour them. The SS guards pushed the prisoners inside the cars and struck them with guns as they passed, then firmly bolted all the doors.

As Chaim remembered it:

All people were left with broken hearts, still not told where they were going. We could not get in touch with any of our families. We were travelling for 24 hours; the Germans didn't give us anything at all to eat in that time.

The train was just a cattle car without windows and ventilation, lit by narrow shafts of sunlight that stole through the cracks in the timber slats of the outer shell.

Conditions inside the transports were extremely inhumane, and for some it was lethal. There was no food or water, and the only toilet facility was a single bucket in the corner (which quickly became overfilled). The smell of vomit, urine and excrement was overpowering, especially without ventilation. As such, many prisoners died en route to the camps from dehydration, starvation or suffocation.

At Lublin, they were made to step out of the train cars and walk down a ramp leading to a big open yard. Forced to sit on the ground, they waited for the trucks to arrive bringing food prepared by local Jews.

Once they were fed, they travelled a further 30 miles to their final destination: Hrubieszow.

Hrubieszow Camp in South-Eastern Poland

As Chaim recalled it:

That place where we were brought to stay was a village where farmers once lived in very small, poor houses until they were confiscated by the Germans, and were no better than stables, with very dirty, empty rooms. There was just straw on the floors.

In January 1941, this forced-labour camp was under the command of three Nazis: Adolf Waldman, Max Stohner and Helmut Waltman.

By the time Chaim stepped off the train, at least 20,000 other prisoners had already arrived. All of them believed they were being taken to the gas chamber. In 1939, the German gas chambers were mostly used to kill physically and intellectually disabled people. But by early 1941, several gas chambers had been built at extermination camps in Poland for the mass killing of Jews.

In August 1941, Winston Churchill, the UK prime minister, spoke of the gas-chamber exterminations in a news broadcast, making it general knowledge to the rest of the world.

Realising they had instead been transported to a labour camp, they considered themselves lucky to be alive. Instead of being killed, Chaim and his fellow prisoners were forced to build a roadway – one stained with Jewish blood.

As Chaim described it:

The first day we were called outside, put in lines of four and taken to a place where they had all kinds of tools. Shovels and wheelbarrows were handed out, and we were divided into many groups, then taken to work in a field to build a highway about 30 miles long. Some pushed wheelbarrows and others filled them so full they were hard to move.

Ukrainian soldiers surrounded us – every few feet, we had those soldiers watching closely that no-one would try to run away from that camp.

Villages along the route were used to house hundreds of prisoners in small shacks, and a single kitchen prepared and served one spoonful of soup for lunch before the prisoners returned to work.

Chaim added:

As soon as we finished that soup, the treatment got worse as the guards started to hit us more and more. I knew right away from our food that we were all in trouble.

For dinner, one loaf of bread would be divided among eight people. It was supposed to last until the next night, but the prisoners were starving and ate it all immediately.

Chaim knew they could not possibly survive on a diet of such meagre rations while doing so much strenuous work. For breakfast, besides any leftover bread from the night before, they were allotted a spoonful of coffee. Actually, it was not real coffee, but they were happy to drink whatever it was as long as it contained some form of water. They got nothing to drink while working.

Water was in short supply, not only for drinking, but for bathing and laundry as well, so their sole set of clothes remained filthy, without any extra shirts or shoes to wear. The presence of lice was rampant, and the infestations of bedbugs and other germs made the prisoners' lives intolerable.

On the daily march to work the prisoners were ordered to "sing Jewish songs". Singing songs, however, was not enough to make the Jews believe they were happy to go to work, and the Germans knew this. How could anyone feel happy when all they could think about was the brutality of being kidnapped, and being away from their homes and loved ones?

As Chaim explained it:

The Germans knew this also and exploited the Jews' heartbreak as a way of reminding them who held the power.

Memories of lost family and friends weighed on the prisoners' minds during the day, but were forgotten by the evening when they returned to the barracks too exhausted to do anything but fall asleep after working solidly for 10 hours each day.

Gestapo commanders pressed the Ukrainian guards to use as much force as necessary to make the Jews work faster and harder. Beating and killing was never off-limits, and the Ukrainians shot and hung prisoners at will.

On one occasion, the Nazis hung a man inside Chaim's barracks. The prisoners were all young, but helpless to defend themselves.

Ten thousand people had already died in this camp in a short time from thirst, malnutrition, hard physical labour, beatings, firing squads and hangings. Should they manage to escape, the Magen David badge on their sleeve would identify them.

A painting job

Adolf Waldman, a Gestapo commandant, entered his barracks to ask if anyone had been a painter before coming to the camp. Chaim raised his arm and was taken to Waldman's farm by a Ukrainian guard to assist another Jewish painter from the town of Hrubieszow so the two of them could complete the work faster.

As Chaim relayed in his memoir:

I started to talk to him about running away from there. Beside that house was the River Bog, where we could see the Russian border. So, I said to him, "Let's run away from here to Russia. We haven't got far to go from there. We will be free from the German murderers."

As soon as I told him this, he got scared that if we did that, we would be caught by the Germans and they would kill us. He did not realise that the Germans would do the same to him a few weeks later.

The man gave Chaim his address, and said if ever he had a chance to escape, he would help him to get home.

When they returned to Hrubieszow Camp, it was deserted. The prisoners had been moved further away as the road progressed. Chaim was heartbroken and feared being left alone at the mercy of a rogue Nazi, or even sent back to those murderers building the highway, so he asked Waldman if there was somewhere else to paint.

Waldman took him to a nearby school to decorate for the next two weeks. The school building was vacant except for the school janitor, who provided a calcimine whitewash as there was no other paint.

As Chaim remembered it:

I had no-one to tell me anything. I was very happy to be working alone without the Ukrainian murderers watching and beating me all the time. The janitor gave me something to eat, but I don't remember what it was.

The satisfaction of painting a school rather than digging a road was disturbed by worries about what would happen after he had completed the painting. He wanted to avoid a return to the camp, being forced to dig ditches by hand with shovels and picks, and facing constant abuse from the Germans, who wanted nothing more than to destroy the Jewish nation. The daily insults of *"Arbeit, Arbeit, du verfluchter Jude!"* ("Work, work, you cursed Jew!") was the Germans' form of fun.

This thought and the idea that guards would kill him when his work was finished finally motivated him to plan his escape.

Chaim's great escape

Carrying a metal pail filled with brush, scalpel and tools in one hand, Chaim tucked a ladder under his other arm, and slipped out of the school unseen.

He then stood at the kerbside with his hand raised to signal he wanted a lift. Hundreds of lorries thundered past one after the other as he waited. He removed his Magen David badge so drivers could not see that he was a Jew. Eventually a truck stopped.

Chaim recorded their conversation:

"Are you going towards the town of Hrubieszow?" I asked the driver, who was a German soldier.

The soldier answered, "Yes. Usually, I'm not supposed to carry civilians and must drop you half a mile short of the city, but since you're a painter and carry a ladder, I'll drop you a little closer."

The soldier helped me to remove the tools from the back of the lorry at a convenient drop-off point and I tipped him with my last five zloty.

"Danke schön," the driver thanked me and drove off.

With the lorry driver out of sight, Chaim dumped the tools. He then walked into the town and asked for directions to the painter's address.

The painter and his wife happily welcomed Chaim inside their home, and invited him to shower and get refreshed; they also gave him fresh underwear and a suit, and then served him his first proper supper in three months.

He went on:

My friend did not expect me, but he took me in with pleasure.
He started to talk about the proposition I gave him while I was working with him in that farm: "It was a mistake that we did not cross that river – we would be in Russia now. I was worried about my wife and children, that was the only reason I did not want to go."

He told him of the Jewish Congress that looked after Jewish people in need, and that they would come by in the morning to help Chaim travel safely back to his home in Kielce. The German order that created the ghettos also decreed that the councils of Jewish leaders – aka the Jewish Congress – were to be established to administer these newly uprooted Jewish communities.

The next day, in the presence of the Congress, Chaim described how he had escaped from Hrubieszow Camp and asked if they could find a way to help him return to his family. They handed him a train ticket and a few zloty, and soon thereafter he set out again.

He recounted his journey years later in his memoir:

I left the Congress in the town of Hrubieszow and went to the train. I had prepared all my tickets to go home. All I had to show was just that ticket at the wicket and they let me right through.

I went inside the train, sat down on a seat and the train started rolling home. In the train all rooms were dark, but I was glad none of the Polish people would recognise me as Jewish. The Poles were talking as usual about the Jews. The whole conversation was only that the Jews are rich. I was even more sick of listening to the Poles than to the Germans.

When the train finally arrived in Kielce, Chaim left the station and could not believe that he was nearly home after three months of detainment. He should have had a permit to walk on the street, but no-one asked for his identification papers because they never expected a Jew to be travelling on the train. Of course, he was not wearing his Magen David armband and knew he was lucky not to be caught.

Home with the family, 1941

At 2:00am the knock at the front door sent shockwaves into Joseph and Dora as they feared it was the SS until they heard the words, "Joseph, this is your brother, Chaim." They flung their arms around his skinny body, relieved to see him alive after his capture. Dora broke down in tears from sheer joy.

Eight members of the family slept on the floor that night as they only had one bed between them. Chaim remembered how it was to return home and then went to seek out his old boss, Mr Gutman.

He wrote:

The next morning, I went to see what is going on in the city, even though I was scared that the Germans might catch me again.

I wanted to see what my boss had done since I left him three months ago. He was still living in the same place as before, on the street Plac Wolnosci. I hoped he would take me back on the job where I was working before.

I was very happy to see him alive, and to learn that he was still carrying on with his painting. And especially that he said he would hire me again.

"I was very happy to see him alive" are eight words that vividly portrayed the world they inhabited at that time, revealing how much more normal it would have been to hear of someone's death.

When Chaim returned to paint the city hall, the Nazis still continued to check their work every few minutes. They shouted vile names and commands at them: *"Ver luchter Jude! Arbeit! Schnell!"* ("Damn Jews! Work! Faster!")

One asked, "How old are you?" to which he replied, "I am 26 years old."

"You've lived long enough. There's not much left for you."

Chaim knew that if he spoke another word, he would be shot on the spot.

Soon, that fear came true, but not for him, as he wrote:

A few weeks later, Gutman and his children were taken by the Nazis; he was shot, but luckily two children ran away.

One went to the Russians and one to another place, but the rest of them were sent to the Treblinka Crema-torium.

Treblinka was a factory of death that was completed in July 1942. A total of 6,000 people were taken on the trains to one of the three gas chambers there. Men, women and children were separated, and those who could work were selected. These were forced to strip naked while the remainder were driven down into the 'bath house', where they were killed with poison gas.

By September 1942, 10 gas chambers had been added, enabling the murders of between 1,000–2,000 people every single hour. Other Jewish prisoners had to drag the corpses out through the back doors and bury them in mass graves.[14]

Sometime later, Heinrich Himmler, the main architect of the Holocaust, ordered the bodies to be dug up and taken to the incinerator. There they were burned, and the ashes were thrown back into the graves.

A close call

On the night Chaim went to visit his Auntie Cyrle, he spotted a German guard standing outside a bank, but he was not guarding the bank – he was looking for Jews.

Chaim recounted what happened next:

Suddenly I passed about 20 feet away from where he was standing. I heard someone calling me, and I turned around and heard that bloody German guard calling me: "You son of a bitch, come here!"

I came closer to him and he grabbed me by my neck and threw me down on the ground and was trying to choke me. He squeezed me so hard that I was nearly dead.

I don't know what happened to him that he let me loose. Probably he was thinking I was already dead. Or else he must have got scared as someone was coming close by to him. It was possible that another SS man was passing by and he was afraid for himself. He was not allowed to do such a thing by himself unless they gave orders to do so.

Chaim raced off to his aunt's home, his heart beating like a machine. "Auntie, Auntie! Open the door!" he yelled as quietly as possible until someone answered. Chaim could not speak for the next half an hour until he was calm enough to tell the story, and it was another two hours before he relaxed completely. After his nightmare experience, he stayed the night with his aunt and cousins, and returned to Joseph's in the morning.

Joseph, meanwhile, spent a sleepless night worrying about Chaim, scared he had been taken by the Nazis. As only government officials had telephones, Chaim was unable to call his brother. Such experiences were common and must have terrified Jews who were left worrying that every time a family member stepped out onto the street they might not return, and there was no way to notify those left behind. Joseph was hugely relieved when Chaim arrived home the next morning.

Chaim decided it was time to leave the city of Kielce and visit his father, who was living with his brother Jacob in the neighbouring town of Lechow. It took most of the next day to walk the 20 miles to Jacob's home, and then for the first time in three years, not since Chaim had moved to Lodz, he and his father were reunited. That was when Chaim learnt that his father's mill and stock of timber had been stolen by the Nazis.

Chaim was thrilled to be with his father again, but here he learned that the terrors of the Nazi occupation in Lechow were the same as he had experienced in other towns.

They took us to work and for the first three months we had to shovel snow every day in the coldest weather, but they didn't give us anything to eat, so we had to go home to eat. We still had some food, but for how long could we have any if we did not earn any money? They came to the Jewish people to take out from our houses whatever we had.

My father was an older man who was forced to carry a sack of potatoes weighing 200 pounds on his shoulder, which he was not able to do, but there was nothing I could do to help.

*Chaim's father Kelman, forced by the Germans
to carry a 200lb sack of potatoes on his shoulder*

The Lagow Ghetto

Then, evicted from our house, we lived outside for a few days, until we were told to go to Town Lagove [sic], where all Jewish people from small villages were gathered into a ghetto.

74

Most of the family's remaining spare clothes were sold to pay the rent for one large room that 20 members of the family shared; they all slept on the floor, and had very little food. Then Joseph arrived unexpectedly with his wife and six hungry half-naked children after the Germans forced them to leave their home, so they ran from Kielce to avoid that ghetto, discovering they had escaped from one ghetto only to enter another.

Chaim's other brother Morris also arrived with his family from Lodz, penniless and desperate for protection, and now just more mouths to be fed. Finally, Auntie Cyrle arrived from Daleszyce with her daughter and son, also seeking help.

At one time, the family had earned a good living, but the Germans had taken it all. Now, there was no extra money, so they banded together and had to do what they could to survive.

Chaim recounted their experiences:

We had one full box of jewellery they took right away. Lagow was a town of 800 families; the majority were poor, some were richer and had a little bit to live on, but the poorer ones suffered. My Auntie Cyrle's son and daughter were working – the son did some tailoring and the daughter was a seamstress, so they both made some money.

My father had been a strong very healthy man, but was made to work so hard that it was a pity to look at him. They [the Germans] *did not care how old he was.*

The Nazis had announced that if anybody would go out beyond the city limit, they would be shot. Very few people took chances to go out of the town Lagore [sic], *except my brother Max. He was captured by the German SS, and was the only one missing from the house. Then my brother Harry was taken from our home to work for them.*

So desperate was the need for food that they risked their lives despite the Nazis' death threats.

Chaim described what they did:

We left together at 4 o'clock in the morning and took huge risks that the Germans would not catch us on the road. We spread out across the village so that we should not be visible because the Gestapo were all over the place looking for Jews to catch and shoot. We ran through forests and hills and valleys, and hid so that the Germans should not catch us. If they caught somebody on the road, they would kill us all.

They slipped through gaps in the barbed wire to evade detection and steered clear of roads.

Chaim recalled the dangers:

The Germans rode with horse wagons and shepherd dogs that could smell a person from far away. Many times, we had to lie down in fields because we heard a horse wagon going down the road, and when we saw or heard a dog barking, we were scared to death, because usually when a dog is smelling somebody he runs to that spot.

By the time we came home, our hearts were beating like machines. But what can one do if he is in need? While we were returning home one day, I had seen the body of a relative laying on the ground. The Gestapo had shot him as he walked home from the same village.

An added danger was the difficulty of differentiating between the friendly farmers, some of whom would risk their lives to warn Jews when Germans were nearby, from the bigoted locals who despised them.

Chaim remembered the anxiety they felt:

Evil farmers did not want to help us, and we tried not to go to those anti-Semites, but one farmer was such a murderer. He locked the door on me and took an axe. He wanted to kill me, but I was very lucky that my brother Morris happened to be outside the house.

Morris heard my scream for help, broke down the door and saved me. We all ran home, afraid that the farmer would point us out to the German Gestapo.

My father had been unable to sleep as he looked through the window all night until we returned, and he was relieved to see us. "Thank God my children are already home!" He was also happy we brought some-thing to eat.

Potatoes, bread and grain became more expensive, and precious possessions were sacrificed for well below their value to purchase the only sources of food.

Three million Jews had thrived in Poland before the war started. But by the winter of 1941, most of those who were still left in the country had to beg potentially dangerous farmers for something to eat.

The Gestapo comes knocking

At around 10:00pm one night, a loud banging was heard at the front door. This was June 1942. Suspecting it was the Gestapo and fearing the worst-case scenario, they did not open the door right away so as to give Morris and Harry time to escape out through the back door, but four Gestapo hammered the door down with their guns and grabbed Jacob.

The Nazis took the youngest male or female from each of the 800 homes in the town that night. Taking the youngest from families was only one part of the Nazis' intimidation plans.

Chaim recalled what horrors came next:

The oldest people were taken to the same lot where the Polish people used to have a huge market, and [the Germans] *shot them one by one.*

My father was 70 years of age and bearded, so he was counted as an old man. Old Jews with beards were despised by the Nazis, so my father was shot right there, watched by my cousin and I, and we saw his body thrown onto a truck and taken away with the others. The man I loved was killed in cold blood simply because he was an old Jew. I was devastated. People screamed, but it did not help anyone.

A few days later they took out all the children and sent them to different gas chambers.

Chaim described how he went to the Jewish Council to ask where his brother Jacob was taken after he saw his father murdered:

The Germans had issued orders that one member of each family had to go to work and the Council must fulfil the order.

They said, "If you would like to go in his place you can exchange for him."

I took his place because I had worked away from home and was used to working for somebody else, but he only worked with my father.

Chaim was put on a windowless truck with 100 others and shipped to Skarzysko–Kamienna, a work camp in south central Poland, although no-one knew where they were being sent.

Despite his fear, Chaim was relieved to leave:

I was glad to leave the town of Lagow [Lagove] because the Gestapo officers were going around looking only to find a Jew. If they saw one with a beard, they cut off the beard with a knife, sometimes with the chin.

They took children from their homes, put them on the trucks and beat their heads against the walls.

At Skarzysko–Kamienna Camp

Several hundred German SA waited at the entrance to Skarzysko–Kamienna concentration camp. The 'SA' Nazi Storm Troopers' violent intimidation tactics played a key role in Hitler's rise to power. The sight of revolvers strapped to the side of the soldiers' trouser pockets was a heinous sight, making the Jews worry that they might simply be shot by the Germans.

Chaim recounted the intimidation:

Finally, we arrived at that camp. We stepped down and could see that we were close to a factory, but that the place we had to stay in was a big, empty school. It was called Ekonomia. As each man was individually selected and put on one side, our hearts beat faster as we thought they are probably going to shoot us.

The Jews were separated into random groups, unaware of how they would be allocated. Chaim was selected as one of the 25 strongest-looking men and was taken to an ammunition factory where he would be working.

He detailed the conditions in the factory:

In that factory itself was lots of buildings, and in those different buildings they produced different ammunitions, heavy grenades and smaller bullets.

Of course, if there is a big production of bullets in that factory, they will need a plumber, an electrician, carpenters and so on. Beside that factory they had two other factories – one in the east, one in the west and one in the middle, where I was supposed to start working.

The next day, Chaim and the selected men returned to the factory and a German SA man introduced himself:

"I am Mr Weber. I am a master plumber and you will be working for me. I have 25 Poles who are already working for me. Actually, these Poles were working in that factory before the war broke out, but did not go into the army as they had to produce ammunition even before the war. The Poles will show you what to do."

On that first morning, they dug ditches in a road for a water pipeline to a new barracks. Yet for all their physical labour, they only received a single spoonful of a coffee substitute for breakfast. For lunch, the 25 of them had to share a can of soup as they were fed nothing else. They received one loaf of bread for dinner to divide among eight of them. How could they survive on such meagre rations?

The Ekonomia School had one large room filled with bunk beds, and four men slept one on top of the other on every bunk. It was so overcrowded they could hardly move around.

Shortly after arriving at the camp, they were reminded that their new life as factory workers was not a vacation from their real lives as prisoners. Nazi guards followed them at all times, and for added emphasis, their boss, Mr Weber, literally reminded them of their subservient positions by talking down to them from his veranda.

Chaim relayed what his boss said:

"Yuden Ihr solt wiesen das Ihr seit jetzt in sin Arbeitslager und ihr must arbeiten gantz schwer here," ("Jews, you should know that you are now in a labour camp and must work hard here. Anyone attempting to escape will be shot,") Mr Weber scolded.

He noticed that the non-Jewish Polish people who worked in the factory went to their homes every evening after work to have dinner and sleep. They were not forced to live on the crumbs the Jews had to subsist on, so they were never hungry.

Chaim remembered how they appealed to their Polish co-workers for help:

While we had been working there for three days, we knew that with this kind of food, we would not be able to exist.

Our Polish foreman, Mr Wdowik, watched us dig that ditch so that no-one should run away from work. We got acquainted with him right away and asked him about our food, explaining that it is very hard to work with this kind of food. He told us that we won't get any more food.

Chaim doubted many could survive such conditions. He did not know how they could sustain the tough physical regime with such poor rations – a single spoonful of a coffee substitute in the morning, a spoonful of soup at lunchtime and a small piece of a loaf of bread in the evening divided among eight men. It was meant to last until breakfast, but being so hungry, they devoured it immediately.

Returning to work after lunch, Chaim recalled his conversation with Mr Wdowik:

"Mr Wdowik, is there any possibility of buying any bread or something else to eat?"

"Yes, if you have money, I will try to get it for you to-morrow."

We said, "We will be glad to pay for loaves of bread."

"My wife will buy bread tomorrow and will bring it right on the job," he told us.

It was exactly as we wished. She carried that bread in a sack on her shoulder, and threw it down it into the ditch where we worked, then went away.

We paid her 16 zlotys beside the cost of the bread. We knew she had taken a big chance, for the Polish people had been ordered not to help any of the Jews. They kept it secret from other workers.

This extra money helped Wdowik to support his family, but he risked getting caught, and when Wlodarczyk, a Polish guard, spotted him, he was warned of severe punishment if caught again.

Wlodarczyk hated the Jews and would quite happily see them starve, so when he saw Mr Wdowik a second time, he reported him to the boss, Weber. Weber was equally afraid of Wlodarczyk, and warned them that Wlodarczyk is a killer.

Following that incident, Wlodarczyk entered their barracks early in the morning, well before they had left for work.

Chaim wrote:

That bloody Polack came in to see us, shouting, "You have to go to work!" and clubbing us over the head with a wooden stick. We ran to our boss, Mr Weber, who had become acquainted with us very quickly. He saw our work was complete and was satisfied with what we had done, but told us to be very careful and watch out for that Polish murderer.

The factory commanders – Dalski, Battenschlager and Blau – instigated a reprisal killing after a prisoner was caught attempting to escape through the electrified fence. Up to 1,000 men and women were lined up in rows of four.

As Chaim described it:

They counted from one to 10 as they walked through the lines to select victims for the firing squad.

Meanwhile, Ukrainian Werkschutz [Plant protection force and concentration camp guards] *waited, machine guns in hand, ready for orders to shoot the 50 men who stood a few feet in front from us. And then they shot them with a machine gun, one by one. No-one could do a thing about it.*

Told to return to work, another order followed: If anyone else will try to escape, they will kill all of us.

Blau was Mr Weber's supervisor, and he was a sadist. Each morning, the Ukrainians and the Jewish police followed his orders, entering the school to beat them with sticks for no apparent reason.

The Hassag Factory was supposedly better than other factories because it had a steam bath. Once a week, Chaim and other inmates washed and steamed their clothes to remove the bugs. One year after they arrived, they received clothes taken from people incinerated at Dachau, Auschwitz, Buchenwald and Treblinka, but these made little difference as the bugs continued to crawl across their skin.

Chaim continued to describe their circumstances:

In spite of having a steam bath, it did not help a bit. The whole day we went around scratching ourselves, picking out lice and bedbugs.

The day that Blau came into the Ekonomia School, he told us: "Juden, get ready – we are going to Germany. Take all of your possessions."
We believed that to be true, but we were still shocked to learn the news. Everything we owned was grabbed. Of course, we did not have many things, but some people still had gold watches, rings, bracelets and other valuables. Besides those, nobody had any clothes or shoes to take.

Lined up outside in the yard, they were counted and told that trucks would come to pick them up from the factory, but this was just a trick. Later, Blau issued another order: "All of you Jews, do you have any golden watches, rings, bracelets or earrings? I have prepared a box for you to put all in. If anyone tries to hide anything, he will be shot on the spot."

Everyone did as they were told for fear of being killed. Then they returned to work.

Blau wanted the gold for their wives, but he also wanted to ensure none of them would have money to buy something to eat. This way they would get rid of the Jews faster.

The volume of gold collected from some 10,000 inmates in that camp must have been huge.

The 40 or so factories produced different types of ammunition, and they worked with 5,000 Polish people from various trades, mainly electricians, carpenters and plumbers.

Chaim wrote about this work:

We were doing mostly plumbing, but also had to keep the drains and sewers clean, working 10 hours a day, but occasionally we did a 24-hour day. After a while, we were transferred to the new barracks.

Chaim lived in Barracks No 62, one of the 100 barracks on site. The men who lived on one side of the row were forbidden from entering the women's barracks on the other side.

Chaim continued:

In that camp was a supervisor named Killiman, another murderer and a Volksdeutscher [those who had German language and culture, but were not German citizens]. *He was a short fellow with a big Shepherd dog. He had nothing to do with the factory, but controlled our food rations to make sure that we should only have bread, which he divided among us.*

Besides that, the Jewish Police worked for him, and followed orders to enter the barracks at 6 o'clock in the morning to send everyone to work, and to make sure no-one was hiding under the bed. Anyone found was beaten. It was terrible that one Jew had to beat up another.

The Jewish Police were well aware that the Germans would eventually treat them just as everyone else, despite their false promises of survival.

Chaim wrote more later:

My cousin ran away with a group of 200 people into a forest. They were all caught and shot, one by one. They would no longer suffer.

Trains often passed along the track about 200 feet from the camp, carrying elderly and the young. Small children were heard screaming, begging the Germans for water. The prisoners had no idea where they went, but Chaim knew they would never return.

Wlodarczyk's bullying got worse day by day, but Chaim took pleasure in writing this note:

One morning we came to work, and as usual waited in the shack for him to come soon to beat us up, but he did not appear. Then our foreman, Mr Wdowik, arrived, looking very happy.

"Mr Wdowik, why you are so happy today?" we asked him.

"Do you know, boys, what I am going to tell you?" he asked us in return.

"No, but we are sure that you must have some good news," we answered.

He smiled. "Wlodarczyk was killed last night. Partisans came into his house and shot him to death."

Every one of us started jumping for happiness. All of the Polish people were happy, and even Mr Weber wanted to see him dead. They had put 18 bullets into his head. He had wanted to see us killed, so he was punished from God.

Weber had always treated them well, but even he was afraid of Commander Blau.

Every Sunday, Blau visited the workshop to select people for the gas chambers, and whenever Chaim was chosen, Weber told him, "You will not take any of my men, including Chaim Goluchowski."

Chaim described the situation:

I was the lucky one. Six of us had worked for him three years. Other bosses took new men every two weeks, but Mr Weber secretly tried to help us whenever he had the opportunity.

Women worked at the machines making bullets, and sometimes poorly made bullets were thrown in the toilet, blocking the drain, so we had to clear toilet drains pretty nearly every day.

Blau and his colleagues, Dalski and Battenschlager, were murdering rapists. For their pleasure, they would pick six of the nicest girls from the women's barracks, rape them all night and shoot them in the morning.

The women were terrified, knowing they could be selected next time.

Killiman was a sadist, without pity for anyone. He searched the barracks hoping he would catch someone who had not gone to work. Anyone he disliked was called 'Kannarek'.

"Hey, Kannarek, you'll be killed tomorrow." And sure enough, that man was sent to Treblinka the following day. He took great pleasure in whipping or shooting a Jew. Every day he had his eye on someone else.

"Hey Kannarek, you will be shot today," he said as he pointed at the others. "You, you, you and you are going to be killed tomorrow."
For two and a half years we went through those threats, day after day.

Siegler, Chaim's friend, got caught stealing a pot of potatoes from the kitchen. Killiman decided to set an example by forcing Siegler to carry two bricks in each hand for several hours prior to his execution, then leaving his corpse to hang until they returned from work.

Chaim described the terror they felt on seeing him:

I shall never forget that incident, whatever I have gone through in all the camps. Killiman was the worst type of Nazi who hated Jews.

Chaim's cousin Mary worked at another factory, Work B, located about a mile from Chaim.

Chaim described her experience:

Mary had worked in Work B since she arrived. Every Sunday she came to the steam bath, so we got the opportunity to meet. Her boss was another Gestapo murderer, by the name of Schlicht. His helper was Laskowski, and she had to also wash his clothes and cook for him.

Every single morning, without exception, Schlicht inspected her work to check she had cleaned up his living space to perfection. He slid his hand across the furniture to ensure there was no dust and that it was perfectly clean.

She carefully hid leftover food in the garbage for friends to collect. When Schlicht found out, he pressed his pistol hard against her face, saying, "Mary if you are ever caught again, you will be shot like a dog." That was in the year 1944.

The Russian advance into Poland forced the Germans to retreat back towards Germany urgently.

Chaim wrote:

They first moved us to another camp closer to Camp B. That was also a very big camp. There was a line of barracks to one side, much worse than the one we left, and we now had to walk two miles to the workplace.

Human bodies had shrunk to skin and bone and become mere skeletons. Many died from starvation while others caught typhoid and dropped like flies. Corpses of men, women and children were piled in the road awaiting removal – all victims of the German policy *'Vernichtung durch Arbe-it'* (extermination through work).

Chaim recalled:

In that barrack, I was sleeping with dead people near me and over me, many dying from typhoid. It was terrible how many died.

We were there for a few weeks, still working in the same factory. After returning from work at night and on Sundays, we sat outside and cleaned ourselves of the lice.

The Germans were now in a hurry. They quickly dismantled the ammunition machines to shift the entire factory.

Mr Weber

Mr Weber was different to other Nazis. He treated Chaim's team respectfully from the moment they arrived at Skarzysko–Kamienna Camp, and he saved Chaim's life many times.

He did so again on another occasion when he arrived at the workplace on his motorcycle, and he heard Chaim scream, *"Don't shoot me!"*

He saw that the *Werkschutz* were holding a pistol pointed directly at Chaim's head, ready to fire.

"What happened here between you and the *Werkschutz?*" he asked, and then he told the *Werkschutz,* "You've no right to shoot without my permission."

"Because he was taking Kaiser buns home," they answered.

Mr Weber told him it was all right because the man was hungry, and he had given him permission to do it.

Chaim wrote:

I was very happy that he came just in time, before that trigger was pulled, for I could not have written my story about the Ukrainian murderers.

Mr Weber saved my life. He had saved me lots of times, but this would have been the last if he had not arrived when he did.

Mr Weber's home was located in a smart residential district surrounded by Nazi neighbours.

Weber had been their supervisor for three years – much longer than some bosses kept workers – and he also protected them. Occasionally, he took six of the prisoners to fix the garden and his wife provided their lunch.

Others were murderers who sent many workers to the gas chamber. Killiman showed surprising appreciation when Weber's team removed a concrete blockage in the drains after the superintendent had failed to remove it. Threatened with death, the superintendent's life was spared after they succeeded.

Chaim wrote:

Killiman was very happy and our boss was happy, too. We were given extra food and some fresh clothes.

As news filtered in about the Russians thrusting into Poland, the Germans fought on in the belief they could not possibly be defeated.

Sulejow, 1944

By June, the Germans were forced to retreat, so the prisoners were moved away from Skarzysko. Leaving camp after the morning roll call, 2,000 men were herded onto a train heading towards Sulejow, and then taken to the camp barracks located on the outskirts.

On the first night, they slept on straw bedding strewn across the barracks floor. Next morning, they were counted again. Chaim questioned how someone could be missing when Ukrainian guards surrounded them the entire time.

He wrote:

They gave us some morning coffee but nothing else, just the same as we got in Skarzysko, and then we were taken to work in the fields. The difference was that here we were digging ditches but nothing else. In Skarzysko, we only did the plumbing, and had just one foreman, Wdowik, who helped us buy some bread. In Sulejow, we were watched only by the Ukrainian murderers.

The Germans considered a three-mile-deep ditch as the best defence against the Russian invasion. Thousands of workers dug with their bare hands or used picks and shovels, only stopping for lunch after four continuous hours of gruelling work.

When they returned, the Ukrainians pushed them to work even harder, yelling, *"Schneller, Schneller, you farfluchter Juden!"* ("Work faster, faster, you cursed Jews!")

Chaim described their work conditions:

The beatings continued every minute until we returned home, and still we got the same supper every night – one loaf of bread for eight men and some coffee – that was all. For the rest of the evening, we sat outside on the grass.

Those ditches were so deep it was impossible to climb out alone. We had to pull each other out three, or four, times a day. The place was like a desert, with no water to drink while we worked. There was also no water in the camp where we lived, so we could not wash ourselves, and the whole day we were scratching from the lice, so it was tough to work properly.

Once every four weeks we were taken to a river. I had never swum and was afraid to enter the water, but got pushed in and nearly drowned. As a matter of fact, a few drowned.

When we got out of the river, the first thing they did was count us again. It didn't matter if somebody drowned, as long as the others did not run away.

German guns were aimed at them all the time – the Germans didn't care if someone was shot as they knew that those who could no longer work would be sent to the gas chamber.

Lieble Feldlaufer, Skoczlas and Weingarten, Chaim's close friends, were nearby. Weingarten's father had been shockingly murdered by a Pole in the street, his head chopped off with an axe.

Chaim also wrote about Germany's fear of the Russians' advance:

The Russians were moving quickly, and the Germans needed to protect themselves. The Ukrainians were also afraid, as they knew that if the Russians surrounded the Germans, they would be caught and the Russians would chop off their heads.

Now the Jews got even less food than they did at Skarzysko, and risked getting 50 lashes if they were caught digging up potatoes from the adjacent fields.

In September, the survivors were transported to the city of Czestochowa.

In Czestochowa

When they arrived, Mr Weber surprised them at the station, where they were happy to hear him calling their names: "Goluchowski,

Harding, Skoczylas, Feldlafer, Weingarten and you three Wagner brothers – you will work for me again."

Work commenced immediately. The machinery brought from the Skarzysko–Kamienna camp was installed and ready to use, and Mr Weber had procured the necessary plumbing materials to fit pipework throughout the camp. Once again, they were supervised by Wdowik, but they were still short of food.

Chaim described the situation:

The food was the same as usual, and more was urgently needed if we were to survive. Trains regularly came to collect ammunition and sometimes brought potatoes for the kitchen.

On one occasion, I stole a pot of the potatoes, but was caught by three Werkschutz. I was dragged inside a building and forced to lay down on the stairs. Each one whipped me. One, then the other, then the third – again and again and again. The brutality was horrendous. When they finished, I was told to stand up, but I could not. Finally, when I returned to the workshop, Weber asked, "What happened? You cannot walk!"

Chaim was warned to be more careful, and told that the next time, the punishment would be worse.

Two weeks later, I again pushed my wheelbarrow close to the train, and my friends half-filled it with potatoes. They told me, "Take them to the shop."

A Werkschutz ran after me, so I also ran and went straight into the shop, but he followed and raised his gun to strike. Mr Weber arrived at the same moment.

"What is the matter? What are you doing here in my shop?" he asked.

The Werkschutz told him I'd stolen potatoes.

Weber replied, "Get out of here. You have no right to come into my shop. You were put there to watch the train, and not here." And then he kicked him in the ass.

Weber told me to hide the potatoes in the basement. Again, he was the only kind German. The others were murderers.

We were thinking he must be a Jew, that probably the Germans didn't know and because he changed his name he was taken to the army, not to the front line because he was a master plumber, and they needed tradesmen in the factory – that's why he worked here.

Chaim thought Weber must be "pretty smart" – he was certainly aware they needed more food to survive and sustain their workload, and his hatred of the Ukrainian *Werkschutz* was reason enough to say, "I am the boss, not you. Now get the hell out of here."

The potatoes might have remained uncooked had Schindler, a master plumber, not had the ingenious idea of taking steam from heating pipes to cook them. Weber permitted them to connect a one-inch pipe to the distribution steam pipe, and within five minutes, one potato could be eaten. Then the pipe was disconnected to avoid suspicion.

Chaim sees Mary

Chaim, surprised to see Mary walk past the workshop, asked, "Mary, how did you come here?"

She said she had arrived at the same time he was taken to Sulejow, so this was a wonderful coincidence.

Chaim then asked her, "Where are you working now?"

"I am still working for Mr Schlicht," she replied.

Chaim described his reflections on this:

I was not happy, but there was nothing we could do about that. Schlicht brought her with him to Czestochowa because she was such an excellent cook, but his behaviour was now much worse. First thing in the morning, he scrubbed his hands after he killed someone to ensure he removed all traces of blood. But worst of all, she was forced to have sex with him, even though he was married, because she looked so beautiful.

Usually, the women were killed after he had had sex, but Mary was saved, not for her looks but because she was such an excellent cook.

[I was surprised to read such an intimate detail about Mary. The telling alone must have been very painful for Chaim.]

She also risked her own safety to bring leftover food for me.

One day Weber saw her and asked, "Who is that girl?"

She was young and very attractive. Weber did not object, but told me she must not be seen with food. After that, whenever she came, he looked in the opposite direction.

Many times, I visited her at the women's barracks. It was a big place, I don't recall exactly how many people, but probably about 5,000.

The Russians

The buzz of excitement quickly spread as the sound of bombing in the distance announced the Russian invasion. This meant the Jewish prisoners could finally pray that the nightmare was nearing its end. However, any euphoria felt was tempered by a sense of dread that the Germans might murder them in cold blood, and Mr Weber was visibly shaken.

Chaim described the scenario:

The Germans, and especially the Ukrainian murderers, were clearly scared and seemed not to know what to do with us.

After the usual morning roll call, we had to line up, six people in a row, and for the first and only time were each given half a loaf of bread, making us suspect something was wrong.

We had no idea where we marched until we arrived at a train and were ordered inside.

The Werkschutz quickly disappeared from view, and left the carriage doors wide open, but we remained inside for fear of being shot. Eventually, one or two crept outside and broke into a carriage loaded with bread and shared it out.

At around 3 o'clock, Chaim suggested to Lieble, "Let's run from here. Nobody is watching."

"No, we're not leaving," Lieble replied. "We will stay because the Russians are close by, and we will soon be free."

As it so happened, the guards reappeared well before they could taste any freedom.

Chaim continued his story:

We got stuck inside the train for three hours and then it started to roll forwards, and gradually moved faster and faster.

We had no food for four days and nights, and just got coffee, but that wasn't until the third day when we still had no idea where we went; the train had no windows, but shafts of light slipped through the cracks in the timber. This was not a passenger train – they would not put Jewish people in a passenger train. Instead, they put us like cattle in a truck. They knew we had stolen the bread and there was no more, nothing at all to eat.

Eventually the train stopped, and we were told to wait on the platform. Women got taken in one direction, and we were led in the opposite direction to a camp they called Buchenwald, and straight into a steam bath.

We were met by a great many barbers waiting to shave our heads and even our bottoms, and we remained naked for the whole four hours.

At Buchenwald

The Nazis amused themselves by handing out the wrong-sized striped clothing to everyone; big people got small sizes and small people were given large sizes.

Then, at dinner, the prisoners received just a tiny piece of bread with the usual bowl of soup, and were then taken to Barrack 52.

As Chaim grimly noted:

We heard that the 1,500 Jews left behind in Czestochowa camp were liberated by the Russians soon after we had left, while we suffered for another five months of hell.

The Jewish Police – Pantel, Tepperman, Friedman, Danziger, Formalski and Markowitz – were taken directly from the train to the crematorium. After a promise of immunity for their roles at the camps, they now shared the same fate as all the others.

Bunkbeds built from wooden slats had been stacked throughout the Barrack like shelves in open kitchen cupboards, with 1,500 men cramped into the space. They had to shove past one other to move around, with little space to sit.

Chaim described a typical day of harsh treatment:

It was impossible to sleep properly on the hard bed frames; four men had to share one bed and snuggled close just to keep warm. Two men had to share one blanket, and that was pulled from one side to the other all through the night, as both tugged at the edge. We had no pillows, not even a straw pillow, and I tore a strip off the blanket just to stop my toes from freezing.

"Raus Ihr ar luchter Juden!" ("Rouse, you cursed Jews!") This order came at four o'clock every morning, and we went outside to stand in rain, or snow or frost for at least two hours. It made no difference what kind of weather, they didn't care.

When we returned inside for a rest, we got no coffee or anything else at all. Then again, three or four times a day, we

*went back outside, and in between we collected dead bodies.
Each day was the same.*

*I would try to push my way to the centre of the group so I could
be surrounded by others, and so that the wind would not blow
at me. At every roll call, the Germans came in and beat us with
sticks over our heads, faces, noses, legs – wherever they could
reach.*

*At lunchtime, long lines formed as we queued to get our food.
Many fainted as we waited, sometimes as much as six hours for
a lousy little bit of soup that tasted more like clear water and a
piece of bread. You had to dive in fast to find one potato in the
soup; by the time we got that bread, someone was trying to grab
it away.*

*And then, moments after we returned to barracks to rest, the
German SS made another roll call: "Alle Juden antratten"
("All Jews stand up"), and so we stood for a further two hours.*

*What was the purpose of all of these roll calls when the
perimeter fence was electrified, guards stood in watch towers
spaced just a few feet apart, and our bodies were now mere skin
and bone? We had no strength to run, nor was there any way
out to escape.*

*Thousands of bodies littered the streets around them, and
although hundreds were burned each day, the ovens could not
take all of them, yet the Nazis constantly brought more victims
into the camp. Can you imagine what it was like to see so many
bodies, to stare at all these dead faces, to constantly be in fear
of recognising one?*

*We were so thin – like skeletons – that many of us even looked
like a dead body. Before someone ate his lunch, his tongue
stuck out from his mouth. There were men so hungry that they
pulled flesh from corpses.*

Chaim saw other prisoners exchange their piece of bread for a cigarette. Were they so desperate for a few puffs? He wondered. While he enjoyed the occasional smoke, he could never sacrifice his meagre rations, especially when there was so little else to eat.

His mind had been tormented over the past four years by the constant threat of beatings and death. He had prayed countless times that he would be dead to bring an end to his suffering. But the will to survive came from his dream that one day he would see the Nazi killers destroyed and revenge taken on those who murdered his family

The Gestapo, or maybe it was SS – at this stage, he could see little difference between the two, for they were all murderers – called out their numbers for the first time, but not the names, just the number. Chaim heard them call his number, 1498. This was six weeks after they had arrived in Buchenwald.

Five hundred prisoners were selected because they were the fittest; they were then marched to the train wagons. He was pleased that he was together with his friends, Naftalin Wagner, Skovzylas and Leible Feldlaufer on the journey to another unknown destination.

They only got food when they arrived on the third day. One eighth of a loaf of bread was handed out, and four days later, on 15 February 1945, they arrived in Friedberg, Germany.

At the camp in Friedberg

Chaim told of the prisoners' horrendous reception:

As we left the train at the stop in Friedberg, we had a 'nice' welcome. Three hundred SS were lined up in two rows, and we were forced to run between them as they whipped us until we could hardly move. Once reassembled, we were counted and sent to the barracks. We were so hungry we could hardly open our mouths when given a bowl of soup.

They had been surprised by the sight of newly built barracks, but had to cross a soft, muddy patch of ground to enter. Their shoes, now caked in thick mud, had to be cleansed by hand using stones before they were permitted to enter. Stones were used because there was no water even to wash themselves, so their hands remained filthy.

The construction of a new factory had already commenced deep inside a densely wooded forest, invisible to the Russians. The building was an identical design to the premises at Skarzysko, but new roads and railway tracks were needed to deliver the materials required for building works to start.

On the first morning, they were given just a small coffee before starting work.

Chaim wrote:

Three hundred SS waited for us, and again we had to run down their line as they whipped us hard around our heads and legs. Then, after they counted us, we walked half a mile to work. In front of us stood a stationary railway wagon filled with gravel.

Just like the Egyptian pharaohs, the Nazis treated the Jews as slaves. When one Jew died from exhaustion, he was simply replaced by another; it was an easy formula for the Nazis.

As Chaim described it:

We were divided into groups of eight. Four shovelled the gravel down onto the ground while the other four loaded it up onto a Lora – a smaller wagon used because large trains could not reach the site. With little room to work properly, we kept bumping each other as we swung around, and two bloody SS men watched us.

If the job was not right, they called us down, beat us and then we returned to work.

Once the Loras were filled, we pushed them wherever needed, accompanied by two Gestapo, and as we unloaded the gravel, they struck us with their guns. Our bodies were paralysed with fear at every strike.

"Why do you hit us, Sir?" Yet the more questions we asked, the more beatings we got. The Nazis were evil, hard as nails.

An empty wagon was much lighter without the heavy gravel, even with two Nazis seated inside. Once refilled, the Loras were pushed back to the site, refilled and pushed again to unload, backward and forward, until the job was completed some six weeks later.

Men were often pulled off wagons, beaten and whipped so hard that some committed suicide. Three men fell down onto the tracks in front of a train, which ran through them, sliced them in half and their blood was poured out like rain.

A clearing had to be created for the factory, so trees had to be removed and the logs were cut to provide railway sleepers. Chaim's job was to tie the end of a rope around a tree trunk while other trees were roped, then 30 men firmly held the ropes, and waited for the order – one, two, three. The ropes were pulled and they shook the tree as it fell to the ground.

"You, *farfluchter Juden,* cut off the branches with these axes!" The Nazis shouted. [The Jewish prisoners must have been tempted to strike the Nazis with the axes.]

The tree now had to be moved, so at the count of one, two, three, they raised the tree onto their shoulders and carried it about a quarter of a mile across an irregular surface. If someone moved too slowly, the load shifted and weighed down on the others.

Chaim described what happened then:

Whenever someone stepped lower than others, the load lay more heavily on the rest of them. The SS told us we were not carrying the tree properly.

After this happened a few times, we were told to lower the tree onto the ground, then the SS pointed at the man not carrying his weight, pulled him down to the ground and struck him for what seemed like 100 times on the back. Sometimes 10 men were picked at the same time.

It was very hard to carry that tree, and we were terrified most of the time. Once the beating stopped, everyone stood up: one, two, three.

"Pick up the tree, onto your shoulder – now carry it properly!" the guards shouted.

Sometimes the prisoners were ordered to strike each other, but no-one wanted to do it. Chaim was whipped for refusing to comply, but he felt helpless.

He told of the trauma:

In that time, we had done so much work it was unbelievable. We were all kinds of tradesmen: electricians, carpenters and plumbers. Whatever you could mention, they had. All were Jewish people.

Then, we had to build the road. First, we carried the stones and laid and paved the road by hand. They never had machines to do the job, and the minute we put down one stone, that bloody SS man said: "This is not the right way, turn it around, Farluchter Jude."

I was struck around the head until I put it the way they wanted. The SS were young and strong like well-fed horses, with the strength to beat us all the time and with an urge to destroy us completely.

Facing our barracks was a large tree. One day we returned from work and saw through the window a man tied to the tree – he had been left to stand for 24 hours until he was dead, but there was nothing we could do to help him. We were not even allowed to leave the barracks.

Chaim reflected:

Where is God? He sees a man bound to a tree in freezing weather and no-one could help him.

This was his only reference to religion in 120 pages.

Passover comparison

The book we read at Passover, the Haggadah, includes a verse that chronicles the Egyptians' treatment of the Jews – words that relate equally to the Nazis:

'And the Egyptians/**Nazis** were terrible to us. They made us suffer and gave us hard work. The Egyptians/**Nazis** set task masters over the children of Israel for them to undertake severe work and they built Pithem and Raamses as store cities for Pharoah/**Hitler**. And Egyptians/**Nazis** made the children of Israel do back-breaking work'.

The killing of male babies by the Egyptians was an early example of genocide – a policy the Nazis implemented with methodical severity.

The return to Buchenwald

The stress of six weeks' hard labour and physical abuse finally exhausted Chaim until he had little strength to continue.

In his own words, he wrote:

They wanted to take out the weakest, and just keep the stronger ones. We stood in line and waited as the SS pointed at the men to step out.

I hid myself not to be picked, but finally a finger pointed directly towards me. I was sure they will send us to the gas chambers, and I nearly died on that spot as I fell to ground. Two hundred of us were selected to leave.

"You are going to the gas chambers. You are dead anyway. We need people who are producing work. We cannot afford to feed those not working," the guard announced.

Graphic images formed in my mind from reading of Chaim's haunting descriptions of the real things that happened to real people. So much Nazi abuse was stuffed into his memory bank: the hatred, constant threats, the beatings from guns or whips or sticks, the gallows, the torment from the moment they left barracks each morning, and then the starvation.

How on earth did these fragile bodies find such inner strength to recover overnight, to start the same routine and go through the same abuse every day and then survive that relentless harm over so many years? Yes, they had willpower, but they were also empowered with a determination to take revenge. I doubt whether any of us can really visualise such a journey.

Chaim was too weak even to climb onto the wagon car, so he rested by the side until eventually a ramp was fitted, then immediately collapsed onto the wagon floor.

He recalled the next steps:

It took us four days with the train – we did not get anything to eat at all, not even one drop of water.

Finally, we arrived at the Buchenwald camp, thinking they will take us straight to the gas chambers. I don't know to this day why they didn't do it. Probably they could not burn so many people at once.

As a matter of fact, as soon as we stepped down from the train, we saw hundreds of dead people on the ground, so that's probably the reason.

When the Jews were taken to be fed, many struggled to open their mouths when they were given a bowl of soup and a small piece of bread.

Chaim described his job of collecting the dead bodies:

They made us pick up those dead bodies, put them on wagons and push them to the ovens where they burnt the bodies. I was lucky I did not work in the ovens because it was difficult for me even to throw a dead man onto the wagon.

But we had no choice, we had to do it every day. Because so many bodies lay on the streets, there was little room for us to walk. Every day, more transports of people arrived.
How many barracks there were, I don't remember. I figured that my barrack number was 52, so there must have been at least double that number. We prayed and hoped that the day will come when we can take our revenge on the bloody SS.

"It was difficult for me to even throw a dead man onto the wagon" – such powerful words expressed the pain from those traumatic memories.

Yet Chaim saw more than slaves murdered by the Nazis. He saw what was now only skin and bone, but had begun life as crying babies, then grown into children than ran in the streets and kicked balls around the park, and then grew up and had lovers and spouses before they bore their own offspring. They had carried their own ambitions inside them until every particle of their lives was stolen by the Nazis. Now they were left as anonymous corpses, with no spouse or child who could be there to bury them, to say a Kaddish or to light the Yahrzeit candle. Here, they just lay lifeless on the road, awaiting collection.

"Thus, the dust returns to the ground as it was, and the spirit returns to God who gave it." (Ecclesiastes 12:7)

A wagon loaded with corpses stands outside
the crematorium in Buchenwald

Chaim continued:

Although it was still winter, the sun had begun to get higher in the sky, but it was still freezing cold in the barracks. We lay on those cold boards at night with nothing to cover ourselves, and still the roll calls continued every two to three hours, night and day.

Black columns of smoke funnelled out of the chimney as the toxic stench of burning skin and sulphurous odour of burnt hair that filled his lungs could be smelled miles away. The weakest prisoners were brought to the camp to die and be incinerated.

Next morning, the guards began with the usual roll call: *"Alle Juden antratten in the reien!"* [All Jews line up.]

No-one there could possibly know who was missing, but they continued giving the roll call anyway. It seemed as if they just wanted prisoners to stand in the freezing cold, so they could walk among them and strike out with an elbow to break someone's teeth.

Despite this treatment, the Jews knew they were better off than at Friedberg, where they likely would have never survived.

Preparing to leave

All 10,000 Jews were assembled on the big lot and left outside for six hours. They had to wait until noon without food, surrounded by hundreds of the Gestapo (or whoever they were).

As Chaim described it:

To me, SS and Gestapo were the same. Their sole plan was to destroy us before the war ended, but [they] were unable to finish here because the Americans were already close by.

Bombing had destroyed the railway tracks, so they could not take us by train. They still had to get us to the nearest station, but it was 10 miles away.

Casting his head around to be sure no-one watched, Chaim slipped away from the lot.

He looked for a hiding place where he could wait for the Americans' arrival, and soon discovered a building he did not recognise. It was not really a surprise, since no-one had ever had the strength to go very far, but he felt much safer as he walked inside.

He described his attempt to hide:

I found a door right next to a vestibule and walked straight into a large workshop, I saw that the vestibule ceiling was lower than elsewhere and thought that it might be a good place to hide.

It was so quiet I really believed I was quite safe, until I heard the front door being opened and then I got scared, especially when I heard lots of people walk inside. It got worse when I sensed that someone had climbed the ladder. I nearly fainted because I thought it was a German who had come to kill me, but it was a Pole. He pulled me down to the floor and struck my back so hard with a hammer that he nearly knocked out my lungs, which caused me to suffer pain for years after, but I was lucky not to be killed.

Finally, I managed to escape from the hundreds of Poles now inside the building.

Chaim knew he had been extremely fortunate to survive the attack. He ran back to join the lunch queue, praying that he had not been noticed.

The Nazis tried to apportion 30 containers of soup to feed 10,000 people, but it took so long that everyone became impatient and eventually surged forward, pushing the tables over and spilling the soup. The SS fired angrily into the crowd and killed many while others got beaten. But no-one got anything to eat.

The death march

The Germans were now well aware that the war was lost but still continued to follow orders and destroy all evidence of their atrocities pursuing Hitler's 'final solution', which meant the murder of every last Jew. As this was not possible to achieve in Buchenwald, they had to march the Jews to the nearest station, which was 10 miles away. The Nazis termed this an 'evacuation march'.

Chaim continued:

We started marching through Buchenwald and into a forest, and soon we heard the first shot. I walked together with my friend, Leible Feldlaufer, and I asked him, "Did you hear a shot?"

"Yes," he replied, "it looks like they will kill us in that forest."

As soon as someone got tired, he was shot where he lay.

As we continued to march, more shots were heard all the time.

Another friend walked close by my side.
He said, "Chaim... I can't walk anymore."

I tried holding his arm for a short distance, but I was too weak to continue and also afraid for myself. The minute he fell to the ground, the SS shot him right on that spot.

Lieble was tall and strong like a horse – unlike me, for although I was strong, I was much smaller and felt so weak I could not believe I would complete that trip. But eventually, I managed to walk the 10 miles to the station.

That shooting was just like thunder – people were shot because they could not walk anymore or were just too slow. I was just happy that I did not hear that shooting any more.

The 10 miles we walked were covered with Jewish blood. How can I ever forget that? That I walked over my own blood, over my brothers' blood. There were no women, only men.

Packed inside the wagon like sardines, 100 of them were cramped so close together they could hardly breathe, and were constantly watched by SS guards at the front and rear. Bodies swayed in every direction. Those in the middle, who were pushed around like footballs, were the first to die. They had to wait two and a half days before they got any coffee or bread. How did it feel to get food finally and be unable to eat, just swallow?

Chaim continued:

British and American planes bombed alongside the tracks as the train continued, and we were lucky not to be hit. We thought it was because the pilots knew we were prisoners.

When the train stopped the next day, we had the usual food, while the Nazis removed dead bodies to somewhere outside, and so the wagons got emptier. On the third day, we were taken to another train that was completely open, but people still died like flies.

Eight days later, the train's route was blocked by a broken rail track that had been badly damaged by Allied bombing.

It came to a halt just by a railway station.

It would take several days for the repair work to be completed. A welcome change in weather conditions brought heavy rain that provided much-needed drinking water, and then once the sun appeared, they were permitted to step down from the carriages.

Spring leaves flourished on an abundance of trees. The mere sight started a stampede of starving prisoners, who grabbed edible leaves from low branches until every single leaf had been devoured.

Chaim continued:

Those who climbed to the higher branches were fired on and many were killed. Blades of grass that we picked could not be eaten raw, so we built a fire from small pieces of wood and cooked in our bowls using water gathered from the rain puddles, even though we were not permitted to do that.

Hundreds of helpless prisoners were murdered at this station alone. Those who climbed a tree to grab leaves were shot as if it were a game, while others died from hunger and thirst. It made the Germans very happy not to waste a bullet. How shocking was that?

Four days later, the Germans prepared to continue the journey. It mystified Chaim when Jews were ordered to stand on one side of the platform, for he knew for certain that only Jews had started this journey. But later he learnt that the others were Polish, Russian, Hungarian and Romanians prisoners who had arrived on a different train and also faced extermination.

Forced to stay out of view as the train continued on its journey for another four days, so they laid low on the wagon floor, watched by two SS guards. Anyone who raised their head was shot.

The prisoners travelled for a total of 14 days and nights. They were soaked by the rain and were given little sustenance.

Their war is over: 5 May 1945

We had no idea where they took us, and it was still dark when the train stopped around 3 o'clock in the morning. We knew something had happened because it was strangely quiet, and so one or two took a chance and stood up.

"Chaim, do you know what?" one asked.

"No," I answered.

"I think the SS have gone, and nobody is here anymore," he said.

The others then stood up quickly, even those with difficulty found the strength to stand to see what was happening. The SS had indeed disappeared, and no-one watched us.

Shortly after daybreak, Czech Police appeared around the train. "You are free. The war is over," they told us.

These were seven words we had been so desperate to hear for so long, but we had at times lost all faith in survival.

From that moment, we were free from those murderers. No-one in the world could believe it was finally over. All of us jumped up and down with joy in the train. The police told us we were in Czechoslovakia, and when we heard voices singing the Russian anthem, I could not believe it myself.

But the truth was, Chaim never really gave up his hope of survival, even during his darkest moments.

The Czechs gave them food before taking them to a large, empty building called Hamburger Kaserne.

Chaim continued:

Our rescuers were disorganised on that first day, with nowhere near enough food for everyone. So, being hungry, we searched the building and found some sacks of corn in a storage room. Close by, we spotted coal-burning ovens and a cooking pot, so took it in turns to cook the corn, but before my turn came, I fainted from hunger and was taken to hospital by a Russian ambulance.

First, they gave me a shower, then I was carried to the second floor of a different building and left with 200 other men. We had to lay on the floor as there were no beds, but we were fed soup and one Kaiser bun there right away, which was very nice, but I was still very hungry.

Meanwhile, many died from diarrhoea and other sicknesses, keeping the ambulances so busy they could not attend to everyone.

On the second day I already felt better, and wandered outside to see what is happening on the road. Hundreds of trucks stood abandoned along the highway; being so hungry, I took a cup of soup from a cooking truck, but it was poisonous from standing in the sun and I chucked it. Others didn't care as they were starving, and a few died from food poisoning.

Finding a piece of bread inside an open truck made Chaim feel like a new person, and thankful that his prayer to sit at the dinner table again and slice his own bread had finally been answered.

Learning that new ovens in Theresienstadt had been built specially to exterminate the remaining Jews, he realised how lucky they had been that the Allied bombing had destroyed the rail track, for had they arrived any sooner, they would be finished. It was truly a miracle they survived.

Chaim continued:

This was the city of Theresienstadt, and being liberated was the biggest day in my life. No-one would have believed 14 days ago that we would have such a miracle, that we would survive after all and be free from those murderers who killed so many innocent Jewish people. Many who had dreamed the day would come to be free were unable to be there.

From the 10,000 people who left Buchenwald, only 500 survived. One day longer and we also would not have survived.

Within a few days, Chaim was taken to a second hospital – not a real hospital, but a large hall filled with 500 beds where they were well-treated by the Russian doctors and nurses.

Chaim described this:

At the beginning, they did not give us so much to eat – they were afraid that if we ate too much we will die. In spite of that, we sneaked into the open kitchen at night to steal food.

The Russians were going slowly with us because people were still dying from dysentery, diphtheria and other infections. We were fortunate they took care of us.

Chaim remained in the hospital for about five weeks. Eventually he recovered his health and was discharged as a free man.

He wrote more later:

I have been here until the Russians dismissed me and I already felt much better.

The Russians surrounded the German murderers in Theresienstadt and killed them like dogs. Many others escaped to Canada, Argentina, Brazil, Spain, the United States and the Middle East, where they continue to agitate the rest of the world against the Jewish people.

Final note

In the Book of Exodus, Moses was called to free the Jews from slavery. He was told this was so that *"you may remember the day of your going out from Egypt all the days of your life".*

"Never again!" we say of the Holocaust, yet nearly a million Tutsi people were murdered in the Rwandan genocide of 1994.

I have re-read Chaim's life story so many times that I have often sensed his ghost at my side, watching as I adapted his words, and imagined his voice whispering the following in my ear:

"You can't leave that out, it's too important."

"Okay, change it if you must."

"Do you have any idea of the pain I went through? The experience and then the struggle to write it all down, and express how I really felt!"

"Mary was so beautiful when she was young, slaving for that murdering Nazi…."

"What will my family think when they finally read it?"

While Chaim's memoir began with the words "Altogether, we are a family of 10," at the end, it was only he, along with his wife Mary, who survived. [There is no record of how he found her.]

Morris: killed 1939, in Moszek.

Max: killed 1940, in Majer.

Leah: killed 1942, in Treblinka.

Kelman: killed 1942, in Lagow.

Josef: killed 1943, in Lodi ghetto.

Harry and Jacob: disappeared without trace, presumed dead.

Mattie: emigrated to Canada in 1929.

Chaim and Mary: married in Stuttgart, Germany in 1946. They sailed to Canada from Cuxhaven Port in October 1948 on the "SS Samaria" with their daughter Esther.

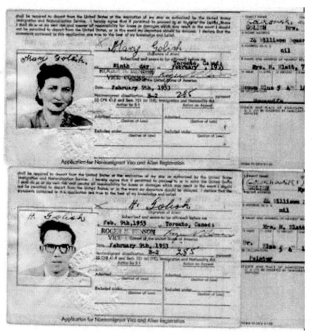

The non-immigration visas Chaim and Mary
used to visit the USA in February 1953

I was surprised to see Chaim's birth and death dates inscribed on his gravestone in Hebrew, and not English, since his only mention of religion had been, *"Where is the God that permitted a thing like this to happen?"* [apart from the mention of a few prayers].

Ken told me that his parents retained their religious beliefs throughout the Holocaust, and lived their lives as religious Jews after the war. His brother, equally religious, had arranged the gravestone to reflect this faith.

That first Shabbat must have been highly emotional, as Chaim pushed open the synagogue doors to hear the once-familiar sound of a Chasan's melodic voice and listened to morning prayers he had not heard in six years. The Torah scrolls were held high as the sound of Hebrew chanting brought tears of joy, and he could finally say a Kaddish prayer for their murdered families.

Revenge?

The Nuremberg Trials were held between October and November 1946. During these, 22 Nazi criminals were tried in the city of Nuremberg for crimes connected with the Holocaust.

A total of 12 defendants were sentenced to death; three received life imprisonment; four received prison terms; and three were found innocent and acquitted of all charges. In all, 199 defendants were tried at Nuremberg; 162 were convicted and 37 were sentenced to death.

The subsequent Nuremberg Trials tried other major war criminals of lower ranks than those in the original trial. Six judges from Great Britain, France, the Soviet Union and the United States presided.[15]

The number of Nazis convicted of crimes in the Second World War is so low – there must have been many others who escaped, and were never caught and tried.

According to Mary Fulbrook, a professor of Germany History at University College London, the number of suspects that have been brought to trial is a tiny percentage of the more than 200,000 perpetrators of Nazi-era crimes.

"It's way too late," she told CNN of the latest trials. "The vast majority of perpetrators got away with it."

Chapter 6

THE WOLMAN FAMILY

Introduction

My maternal grandparents joined the mass exodus from Russia in the early 20th century, when many Jews fled, desperate to escape poverty and anti-Semitic pogroms.

My grandfather Isaac left first in 1912 – one of 100,000 Jews escaping Eastern Europe at that time. My grandmother Ethel followed in 1914, just before the German invasion.

Starting a new life in London was a major challenge for them – their first language was Yiddish, so they had to learn to speak English. Hearing the endearing Yiddish words *Bubba* and *Zaida*, which translate to grandma and grandpa, revives strong family memories.

Isaac

Isaac, aka Zaida, was an archetypal grandpa – he was a natural prankster, especially in the eyes of a seven-year-old Barrie.

Born in February 1884, Isaac was raised in Grodno, one of the oldest Jewish communities in Lithuania, which was at that time part of the vast Russian Empire. Although Grand Duke Witold granted rights to Lithuanian Jews in 1389[16], these made little difference over the long term, as many Jews were still expelled in 1495 and children were kidnapped for forced conversion in 1616. But eventually, because the Lithuanian Jews had contributed to the local economy substantially, this helped to improve relationships somewhat.

By 1887, 80% of the local commercial undertakings were owned by Jews.

Vast numbers of Lithuanians had emigrated to the United States in the latter part of the 19th century due to a lack of development and job opportunities, as others left to work in the industrial towns of Riga and St Petersburg.

Ethel

Ethel Kirszenbaum was born in July 1882 in Kielce in the southeast of Poland. Her eight siblings included Raizl (the mother of Chaim Goluchowski), and Chaya Sarah (the great-grandmother of Genevieve Pasternak [de Cointet], whose story is told later.)

The so-called 'Royal Privilege'[17], whatever that was supposed to be, prohibited Jewish settlement in Kielce in 1535, but the Jews still tried to return. However, the small number that had settled in 1833 were expelled in 1847.

By the time Ethel was born, the Jewish population of Kielce was 2,600, but it is difficult to comprehend why Jews persisted in living in a place where they were clearly not wanted.

Since Ethel and Isaac lived 340 miles apart, their marriage on 27 Tishri 5666 (Thursday 27 October 1905), was probably 'arranged' by a matchmaker.

Their *Ketubah* [Jewish marriage certificate] reads: *The Chatan, Chaim Avraham Yitzhak ben Berck, married Etel, daughter of rav Eliezer, a Maiden/ virgin, just after Succoth and at the end of the High Holiday period.*

In those days, a marriage consummation was expected to take place immediately after the service; in order to verify the bride's virginity, the bloodied sheet was brought out for all to see. It seems a barbaric, humiliating act for young couples to have to go through; whether or not my grandparents went through it, I don't know.

Isaac and Ethel's journey to London

Isaac travelled alone in 1912 to find a job and make a home for the family in the East End of London. He almost certainly caught the train to Gdansk, Poland, and then boarded a crowded ship, disembarking a few days later.

He had to send money to Ethel for her to pay her bills, so he wrapped cash inside layers of brown paper and posted it, and she saved enough to pay for her passage to join him in 1914.

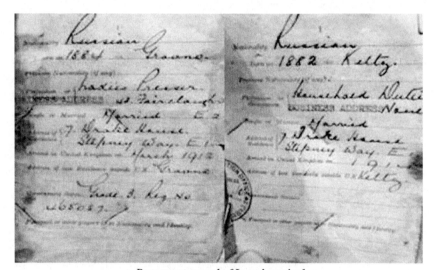

Document record of Isaac's arrival
in the UK in 1912 and Ethel's in 1914

Ethel's journey to London was cumbersome. She was bringing three young daughters; a one-year-old Mariam (Mary), three-year-old Leah, and seven-year-old Lieber, plus their luggage and her precious *dak* – an enormous, bulky, white-cotton bed cover packed with the finest-quality Polish/Hungarian goose down –the perfect hiding place with which to screen Leah from the ticket collector.

These strange bed covers were unknown in England until one romantic evening when, allegedly, Terence Conran discovered them:

In the 1950s, before the halcyon days of the Swinging Sixties,
Terence Conran was in Sweden, and found himself lying under

a strange cover – a bit like an eiderdown but with no sheets or blankets between him and it. Years later, he became the first person to sell duvets in Britain, in his new shop on the King's Road.[18]

The Wolmans in London

Pregnant Jewish mothers back home usually took it for granted that family would help with childbirth, but in London, Ethel's husband was the only family available.

Medical resources were sparse. Doctors and nurses were urgently required for the war effort and the Spanish Flu epidemic; as a result, it was mostly uncertified and untrained midwives, aka 'handywomen', who helped the needy, despite their supposedly being outlawed. The working-class community in London had little choice; these women were much less expensive and were also more available for employment.

Therefore, one such 'handywoman'[19] helped with the birth of my mother Rachel at their home in Christian Street, Whitechapel, in August 1918. Wally, the youngest, was also born at home two years later in November 1920. Another baby did not survive.

Two months after Rachel was born, at 11:00am on the 11th day of the 11th month of 1918, Germany surrendered, thus bringing the First World War to an end. By then, 65 million mobilised forces had fought in the war, and 25 million had died.

Rachel, my mother

The end of the First World War hostilities saw the start of the peaceful life the family had relished when they first came to London – a peace that continued for the next 21 years.

Educated at the local senior school, Rachel excelled in the English class, and easily made classroom friends.

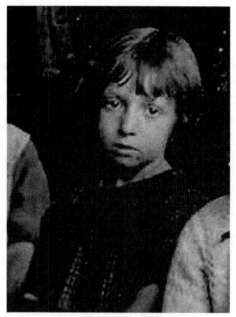

Rachel, about six years old

Rachel in class, second row, fifth from the left

Lilly Coffer was one of Rachel's childhood friends. She frequently drove to Brighton on hot summer Sundays during the 1950s, bringing her family to spend a day on the beach. My mother dragged me along when they met on the pebbles for a chinwag.

Rachel in 1933, aged 15   *Rachel shopping with Lilly*
in London's West End

The family on Margate Beach, circa 1935

Cable Street

Cable Street, in the East End of London, was originally a long, narrow path, the standard length of hemp rope, where workmen twisted hemp into long cables [ropes], that were then sold to ship captains moored in the Pool of London. Hence the path acquired the name 'Cable Street'. [20]

The Pool of London, circa 1938

East End home

Christian Street, a side turning off Cable Street, was transformed into a hub of Jewish life by immigrant tailors. It featured delicatessens and kosher restaurants reminiscent of the streets of Poland.

For the Wolman family, this familiar way of life was now so much more enjoyable, especially with their three daughters working in the business – that is, until their peace was disturbed in the early 1930s with the ugly face of fascism.

The political disruption of the 1930s coincided with Hitler's ascent to power; his introduction of toxic anti-Semitic race laws became their worst nightmare. They worried about the families they had left behind.

The rise of fascism and anti-Semitism in the UK

Sir Oswald Mosley did not earn his title; it was hereditary, inherited from his father on his death. This anti-Semitic leader of the fascists led the fight for fascism in Britain.[21]

Four years after being expelled from Sandhurst Military Academy, he was elected Conservative MP for Harrow. Then, in 1931, he founded the fascist 'New Party'. Joining forces with other UK fascist movements in 1932, the party became the 'British Union of Fascists', using the slogan 'Fascism can and will win Britain'.

UK Jews were horrified when both the *Daily Mail* and the *Daily Mirror* national newspapers backed these fascists, and even more so when the *Daily Mail* published an article with the banner 'Hurrah for the Black-shirts!' The then-*Daily Mail* owner, Lord Rothermere, had befriended both Hitler and Mussolini, so while the headline was shocking it was not unsurprising.[22]

Mosley's creation of the Fascist Defence Force [aka the Black Shirts] – a corps of a black-uniformed paramilitary troops inspired by his visit to Italy to meet Mussolini's Italian Fascists – was the largest-ever organised anti-Semitic force in Britain and a serious threat to the Jews.

As anti-Semitism was the main thrust of Mosley's manifesto, life for Jews in London hit rock bottom when arrogant gangs of Black Shirts roamed East End streets seeking to molest Jews physically, reminiscent of the violence simultaneously being perpetrated by Nazis in Germany.

Mosley was passionate in his drive to change English politics to align with Nazi Germany. Five thousand Black Shirt supporters followed him down Cable Street on 4 October 1936, marching to celebrate the party's fourth anniversary, and to canvas others to join his evil forces, intimidating the Jews who barricaded streets to block their way.

A plaque commemorating the Battle of Cable Street

One such barricade was positioned at the corner of Christian Street, close to the Wolmans' home. Violent hand-to-hand fighting erupted, Mosley's car was attacked with bricks and a London tram was even used as a barricade.

Irish dockers joined the Jews in solidarity because of their support during their strikes of 1912, and helped by ripping up paving slabs to add to the barricades.

The fascists soon discovered they had underestimated the power of the Jewish, Irish, Communist and Trade Union communities who spurred their cohorts with the slogan, 'Mosley shall not pass!'.

Mosley was eventually forced to give up and run after nearly 300,000 people on the streets had collectively rejected the presence of the Black Shirts.

Mosley's Nazi wedding

Mosley's blatant relationship with the Nazis was exposed two days later when he secretly married Diana Mitford in Joseph Goebbels' Berlin home on 6 October.[23] Adolf Hitler was the guest of honour at the wedding. Goebbels, Hitler's most devoted associate, was renowned for his deeply virulent anti-Semitism, which called for harsh discrimination and full extermination of the Jews.

These evil people were all inextricably linked. God help us if Mosley had succeeded in Britain, but both he and his wife were detained in May 1940 under the Emergency Powers Act, and interned for the duration of the war.

A difficult time for my grandparents

It is impossible to imagine the living hell my family went through. They had run from a country rampant with anti-Semitism to make their home in a safer environment, and now they had to worry how the British would respond to the rise in fascism. But at the very least, it did provide them with the opportunity to join the fight and not be mown down by machine guns.

I would love to know how my 18-year-old mother responded to this event being right on her doorstep. Sadly, that is yet another story we never discussed together.

Moving in response to the war

The Second World War broke out in September 1939, but the first bombs did not fall on London until August 1940, and the resulting bomb damage was intense. Families had to be rehoused time and again, often to different parts of the country, and it was no different for the Wolman family.

Sometimes the properties they moved to were uninhabitable; on one occasion, my family had to be relocated again because the slum flat they were given in Bethnal Green was immediately classified as 'dilapidated'.

They first moved to Northampton, then to Nottingham, then to Stepney and then finally to their own home in Old Coulsdon, Surrey.

The workshop

The sound of clattering Singer sewing machines reverberated across the battle-worn wooden floor in their workshop in the East End of London to flow down the timber steps as we slowly climbed the steep staircase, pushing me as a young seven-year-old even harder to scramble up to the first floor.

Finally, I had arrived, feeling very excited to see my family working in this much-talked-about hub – the workshop.

As the 'Music While You Work' programme blared live popular music continuously from the radio speaker, my two aunts Lieber and Leah laboured in their flowery aprons, and my *Zaida*, tape measure draped around his neck, pressed dresses.

Machinists pedalled and cotton threaded through timeless Singer sewing machines as a buttonhole maker worked close by and my uncle Usher leaned against a large wooden table as he cut fabrics. Right behind him was the small kitchen, fitted with a miniature electric stove to make food and tea.

Lieber was the brain behind the business; she and my *Zaida* started the workshop together as 'Outworkers to the dress trade'. Their job was to convert rolls of fabric into clothes, primarily for retailers.

Clients provided the roll of material together with a template for the dresses. The workshop was paid a fixed sum to manufacture a certain number of garments from that roll.

Usher guided the thin wedge of white chalk along the outline of a template to mark the pattern onto the fabric. His special skill was the ability to elicit more garments than ordered from the roll. Any surplus garments were then sold to private customers, often bringing much-needed additional revenue. If the client ordered 12 garments and Usher extracted 14, the two extra garments were referred to as 'the cabbage'.

Sewing machine typically used in workshops
(Photographed at the Jewish Museum, London)

Tailor's chalk

Dressmakers in a typical 'outworker' workshop

The Wolman family's trading difficulties, noted by Wally

Wally's wartime letters and diaries provide an insight into the family's financial difficulties at this time. His letter of 2 October 1941 as below is an example:

My dear family,

Unsettled, appears to be the gown business condition, for each report I get contradicts its predecessor.

Perhaps I will be so fortunate to learn from your next letter of the seasons really having started in full swing.

When you mentioned having sold more of our own made-up stuff, I gaily pictured your having sold it to some retail shop but as it is, provided the cash is O.K. there is cause for congratulation.

Is it not possible that another manufacturer would be interested in our cheaper type of good work? Failing mutual satisfaction might there not be someone in the West End with whom we can commence business? Is Lustigman a thing of the past? What of E.G. Myers & their two pieces?

I cannot believe that Mr M.P. is dropping Mr Gold for he has oft times made the same statement. Why is it that the other P's are not giving you much work?

In a diary entry from 29 December 1941, Wally mentioned that he was:

Concerned both over the difficult straits my family find themselves in and the way they appear to be worried over me.

In another letter, dated March 1943, Wally wrote:

Dear family,

Perhaps by now Lieber has got the 'gen' on 'the racket'. If she has, you know I am very interested.

About that dress for Harry's aunt, I leave the matter in your very capable hands. Harry's aunt wants a dress, if you can do so profitably, do so, otherwise I shouldn't be too concerned about it.

You seem to have your hands full and more at the workshop. Let the manufacturers do the worrying, you just carry on like normal human beings by which I mean I hope you are not working outside of normal hours.

Before the books are next brought up to date, I should like to offer some advice. Perhaps I shall be able to get some leave in a month's time, at which time I will advise you.

From left to right: Mary, Bubbah Ethel, Lieber, Rachel, Leah, Wally (seated) and Zaida Isaac, circa 1925

Coulsdon

The house in Old Coulsdon Village remained the Wolman family home until it was sold in 1953. After that, my favourite childhood holiday place was gone.

Memories are etched in my mind from the happy times when I was dumped there while my parents gallivanted on their holidays.

I was probably eight or nine when I ventured alone down to Coulsdon town, bought a white balsawood model airplane kit in Woolworths, assembled it back home, then wandered for over one mile through Hillside Road and the back streets to reach the Farthing Downs, where I played with my imaginary fighter aircraft on the hills – I would have been only a distant tiny figure just about visible from the house.

The Luftwaffe had flown at a low level across the same hills just a few years beforehand to avoid detection. No-one today would permit a young child to enjoy such an adventure alone.

Lychgate entrance outside 76 Marlpit Lane

Shirley, my first cousin

Shirley was my mother's niece, my first cousin. She had lived in the Wolman family home in Old Coulsdon from 1941 when she was six years old. The house remains instantly recognisable from the old quaint 'Lychgate' on the corner with Hillside Road.

Shirley shared her childhood recollections of living in the house with their large family:

Bubba and Zaida took the front bedroom downstairs, right next to the entrance door. The rest of the family slept upstairs. My room was the small bedroom immediately above the garage. I wrote homework seated up high on the fixed shelf of the small bay window and watched people walk along the road.

Mary helped keep house with Bubba, cooking together in the large kitchen/breakfast room at the rear with its expansive view of the Farthing Downs. A coal-fired boiler heated the hot water and made delicious toast. The living room, backed with a large glass-walled sun lounge, also faced the Farthing Downs, and got hot like a greenhouse so Zaida grew his tomatoes inside.

Hidden beneath the carpet, a trap door led down to our air-raid shelter, waiting to protect us if bombs fell. There were beds down there, and Zaida stored his cherry brandy in large clay jars. (This was fabulous and it smelt amazing.)

Auntie Leah got fed up hiding in the shelter, so stayed upstairs to watch the planes. Bombs rarely dropped in our proximity, but random bullets or maybe shells from anti-aircraft fire fell, and every morning she collected the remnants from the garden and around the house and threw them in the garbage bin.

We went for walks up on the Farthing Downs, and occasionally German planes flew over at low altitude to avoid detection, so we jumped into trenches very quickly until they had passed.

Zaida loved to nurture his fruit – the rhubarb, gooseberries, and redcurrants in the rear garden – and the vegetables – carrots, potatoes and lettuces. The gooseberries were particularly memorable.

Five chickens were kept in a pen he made, so we enjoyed freshly laid eggs most days. Then, every morning, Zaida and I chased after the milk horse and cart to shovel up the horse faeces [that's rounded balls of horse shit] into buckets and laid this beautifully smelly, fresh manure in the garden.

Shirley described what it was like for my grandfather and aunts to travel to work in London:

> *My parents worked in the East End so took the train every day, along with Zaida and Leah. Coulsdon South station was a ten-minute walk down the road, but slower on the way up because of the steep hill. From London Bridge Station, they caught a bus to the factory in Whitechapel.*
>
> *Well, it was more like a workshop, really. They were 'outdoor dressmakers' in Fairclough Street.*

Life in Old Coulsdon

Shirley also wrote about what life in Coulsdon was like for the Wolman family:

> *Like most other people, we never had a car. In the evening we stayed home and played cards – Chase the Ace or Bingo. In 1952 we got a tiny 9-inch TV, housed in a large wood cabinet, and lots of people came into our house to watch the Coronation of Elizabeth II.*
>
> *Neighbours viewed us with some suspicion, probably because so many of us lived in the one house.*
>
> *Other Jewish families lived nearby, so they arranged a Cheder [a Sunday school for Jewish children] in a local church hall in Coulsdon. The rabbi travelled from Croydon Synagogue to teach us, and so I met my now oldest friend, Frances Rabin.*
>
> *On special days we went to Croydon Market to shop for fruit and vegetables; kosher meat was bought from the butcher at the back end of a non-Jewish butcher shop and Zaida bought chickens from Hessel Street Market in the East End.*
>
> *Gordon Pirie, the runner, winner of the silver medal in the 1956 Olympics, lived close by, and was frequently seen jogging the local streets or up on the Farthing Downs.*

Synchronicity

According to Carl Jung, events that appear a coincidence are synchronised in a coming together that is difficult to explain. Such synchronicity showed with perfect timing at the first *Shiva* [mourning] service after my mother's death, for on the front cover of the prayer book handed to me to read the *Kaddish* memorial prayer was Lilly Cooper's name, the namesake of my mother's closest childhood friend had dedicated this book to the synagogue.

The coming together of those inner and outer events was extremely comforting.

Chapter 7

WALLY'S 1941 DIARY

Introduction

Regretfully, my mother and I never meaningfully discussed my uncle Wally Wolman. I do wonder why the act of sifting photographs with my grandchildren never prompted that discussion, but it didn't.

Just a few years before her memory began to recede, my mother asked if there was anything I wanted to know. Regretfully, being somewhat embarrassed by the question and suspecting she knew her memory was fading, I did not continue with the dialogue.

If I had only known about the RAF box then, we could have explored and discussed its contents together.

Cousins fighting the same war in different battlegrounds

First cousins Wally (20) and Chaim (25) faced the same enemy in different circumstances. Wally fought to defend his country, to defeat Germany and the Axis powers, while Chaim battled to stay alive in Polish concentration camps. But neither knew of the other's battles.

Wally

Wally was my mother's brother, the youngest of four older sisters born to Isaac and Ethel Wolman: Lieber (the eldest), Leah, Mary and my mother Rachel, who no doubt spoilt their newly born brother like crazy, for Wally, born on 7 November 1920, was the Wolman's only boy. I guess the nickname 'Wally' derived from his surname; his full name was Morris Louis Wolman.

Wally's name was rarely mentioned in our home, and sadly my grandchildren, although fascinated by his old black-and-white photographs, smartly dressed in uniform or flying the BT-13 basic trainer aircraft in America, never explored his history with their great grandmother. But then, neither did I.

However, my daughter once showed me the note she wrote while chatting to my mother about her life:

"Did you know about my brother?" my mother asked her. *"Such a waste. Such a lovely man. But let's not talk about sad things".*

Wally in uniform, 1940

Wally's conscription into the Royal Air Force (RAF)

Wally was 20 years old when his enlistment notice arrived in November 1940 with a postal order for four shillings – an advance on his service pay – together with a warrant for a train ticket, and instructions on the small amount of kit he was permitted to take. This was after an act of Parliament made it compulsory for males of a certain age to serve in the military for the "duration of the present emergency".

At that time, 500 young pilots – with an average age of 22 – had been killed and hundreds of aircraft destroyed during the infamous 'Battle of Britain' in that first summer of the war, hence the RAF was desperate for more pilots to join the fight to defeat Germany.

Seven days later, Wally found himself leaving Euston Station and crossing to the other side of Eversholt Street, following signs to the Recruiting Centre in Euston House and looking for the RAF office.

That short walk began the most defining moment of his young life. Up until then, he was merely the baby of his family – now he was an only son about to embark on a journey that would transform him from an immature lad to a man, from an innocent youth to a warrior and from a peace-loving, happy adolescent to a killer.

His skilful coordination will see him master weaponry as he learns the art of releasing bombs accurately to cascade over the enemy, to strike strongholds, towns and villages filled with families just like his own. On this day, he is still a mere child, yet soon his childhood memories will blur with the blood of war.

Wally sets off

Wally's dream of becoming a pilot came a little closer when he was accepted by the Selection Board with a recommendation that he be trained as a pilot/observer. Next morning, he was told to board the Cardington, Bedfordshire train, which would take him to join the No 24 (Training) Group of Technical Training Command.

The family's tears flowed as he closed the small bag, and his father Isaac blessed him with his prayer book in hand – the *talith* (a prayer shawl, a Jewish religious symbol that covers the shoulders and envelops Jews physically and spiritually in sorrow and joy, in celebration and prayer) covering his shoulders as he hugged his son and said farewell.

Bidding farewell with words of "good luck, stay safe and say your prayers", my grandmother Ethel also slipped a strip of red ribbon into his bag before he left home for St Pancras station [a red ribbon is a traditional type of talisman to ward off misfortune brought about by the 'evil eye'].

Training at the Cardington Bedfordshire RAF camp

The RAF camp was buzzing with the excitement of young recruits keen to fly. Yet there was so much to learn before anyone would be able to climb inside an aircraft.

After passing his physical check-up, Wally easily completed two competence tests for 'General Intelligence and Elementary Maths'. He was then given the standard RAF kit issue – greatcoat, uniform and boots – signalling that he was now ready to commence his training.

Soon, he and his young comrades-in-training were engaged in 'Square Bashing' – learning the intricacies of marching and saluting – followed by training in how to fold blankets and polish boots and every single button until they reflected the sun. This "bullshit", as Wally described it, continued for eight more weeks until he was transferred to RAF Waddington in mid-January 1941.

Unlike many of his contemporaries, Wally had more than a fierce commitment to fight for his country. He also battled for close family members – uncles, aunts and cousins – now living under Nazi rule. His parents had spoken with much love for their family in Poland ever since he was a child, and even though Wally had never met them, he was dedicated to fighting for them.

Author's preface to the diaries

Wally kept diaries regularly to record his experiences in the RAF. His first diary, begun in 1941, was given to him by his friend Charlie on the understanding that he would meticulously record his daily activities throughout the war.

The tattered edges suggest it was stuffed into a pocket wherever he went – indicating a real love for the diary rather than neglect – but due to its fragile condition, I need to handle it very carefully.

Wally's 1941 diary with its tattered front and back covers

I was mindful that these diaries held the very personal and private thoughts of a young man. I invite the reader to do the same.

Did Wally record his experiences to revisit memories in later life, to get nostalgic about the conversations he had had with his diaries? Would he be horrified to learn that I read them and was about to expose his personal scribes?

Yet – whatever his true personal thoughts might have been – I selfishly wanted a genuine sense of his life, even though it may have been private writing never intended to be read by anyone else. I recognise my guilt of trespassing on private thoughts that his family were too grieved to read, and acknowledge that I am probably the first person in 77 years to study them in detail.

I have meticulously copied extracts of Wally's diary entries, but not every hand-scrawled word was easy to read, so there may be errors in the transcription. Some of the major events of the war that he casually references in short-hand form have been amplified, with added comments from me to bring further relevance to his story.

The opening pages were written when Wally received the diary on 8 January:

Jan 8 Wednesday
Charlie sent me this diary this day & I shall endeavour to recall events prior to this date

He then began to add his recollections from the start of the month, and eventually recorded at least 2,000 events that tell stories for 1941 and 1943; these provide an insight into his deepest thoughts and feelings as he endeavoured to travel through this new world. So perhaps it's best to start with his early reflections.

Apart from the day-to-day mundane events, we learn of his relationships with girls, the business difficulties his family faced, troubled flying mishaps and world wartime events.

So let us join him on Day 1 as he excitedly writes his first words, two months after he enlisted:

Jan 1 Wednesday
15 rounds on Lewis Gun
A pair of gloves arrived from my sister Mary.
Quietest New Year's Day I can recollect.

Jan 2 Thursday
Snow prevented us passing out in P.T. [Physical Training]
75% of the chaps in T. Wing posted.

Jan 3 Friday
All chaps posted went this morning, & I was especially sorry to see Jack D, Bill, Charlie J & Bill SL go.
The remainder were moved into 457 squadron.

Jan 6 Monday
Was amazed to hear of the experiences of George, of his thrills in his 18 months with the Spanish Government & having been Southern London Diving Champ.

Why did Wally enjoy George's thrills with a Fascist anti-Semitic government?

At that time, Fascist Italy and Nazi Germany were supporting Franco,[24] and Franco reciprocated by sending volunteers to fight for the Germans against the Soviet Union.

Jan 10 Friday
Played table tennis with Cyril.
Bertie had his 30/- [shillings – £75 in 2020] stolen, so we had a whip-round and collected 23/-.

Wally must have felt so great establishing such camaraderie. He loved his sport and frequently wrote about playing tennis, soccer and badminton.

Went up to gym & played some most enjoyable badminton with Maurice, Don & Ginger after Parade.
Bad London Air Raid.

The Bank underground station, so named because it is situated close to the Bank of England, had been bombed [25] and at least 50 people had been killed. Wally was seriously concerned for his family, who were living and working on the east side of the city.

Jan 12 Sunday
Younis passed the most foolish ill-mannered remarks imaginable, & I told him off. Upset.

Clearly not everything was so peaceful in the barracks; being a Jew, he was sensitive to stupid remarks. This may of course not have been the reason for him being upset on this occasion.

Table tennis & Billiards with Charlie.
Chess in the hut.
Bertie Blacked.

Bertie messed up his work and it got him into trouble.

French beds from Charlie, Norman & Collier.

Mischievous youths folded a sheet, thereby preventing occupants from slipping under the covers at bedtime, so the bed had to be remade.

Jan 13 Monday
Shelter fatigue proved quite enjoyable in spite of the
fact that I put my foot in a hole.
Trench digging in the afternoon.
Annoyed because I worked the whole day.

Jan 14 Tuesday
Mum is unwell? [Ethel, his mother and my grandmother, suffered with ill health for many years. Flu, tinnitus and nose bleeds were a constant problem.]

Trench fatigue.

Long periods of boredom, terror, poor living conditions, lack of sleep and a few rats could fatigue anyone.

Jan 17 Friday
Posting came through. Waddington.

Located just south of Lincoln, RAF Waddington had been established as a bomber airfield in 1916,[26] and was used as a training base from the start of the Second World War.

Wally described his journey from Cardington:

Jan 18 Saturday
04:00 hours House woke. Took the 6:35 train for
Hitchin–Grantham lines.
Bus to Waddington.
First impression miserable dump, although it's Real Air Force.
We are all in for tough time, daily guards.

Jan 20 Monday

Nazi leaders met on this day in the Berlin suburb of Wannsee to discuss the 'final solution' of the 'Jewish problem'. Minutes of the meeting were recorded by Adolf Eichmann.[27]

Eichmann was eventually found in Argentina 15 years after the war had ended; he was captured by Mossad agents and flown to Israel in May 1960. Eichmann stood trial in Jerusalem, where he was found guilty of war crimes and executed in 1962.

Jan 21 Tuesday
Snow shifting in the morning.
Received letter from home. Mum has flu.
My first duty at Waddington Gun Post. Due to it snowing heavily, we did not go out to gun post.

Jan 22 Wednesday
Feel very important standing about with my rifle at the ready.

We are already getting a feel for his life in the RAF, but so far there has been no flying.

Hand-written pages from Wally's 1941 diary

Jan 23 Thursday
Tobruk ours.

The Libyan port city of Tobruk[28] was captured after fierce fighting against the Italians in the first Allied offensive of the Desert Campaign. It was subsequently recaptured by the Germans.

Jan 24, Friday
Mum appeared to be better.

Jan 26 Sunday
Stood by in hangar.
Got out early, lift into town. John went to his church.
Don & I went to Lincoln Cathedral, cursory view both inside & out, very thrilled.
Interested by Jews house.

Wally was fascinated by Lincoln's Jewish heritage. There is nowhere else in the UK with so many surviving Medieval Jewish houses. 'The Jews House',[29] one of the earliest extant houses in England, is Grade I-listed.

In 1290, a century after Jews were murdered in the York pogrom and expelled from England, the house was seized from its Jewish owner.

A disturbing piece of anti-Semitic history is that the roof of 55 Steep Hill in Lincoln is covered with copies of original 'Mediaeval anti-Semitic roof tiles'[30]. One of these original tiles is displayed at The Collection Museum as an example of the growing anti-Semitism of the 13th century.

Jan 27 Monday
Parade held in hangar.
Investiture in No 4 hangar which I missed. Cheered King as he left. Very impressed by his regal appearance.
John lent me 3 books including 'The Citadel' by A.J. Cronin.

Did Wally read this book because it had won the National Book Award in 1937? The book follows the life of a young Scottish doctor, and it became an inspiration for the UK's National Health Service (NHS).

Early on in the diaries, Wally gives us an insight into his struggle with girls; the poor guy suffered from a distinct lack of confidence, no doubt like many other 20-year-old youths of this time.

Evening Lincoln Dance. Fine. I am certainly not a Gigolo.

Feb 4 Tuesday
Received letter from home telling me Mum had just come out of hospital. [Her flu had been more serious on this occasion.]

Feb 5 Wednesday
Blizzard.
Airplane crashed at a mile away.
Crew came into our hut at 11:00pm

Feb 7 Friday
Practised sending Morse code while on gun post.
Benghazi ours.

Benghazi was captured from the Italians[31] following Lieutenant Colonel John Combe's successful North African campaign. Foreign Secretary Anthony Eden quipped "Never has so much been surrendered by so many to so few."

John Combe himself was then captured two months later, and was held as a prisoner of war in Italy for the next two and a half years.

Feb 8 Saturday
Range 200 x 4/10. [Shooting practice in the rifle range.]
Flip [flight] *in the afternoon Manchester–Bicester – 1 hour.*
Great thrill. Exhilarated – no other sensation like it.

It's early days, but Wally has quickly developed a love of flying.

Feb 15 Saturday
Went to Lincoln City Cafe, met two girls from Wapping, took them to pictures and saw them to the bus.

Action on station. A Bristol Blenheim & Wellington aircraft both damaged.

Feb 19 Wednesday
Received letters from my sister Leah telling me Mum's nose bled in Northampton. Worried.

Ethel's ongoing health problems are frequently mentioned throughout Wally's diaries. Stress was a factor – she worried about the dangers he faced in the RAF and her family in Poland who were suffering under the Nazi regime, and he worried about her, too. As he was away so much, he rarely saw her. Strangely, Wally doesn't actually mention his father, despite their close relationship.

Feb 20 Thursday
Worked at Bomb dump.

Bomb-storage areas had to be camouflaged with netting to keep them from being seen by enemy aircraft.

Feb 21 Friday
Took out 'German War Birds'.

Wally had a particular interest in historical stories, and this book was no exception as it told dramatic tales of air combat fought by the best German pilots of the First World War.

& Macaulay essay of Lord Clive [in India].

Macauley influenced articles in the best journals and periodicals, as he wrote in a clear, direct and resonant style.

Feb 28 Friday
Education class. V.G. Took out 'R.F.C. H.Q.' By Maurice Baring

R.F.C. H.Q. was a biography of the Royal Flying Corps in the First World War.

March 1 Saturday
Bulgaria invaded.

Following a period of neutrality, Bulgaria signed a pact with the Axis countries on 1 March 1941, but three years later, it switched sides and joined the Allies.[32]

March 3 Monday
Lambing season. [How sweet!]

March 6 Thursday
Am beginning to think I must stink.

An early indication of his lack of confidence.

March 11 Monday
The very middle of lambing season.
Best barrier I've ever done.

March 13 Thursday
Pinched Merle Lieberman.

Oh what a cheeky young man! Such behaviour might have been acceptable in 1941, but it would not be tolerated nowadays.

March 18 Tuesday
Date with Dorothy?

March 23 Sunday
'Day of National Prayer'.

The origin of the 'National Prayer'[33] day, dates back to the 10th century when King Ethelred ordered the British nation to say prayers, and appeal to God for help to defeat the Danish invaders.

Centuries later, Germany's inexorable advance into the Balkans caused King George VI to ask his countrymen to join him in asking for divine help. Queues formed outside Westminster Abbey as crowds lined up to pray, and then four days later, Yugoslavia turned against the Nazis. Was this a miracle in answer to prayer?

In May 1940, the entire British Expeditionary Force and other Allied forces were trapped at Dunkirk and faced annihilation. Churchill was fully prepared to announce details of an unprecedented military catastrophe: the capture or death of a third of a million British soldiers. However, after George VI called for another day of National Prayer, 338,226 troops were rescued, including 125,000 French troops. Churchill hailed their rescue a "miracle of deliverance" in his famous "We shall fight them on the beaches" speech.

Prayers were also credited when an earthquake below the Atlantic seabed caused storms across the English Channel, throwing Hitler's ships 80 miles off course, and forcing him to abandon his planned invasion that September.

Ray's wedding. [My parents' marriage.]
Flowers. Guests. Synagogue. Service. Dinner tipsy.
Sadie 'pissed' etc, etc. Maxine's.

March 24 Monday
Workshop

The family business of 'outworkers to the dress trade' was referred to as the 'Workshop'.

Hamburg, Berlin & Bremen bombed.

Berlin became the focus of this night's offensive, which included Kiev and Hanover, and particularly on their docks and shipyards. It was a rare occasion when French fishermen cheered British airmen.[34]

March 27 Thursday
Yugoslavia la-de-da declares for us.

The pact Yugoslavia signed with Germany on 25 March attracted fierce objections with its slogan, 'Better the war than the pact, better the grave than a slave'.

After a *coup d'état* on 27 March, Yugoslavia sided with the Allies, an action welcomed by Winston Churchill, who said: "Yugoslavia has found its soul." [35]

March 28 Friday
Harrar & Keren ours.

Harrar in Italian East Africa, present-day Ethiopia, and Keren in Italian Eritrea, present-day Eritrea, were both captured by the British.

March 29 Saturday
Italian fleet K.O. [knocked out]

An interesting war story of a British success was hidden behind these few words, which recorded the defeat of the Italian Navy by the Royal Navy in the Battle of Matapan.

Mavis Batey, a cryptanalyst at Bletchley Park, successfully broke the Italian enigma code to learn of an Italian battle force sailing to attack merchant convoys in the Mediterranean.[36]

The British fleet commander, Admiral Cunningham, created an audacious plan to deceive the enemy[37]: arriving at his golf club in Alexandria in the afternoon with a suitcase as if for an overnight stay, he spent time on the golf course within sight of the Japanese consul before making a surreptitious exit after dark to avoid being seen boarding his flagship. His fleet sank three heavy cruisers and two destroyers – most of that Italian force.

March 31 Monday
Went to Lincoln with Fox & was told of our being posted.
Very excited.

April 1 Tuesday
Dispersal.
Duck Shoved [slang for 'to get rid of responsibility'].

April 5 Saturday
I'm now amidst intellectual company and have found a happiness granted few, and yet I don't feel out of place.
Farewells to everyone.
Yugoslavia invaded.

Germany's attack on Yugoslavia, which began with the bombing of Belgrade, was followed with a land invasion culminating in an unconditional surrender on 17 April.

Derby–Birmingham.
Some 70 pilots left on the train.

Wally was transferred to No 6 Initial Training Wing, Aberystwyth, Cardiganshire, in Wales, to train as night fighter crew.

He describes the transfer:

8:30 Off & took 6 No back bag [kit bag] *then marched to H.Q.* [Headquarters].
Filled in entry forms & had tea at hotel.
As cadets, according to corps, we are super, the A.C.I. [Aircraftsman First Class] *told us we are the goods.*
In general, it is the RAF I had hoped to find 4 months ago.
We were given a talk on sex.

April 6 Sunday
Up 6:30 feeling absolutely tip top, even had shave though I didn't need one.
Received new tunic trousers & cap but the trousers don't fit.
Canteen lovely.
The family's financial situation bothers me.
I know that if hard work alone will get me through, I will get my wings.
I hope there is sea school too.

April 7 Monday
Small wonder Shakespeare took up Ink Pen.

Wally wrote so many of his entries using a pencil.

Freddy Fish are fine Picquets.

This was slang meaning "new recruits made fine guards".

April 8 Tuesday
Salonika falls.

The German Wehrmacht army had successfully invaded Greece.

148

April 11 Friday
Passover

Jews celebrate the eight-day festival to commemorate the Israelites' escape from slavery in ancient Egypt. Wally does not mention a Passover service at the Air Force base.

April 13 Sunday
In the afternoon strolled by river, tea – letter – supper – Red Lion with Charlie – met Wendy & Sylvia at 'Dirty Duck'. [Must have been a pub].
Wendy 'fine'.

April 14 Monday
WENDY IS A BITCH.

Yesterday Wendy was 'fine', but today she is a bitch. Did she flirt outrageously with some other innocent young man? Maybe she became a bitch after his further advances were rejected?

Terribly worried as to how to procure tickets for dance in order to meet Wendy.

What! I am confused – why did he still expect to meet her?

Pat got two tickets for me. I like Pat.
Further embarrassment at Dance. Sylvia sizzled [glared with anger] *at us at bar – hate them both.*
Wendy – bitch.

Was he rejected again? Did he feel confused and foolish? Wally, for goodness' sake, leave that girl to others!

April 16 Wednesday
Where Yankees?

A slang word used to describe Americans. Did he question why they had not come to the aid of Britain?

Corporal leads me to believe we are all being posted.

Slid down rope from Charles window and twice nearly broke my neck.
Discarded greatcoat from 12:00 hrs.

Large woollen overcoats were standard issue for most armed services around the world, mainly because of their protection against extremes of weather conditions.

Collar and cuffs could be turned out to protect the face and hands from cold and rain, the long coat hung below the knees, and its deep pockets were useful to keep letters and food dry.

April 17 Thursday
ABERYSTWYTH – SAT
Yugoslavia army gives out.

Yugoslavia surrendered to the Germans after a massive invasion.

London's worst air raid.

Historic buildings including St Paul's Cathedral[38], the Houses of Parliament, the Law Courts, the National Gallery and Selfridges were damaged during a nine-hour bombing spell.

Posted to Aberystwyth
Drill – P.T. – X. Country run (came 12th)
Got registered letter containing 30/-0d from home.

Thirty shillings was the equivalent of £75 in 2021.

Met Pat & took her home, she is more beautiful than even my imagination had pictured her. I was foolishly dumb struck. She wasn't eager to have me write but accepted.

Poor guy probably felt rejected, but in reality, she simply was unenthusiastic. I've engaged with Wally's experiences from his private thoughts in the diary, and they sadden me.

April 18 Friday
Packed. HARRY?

F.F.I. [Following a medical check-up, he was graded 'Free from Infection'.]
Went to dance with John, danced very little, hurt as Pat never came, danced with another.

April 19 Saturday
Received letter from John at last. Said farewell.
Special train.
Wales is beautiful.
Aberystwyth looks green.

He was moving to the training wing at Flying Training Command in Cardiganshire, Wales.

Disappointed at not being able to billet with John and have four none-too-pleasant roommates instead.

April 20 Sunday
Went for stroll on my own. Kangaroos profuse.
['Kangaroos' was slang for Australians.]
Bed early after borrowing the book 'Richthofen'.

The German First World War fighter pilot Baron von Richthofen was considered the 'ace of aces' of war, and credited with 80 kills.

April 21 Monday
Disappointed to find myself in lower form in Maths. Stinks.
Must not spend so much & must be careful in future exams.
Resolved to work harder.

April 22 Tuesday
Went x-Country running & did poorly, but had fair time.

April 23 Wednesday
Greek army capitulates and surrenders to Nazis.

April 25 Friday
C.O.'S [Commanding Officers] *inspection fiasco this morning.*

Was pulled up by W.O. [Warrant Officer] whilst going to dance where I met Blue Trousers who no doubt I shall see again.

April 26 Saturday
Have arrived at that congenial stage where I lend Bob a bob.

'Bob' was slang for one shilling – UK old currency.

A one-shilling coin

USA will convoy shipping.
[USA had started to protect UK shipping.]
Field Marshal Jan Smuts quoted as saying 'Germany is winning the battles but losing the war'.

Jan Smuts was twice prime minister of South Africa[39]; he was also instrumental in forming the UK Royal Air Force in 1917 together with Lord Trenchard. In 1941, he was appointed field marshal of the British Army.

April 30 Wednesday
Squadron Parade
Went to dance met 'Trousers'.

May 1 Thursday
Greece evacuated.
[The evacuation of 50,000 British Expeditionary troops.

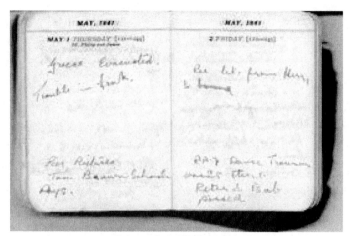

Extract from Wally's diary

Trouble in Iraq.

We can either gloss over words in a diary or we can investigate. I delved to discover an amazing victory for a small band of RAF servicemen at the local airport base.

The base at Habbaniya in Iraq was constructed by the British on the west bank of the Euphrates in 1935, part of the Anglo-Iraqi Treaty of 1930 to support the Iraqi Army. The Iraqis, in return, provided endless oil supplies, and in 1938, the base was renamed RAF Habbabiya. Oil had become essential to Britain's involvement in the war.

Following a coup at the beginning of April by anti-British Rashid Ali, Iraq switched sides to support the Nazis, and by 30 April, 10,000 heavily armed troops and 122 Iraqi aircraft had besieged the base in readiness to attack.[40]

Sparsely manned by just 39 pilot instructors and their students, of which only three had combat experience, the RAF, armed with just nine obsolete Gloster Gladiator biplane fighters and 65 other training aircraft, took the initiative and attacked the huge Iraqi army.

By 7 May, the Iraqis finally retreated, providing a magnificent victory for the RAF and a humiliating defeat for the Iraqis.

Following signature of the armistice agreement, Regent Prince 'Abd al-llah restored his government.

Three weeks after their defeat, the Nazis inspired a pogrom of extreme violence in Baghdad. Hundreds of Jews were murdered, ending 2,000 years of peaceful existence between Jews and Arabs that dated back to the time of Babylon.

May 5 Monday
All Iraq & Iran turn more pro-Nazi as the oil pipe line has been cut, the situation is by no means favourable.

May 6 Tuesday
Sports. Best game of football in my life.
Went to flicks with John. 'Strike up the Band'

Mickey Rooney and Judy Garland starred in the 1940 American musical film *Strike up the Band*.

May 9 Friday
Received letter from Dinah which pleased me no end.
Dance. 'Trousers' refused my invite to dance. Most peeved.

He continues to have little success with the ladies.

May 10 Saturday
BOMBED OUT AT HOME

The family home and surrounding area were badly damaged, so the Wolmans moved to temporary housing.

Bad London Raid.
1,400 people were killed during this final major bombing raid on London.

May 11 Sunday
Night fighters setting up a fine score.
[A reference to recent successes of the RAF.]

May 12 Monday
Pamper did not come out.
Rudolf Hess Dead.

Wally was mistaken on this point, for Hess was still alive. Hitler's deputy führer flew solo from Germany to Scotland in his personal twin-engine Messerschmitt Bf 110 on an ill-conceived peace mission, but when his plane crashed on Scottish farmland, he was immediately arrested and imprisoned until the end of the war.[41]

At the Nuremberg trials, Hess received a life sentence for his 'crimes against peace'. He committed suicide in 1987, aged 93, while still serving his sentence in Spandau prison.

May 13 Tuesday

A few days after being appointed prime minister in 1940, Churchill told his cabinet: "I have nothing to offer but blood, toil, tears and sweat." 42 He repeated the line later that day when asking the House of Commons for a vote of confidence in his new all-party government.

May 14 Wednesday
Learnt of my flat being uninhabitable.

His accommodation, provided by the council in London, was deemed to be a slum.

Complimented upon the way I folded my G.C.
[I guess that was his army greatcoat.]

Made P.T. [Physical Trainer] Leader.
100% in maths. Flight over 94.3%
Squadron Dance very, very gay.
Megan. Mary.
Must not become swollen headed.

May 15 Thursday
Resolve to act as Wally and not one of the lads.
Mum & Dad are with the Tankels in their country house.
Lew (Lily) discharged from Navy. The stink is suffocating.

I was greatly surprised to learn here about a 'country house' owned by my paternal grandparents.

Sadly, no member of our family remains alive who can tell me anything about it.

May 16 Friday
Dance – I got rid of 10/- [shillings].
Mary & Meghan were there. Megan didn't allow me to see her home.
Mary was escorted by someone else.

Oh dear, I feel this is so sad, as his romantic life is worsening. I wish I could help him.

May 20 Tuesday
Nazis try to invade Crete.

The airborne invasion of Crete had commenced, and despite heavy casualties, the Germans eventually took control of the island.[43]

May 23 Friday
Met Mary at Dance.

May 24 Saturday
Took Mary to dance & cinema. Withdrew £7.

The £7 he withdrew is the equivalent of £350 in 2020. Why did he need so much money?

Training to be a pilot involved more than 'square bashing' or technical training, it also required team building. And so they climbed 'Cadair Idris', the second-highest peak in Wales, with great enthusiasm.

The Cadair Idris peak in Wales

June 1 Sunday
4:00am Coach for 'Cadair Idris' ugh.

He evidently did not enjoy early starts any more than I do!

12:30pm Sandwiches, climb. Cadair Idris is, though basic, on a day as fine as today, a thing of rare beauty. Dickie was champion.
We swam in a very cold lake halfway up & again in a far warmer lake when we got down.
What with riding & some awful climbing I am tired no end.
Mary was not there at 8:30pm and was to be.
    [I cannot comment any further!]

June 4 Wednesday
4.45 Armaments exam. 95% result, very happy.

June 5 Thursday
New hygiene exam. 98% result, very happy.

June 6 Friday
10:30 Navigation. Farce.
Caught 6:10 train for Northampton.

Most fatiguing trip with no sleep all night.

June 8 Sunday
I talked with mum.
11:55 from Northampton.

June 13 Friday
Date with Betty was a poor show.

June 16 Monday
Kitted out.
[Got his uniform and equipment.]

June 22 Sunday
Went for a Swim at V.P Lido in Purley, Surrey.

The Lido, which opened in 1935, was hailed as a 'masterpiece of science and skill'.[44]

Went to Kimpton to see Shirley.

His niece attended a boarding school in the village of Kimpton in Hertfordshire, about 50 miles north of London; her parents wanted her to be well away from the London bombing. Houses along the High Street in this pretty village date back to the 16th century.[45]

June 23 Monday
Film in West End. 'The Lady Eve', a comedy very enjoyable.

The 1941 film *The Lady Eve* starred Barbara Stanwyck and Henry Fonda.

June 27 Friday
8.15 from Euston.
Dismal return as I learn that 80% of the other fellows have left, John being amongst them.
(Would have liked to have met a woman during the week but didn't).
[The saga continues.]

June 29 Sunday
Germany doing far too well. Have feeling we will all go event-
ually.

Wally felt pretty pessimistic about Britain's chance of winning
the war after the encirclement of 300,000 Red Army troops in an
area near Minsk.[46]

Rumours so vague that they cause serious disease.

July 1 Tuesday
No 'Gen'.

The 'Gen' referred to a lack of information about their
forthcoming move to train in the USA.

July 2 Wednesday
'Gen' is that shall go on Saturday.
Table tennis with Wells & Robert.
Have for the most part in U.K. flown solo.

July 3 Thursday
Rec letter from Henry – most aggressive in which he tells of his
trying for matrix & a degree.
And from Rose T, who has broken off relations with her fiancé
and requires sympathetic companionship.

Rose Tankel was my father's sister, remembered for her strong
personality. She sought companionship after the recent break-up of
her engagement, and had taken a shine to Wally. However, he was
not keen, for they had very different personalities.

July 5 Saturday
Told we are going tomorrow.
Getting excited.
Confined to Camp.

Wally was very excited to know for sure finally that they were
travelling to the USA, and started to write diary entries in more
detail, describing the long trek from England to the base in Alabama.

July 6 Sunday
10:30 train Wilmslow–Liverpool.
Northumberland troop ship, accommodation most cramped.
Ferry's galley crowded sailed past all afternoon & evening.
Lots of Cadbury's milk procurable.
Wrote Charlie & home & like a fool put stamps on both.

Letters from serviceman were exempt from postal fees – they just had to write the letters 'OHMS' ['On His Majesty's Service'] on the envelope, so it was unnecessary to affix postage stamps.

Tug took us out to centre of river but we stayed there all night. Hot night due to crowd.

July 7 Monday
Sailed 9:00am.
Slow crawl, some eleven ships with us.
For the most part appear to lie stationary but around tea time the sea broke a bit & we began to feel queer. Thick mist & calm followed & it is suggested we are doing 8 knots.
Horns & surf keep ships in two boat drills.
Distressingly slow. Surprised there is no escort so far.
Watching the surf is most fascinating.
Roll far more noticeable below.
Ate pound chocolate today – Pig.

July 8 Tuesday
Ship definitely more lively
Joined convoy. Same 4 destroyers, 3 corvettes?
Few fellows sick.
Lunch. I missed as I was queer & spewed twice.
Was silly & ate some chocolate after, & am now undecided inside.
It has been an extremely fine day, & a South Westerly has made sea swell.

July 9 Wednesday
Slept pretty well apart from falling on my head.

Pretty queer this morning & so walked up & down the windward side of upper craft for a couple of hours & felt quite well.

Dined well, sunbathed top of butcher's store.

Sing song on starboard upper deck & in fact was in best of spirits.

Shoal of porpoise caused a stir.

Threat of submarines twice today.

Shared tin of peaches with John Wells.

Caused almost an uproar by polishing my buttons.

Have found my sea legs.

July 10 Thursday

Slept very well.

Convoy has changed format again & we are now on the outside. Destroyer 186 very close.

Weather miserable & wet. Eventually had to take my coat out of my pack to wear it.

'Northanger Abbey' [by Jane Austen] *from library.*

Impression is that we have travelled some 1,000 miles.

Towards evening it gets extremely squally & ship was the most violent since start of trip.

Sat in bows and wind blew strong.

July 11 Friday

Poor weather.

The a/c [aircraft] *and 2 destroyers turned back.*

Forecastle [the front part of the ship] *is our favourite haunt.*

Took out 'To You Mr Chips' [by James Hilton].

Rumour that we (500,000 troops) had invaded Holland.

[There was no evidence of this invasion.]

Why is it that I feel poorly at night?

Bullshitted.

Hope they are not too worried at home.

July 12 Saturday

Forecastle. Wed? Tue? Mon? Thu? or Friday?

Had he lost track of the days of the week while at sea?

Took out 'Goodbye My Chips' [by James Hilton].
'High Wager' a good book.
Whole week board ship.
Did fair amount of walking & had long chat with 'Perce the Pig'. [He meant Percy the Pig.]
Holland rumour groundless. Pig in a Sty. [Slang for incorrect rumour.]
Mist – 50 yards vis.
It is suggested we will sight Newfoundland on Monday.
Blowing aft.
Will continue my letter tomorrow.
Gone are our carefree dinger quarrels.

July 13 Sunday
Dull morning.
Church services B. Deck.
Continued letter home.
Evening turned out quite pleasant & few of us sat in forecastle sang & chatted.
Thrill in seeing a whale blowing almost caused a resurrection.
Bought couple of Penguins [milk chocolate biscuit bars].
Evening was extremely pleasant & didn't go below till 9:30.
Reminiscing on school days.

July 14 Monday
Forecastle, but as it is very misty, we couldn't even look for land.
Anticipated the fun of our trip through 'the states'.
Misty all day so land was not to be seen.
D.R.O's show promise of our landing by Friday.
Cheese & biscuits.

July 15 Tuesday
Mist in morning cleared. Is brilliant sunshine.
Slipped down hatch steps with lunch.
Land?? Cloud?? In sight.

Handed my £5-10-0 in.
Got webbing out of store. [Webbing was the set of essential containers used by servicemen.]

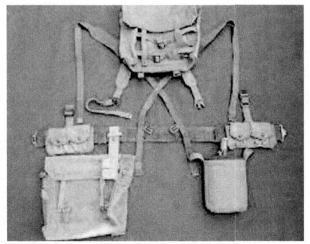

What Wally described as 'webbing'

Saw two ships going in opposite direction today.

July 16 Wednesday
Thick mist all day.
Boxing match in the afternoon fine.

July 17 Thursday
Docked 2:15.
Disembarked 4 o'clock.
No end pleased to see "R.M.S. Empress of Canada" & "Revenge" in Halifax.
Called home (3 shillings and 8d cost to phone).
Rec $34.36. ($10 pay). Big one, little one, proud one!!!
Piss balled around until 4 o/clock in morning.
Train great. Bought bar of choc for 5 cents.
Queer no Black Out here.

Blackouts were obviously not required in Canada because there was no danger of aerial bombing attacks there. In Britain, they had become a legal requirement, hence it seemed strange when he first arrived.

July 18 Friday

Scenery superb. Timber, lakes, forests, streams, Cars!!!
Left Halifax 6 o/clock.
Grand forest country to Toronto.
Woman gave apple to each of us. Forests!!!
Grand breakfast.
Bought pics at every stop & in between stops too.
Kiddies ask us for pennies.
Halifax–Truro–Moncton–Charlo–Campbellton–Newcastle–
Toronto [a 29-hour train journey].

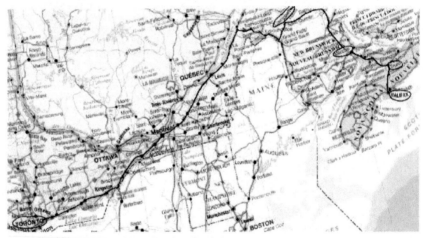

Map showing the train route

Browned off with train vendor who keeps walking by.
Most jolly simple French Glace [ice cream].
Grand dinner.

July 19 Saturday

Montreal 8 o/clock.
12 peaches for 25 cents.
Large proportion of French makes too effusive reception.
30 minutes stay. 10 cent service.
Toronto.

We are going to Arcadia, Florida. John has gone to S Carolina.
Photograph town 9:30–1:30.
Dance. Canteen 'Queensway' of dancing here.
Smart suits Canadians have.
Food great.
Hearing good 'Swing' [a style of jazz].
Free 7 hours.
Lots of Scots here. English Cadets respected!!!

July 20 Sunday
Beverley St/Dundas St. Toronto.
Did bugger all due to their blasted documents keeping us
in this pig hole.
Browned off. Got out at 10 o'clock again.
Huge Silverstone Store here. Big chocolate fan.

July 21 Monday
Great day.
Busied with finger paints in morning.
Went on trip arranged by the Active Service Canteen through a
Mrs Marrow.
Grand trip & thoroughly good afternoon.
Jean McPhee good fun in sing song coming home.
Learnt 'Far-away'. 'General Brack Hotel' – Grand Fruit
Country all the way down to Falls.
Bought 6 cards

July 23 Wednesday
No sleepers 'Propaganda'.
Detroit terrific industrial town.
Raven my travelling companion.
Americans less effusive than the Canadians.
Crisis over Japan both for U.S.A. & G.B.

Japanese troops entered parts of Indo-China in 1940, and took control of the entire country, which is now divided and known today as Vietnam, Laos and Cambodia. Three days later, President

Roosevelt confiscated all Japanese assets held in the USA in retaliation for their occupation.[47]

July 24 Thursday

Some fine country to be seen. Georgia & vicinity has bright red earth.

'Gone with the Wind' [a 1939 film watched by 200 million people].[48]

Negroes profuse perhaps 90%
Turpentine cups on trees.

Tree resin (what Wally calls turpentine) was distilled and sold by the families who had lived in the woods for several generations.[49]

Jacksonville has lots of fruit & saw 2 kosher shops.
Most brilliantly 'tit' town I've seen.

July 25 Friday

Arrived in Arcadia. Fleet of neat cars took us to Drome [airbase].

Wally had arrived at the Carlstrom Field airbase in Florida. Such excitement!

Good billets & food. Bullshit Pukha cadets.
High % have failed of previous late.
We are training on Stearman P.T.17s. [Biplane].

The Biplane was a fixed-wing aircraft with two main wings stacked one above the other and was originally used as a military trainer aircraft. At least 10,000 were built in the United States during the 1930s and 1940s.[50]

President Roosevelt's signing of the Lend-Lease Act[51] in March had enabled British pilots to train safely in American air space, and they were based at several special schools throughout the South and Southwest of the USA. The US Army Air Corps provided the aircraft, and the pilots were supervised by British flying officers.

The most successful students became sergeant pilots; Wally was one such pilot.

Senior Cluster & Senior Class-men etc most peculiar.

July 26 Saturday
First Saluted Yank flag.
Concerned for family reaction to my safety as a pilot.
Medical Inspection.
Kit issue.
Arcadia for some shopping got shirt & pants & vest.
In all got about 6 books of routine to read.

July 27 Sunday
11:45 P.T. & games (baseball & medicine ball).

Solid-weighted medicine balls – manufactured using hand-stitched leather – have been used to achieve high levels of fitness since Roman times.[52]

2:45 Flying Dual for 45 mins. Disappointed in my performance.

July 28 Monday
Ground school introduction.
Calisthenics.

Calisthenics involves rudimentary fitness activities like hopping, lunging and stretching. The full-body movements focused on muscle groups like biceps and quads, and engaged secondary muscles for stability and balance to provide a well-rounded workout.[53]

Volley Ball.

Volleyball was invented in 1895 at Springfield College, Massachusetts. It was considered to be a less-strenuous sport for older people. Originally called 'Mintonette', it was subsequently renamed volleyball after a local professor noted the ball was being volleyed over the net.[54]

34 mins Dual [flight]. A little better than yesterday.
Borrowed Billy's helmet which proved much better.

July 29 Tuesday
Ground school.
Bathing pool opened & so had fine 15-minute bathing.
Tailor instead of calisthenics.

'Tailor' is a 'sitting' exercise that makes the thigh, pelvic and hip muscles more flexible.

These are the exercises and the order in which they were to be done:[55]
    1. Sit on the floor with the soles of your feet together, keeping the back straight.
    2. Gently lean forward until a mild stretch is felt in the hip and thigh muscles. The back should remain straight. Do not push down on legs with the hands.
    3. Hold and count to 5, then relax.

July 31 Thursday
Meteorological quiz O.K.
Bags of swimming.
Flying poor.

Aug 1 Friday
Tried a few landings.

Aug 2 Saturday
Broke my frontal filling on coconut.
5:30 Sarasota. Dead cow on way being eaten by vultures.
Strolled about & bought lots of fruit.

Aug 3 Sunday
Pleasure Beach. Beautifully fine sand with lots of shells.
Tried catching fish which swam in shallows by throwing stones at them.
Swam all day.
Vultures still eating stinking cow.

Aug 4 Monday
Landing's a little better.

[His landing skills have improved].
Bags of Bunting.

'Bunting' describes small decorative flags more commonly used by ships to send messages to other ships.

Flying in morning this week gives us lots of time to ourselves.

Aug 5 Tuesday
Sick Parade – Toothache.
Must parade tomorrow.
9 boys soloed.
9 boys in pool.

Trainees were traditionally thrown into the swimming pool after a first successful solo flight.

My landing is a little better.

Aug 6 Wednesday
Landings – poor.
Lots – (16) Chaps soloed & were thrown in pool.
Upper classroom.
Bunyan bailed out [he jumped out of his aircraft with a parachute] *onto the apron* [an area where planes could be parked].

Aug 7 Thursday
Lots more chaps soloed.
First washouts [heavy rainfall].
Disconcerted. Will have to pay for my own dental repairs.

Aug 8 Friday
50% at least have soloed.
Fine splash game in the pool.
No of upper class-men thrown in pool.
Found check [American spelling of cheque].

Aug 9 Saturday
Sarasota. Flicks [the American term for cinema].
Taxi to Lido Beach, 'I can get you anything.'

I was amused by his throw-away line, for the taxi driver inferred he could arrange anything, from nylon stockings to girls!

All the women appeared to be married. Two proved good fun.

Aug 17 Sunday
Speedometer gag!!!

The car speedometer was 'fixed' to mislead the driver about the car's actual speed!

Woke up late & sat in bed reading.
Outside was a severe rainstorm.
At 11:30 I went out for breakfast & started hitch back to Carlstrom.

As Wally had no access to transport, he and his friends hitch-hiked around town.

After half an hour on wrong road I got a 5-mile lift & after a further half hour a car containing Sull, Kane & Gavin gave me another lift. The four of us then got a further 5-mile lift, followed by a 10-mile lift in a garbage van. From here we (after 3 hours wait) met some of our fellows in car and they brought us home.

Aug 18 Monday
Up for 20 hours. Check with Mr B & although I flew pretty badly, I passed.
Received a letter from Home & Rose Tankel!!!!

Aug 19 Tuesday
90 Degree stage which Mr G tells me I passed with a good grade.

Aug 21 Thursday
60% in Meteorological test. Just gave me another paper and got 70%
More bullshit, we now have 14 officers.

Aug 23 Saturday
Four demerits for being out after lights out.
Chatted with some Yanks on relative merits 'Tommy v Yank'.

'Tommy' was a type of slang used to describe British soldiers – it was first used after a mutiny in Jamaica in 1743, and then commonly used during the First and Second World Wars.[56]

Went to both Cinemas & then to Tropical [a bar].
Ate watermelon by the road at 2am.

Aug 26 Tuesday
180-Degree side approach (Passed).
'March of Time' photographs. [The American newsreel *The March of Time* was shown in cinemas from 1935–1951.]
Had really good time in the air today & thoroughly enjoyed it.
Had my first game of tennis.

Aug 27 Wednesday
180-Degree side approach, passed.
New lot of chaps came in.
Will have to, but dislike replying to Rose's letters.

Aug 28 Thursday
Gave Mr G a fair ride & nearly made myself sick doing 'Lazy Eights'.

The 'Lazy Eight' flight manoeuvre consisted of several S-turns flown across a road. The first, a 180° turn, was taken to the right, and immediately followed by a 180° turn to the left.[57]
The Lazy Eight adds both a climb and descent to each segment, the first 90° being a climb; the second 90° is a descent. [I feel airsick even as I write this!]

Mr G gave me some aerobatics.
Lent Tommy Blenheim 50 cents.
Laval shot.

The quisling of France, Pierre Laval, was a recognised collaborator with the Germans. He was wounded during an assassination attempt on his life. After the war, he was found guilty of treason and executed by a firing squad in 1945.[58]

Aug 29 Friday
Sarasota.
Bought 'March of Time' by E.C.T. Horniblow.

Sep 5 Friday
40 hours flying.

Sep 6 Saturday
Bus to Sarasota.
Bought pair shoes & trousers.
Lido.
Went to surf club.
Went to Big House. Mike's thin bitch slept there.
Was he jealous of Mike's girlfriends?

Sep 10 Wednesday
Day of Revolution.
We all sang "Why are we waiting" for officers at breakfast.
Piss balling in General. [Piss balling – messing around playfully].
Adolf Wolman. [Wally, a little Dictator!]

Sep 11 Thursday
Received a letter from home & one from Rose.
We have a house in Surrey.

The family home in Marlpit Lane, Old Coulsdon, was finally purchased.

No flying due to wetness of field.
Played tennis.
Came back, had haircut & lots of fun in barracks throwing socks about.
President Roosevelt speaks. War?

President Franklin D. Roosevelt appreciated the power of communicating through mass media, and in March 1933 gave the first of his 'Fireside chat' radio broadcasts to connect the White House to ordinary Americans as never before.59

He was introduced with the words: "The President wants to come into your home and sit at your fireside for a little fireside chat".

'Fireside chat', a term coined by a CBS station manager, referred to the President's conversational casual style. He gave around 30 talks over the four terms he served, starting with the words "My friends" or "My fellow Americans".

His first address spoke of the problems and successes of the Great Depression. The 'Fireside chat' broadcast on 11 September was used to tell the nation of a German U-boat attack on a US destroyer:

"My Fellow Americans, the Navy department has reported to me that on the morning of September 4th the US Destroyer Greer, carrying American mail to Iceland... flying the American flag, was attacked by a German submarine. In spite of what Hitler's propaganda bureau has invented, and in spite of what any American obstructionist organisation may prefer to believe, I tell you the blunt fact that the German submarine fired first upon this American destroyer without warning, and with the deliberate design to sink her."

Sep 15 Monday
Flew 1 hour.
Marine killed.

Sep 20 Saturday
Flew at Parker.
Started out for Miami.
Impossible to get to Tampa so landed up at Sarasota instead.
Flicks, popcorn & grapes.

Sep 21 Sunday
Exam results out, passed O.K.
Upon going off met gang, went to Museum.
Fine collection of Reubens & some of Gainsborough,

Snyders, Van Dyke, etc. Interesting
Fine farewell from Mr & Mrs Reynolds & Grace.

Sep 23 Tuesday
Still no letter from home.
Wrote home and enclosed photos.
Weak on Chandelles.

A Chandelle was an aircraft-control manoeuvre where the pilot combines a 180° turn with a climb.[60]

Sep 24 Wednesday
Flew 3 hours today, all acrobatics & amazed Mr G by my snaps & a half & half slow roll when I took him dual.

Sep 26 Friday
Snaps not at all good, only 30 out of 70.
Girls promised from Miami did not turn up
I was tucked away in the corner of the stage doing a sort of automatic jig during chorus.

Sep 27 Saturday
Received Diplomas.
Bought view scope [a telescope] *for Mr G.*
Bags of fruit.
Went to dance at Elks Club where Mr & Mrs G wish I have a good time.
'A coca cola not a dance' [maybe he just drank cokes and did not dance?].

Sep 28 Sunday
Shite-poke [oh dear, now he had had a poor sexual experience!].
Mr G called at 7:30 when we gave him View-Scope.
'Kissengen Springs' fine boating, swimming, eating, ball games & extremely good fun.

The spring waters in Polk County, Southwest Florida, were a significant tourist spot for picnics and water sport, used for parties and dancing, and now this band of RAF pilots also enjoyed the spot.[61]

> *Mrs G's flat for a while & then we were given lift back. Dot would play*!!! [Ahah! Was he having fun at last?]

Sep 29 Monday
Sing-song in Mess Hall, snake march in Carlstron.
Panties (hoisted) up flag mast.
Mr & Mrs G & Ada came to see us off.
Left Arcadia.
Mrs G kissed us goodbye. But not kiss???
[Suggesting that he wanted something more sensual.]

Sep 30 Tuesday
Jacksonville for about an hour.
Rather uninteresting trip. Arrived Gunter.

US Air Force poster

Wally flying a BT-13 from Gunter Field

Vultee BT-13 Valiant aircraft were now used to train in friendly US skies without fear of attack. The BT-13 was nicknamed the 'Vultee Vibrator' due the amount of shaking. I don't like shaking when I fly![62]

Good gzab. [Meaning a friendly atmosphere among the airmen in Gunter Field].

The typewritten sheet below, headed 'CROSS COUNTRY RULES', was discovered among Wally's papers:

GUNTER RULES

1. STAY AWAY FROM THUNDERSTORMS AND WOMEN.
2. DO NOT FLY IN OR ABOVE CLOUDS, ESPECIALLY CIRRUS.
3. IF THE CEILING GETS DOWN TO 800 FT ABOVE THE GROUND, IT IS TIME FOR A 'BURTON'.
4. DO NOT FLY LOWER THAN 1,500 FEET UNLESS THE HUMULUS BECOMES TOO CONGESTUS.

Humulus is a plant, cumulus is a cloud, so this was either written in jest or it was just a simple spelling mistake.

Oct 1 Wednesday
Had this first day for bedding down.
Went swimming in the extremely filthy pool they have here.
Fine post exchange.
Serving bags of ice cream.

Oct 2 Thursday
They have a fine system of automatic drink selling machines.
25 mins sightseeing in [Vultee] BT 13. I was thoroughly shaken in landing for this ship rattles no end.

Letter from Wally to his family

There were a few letters among Wally's possessions, mostly written by him, plus one other. Extracts follow.

Thursday 2nd October
F/C Wolman M.L.
Flying Cadet Detachment
Gunter Field
Block 215
Montgomery Alabama U.S.A.

My Dear Family,
I have delayed this letter in order that I might write to you from this, my present address.
    After going without a letter for over a fortnight in Arcadia, I was pleased to receive four letters from you in as many days. These letters have considerably enlightened me as to what our new house is like & none of your points mentioned seem detrimental.
    I'm glad that Lieber is with you, that the train service is so good, that the hill climbing can be avoided & that the house appears to be quite central.
    Lieber, by now you should know whether sending Shirley to an elementary school will be to her detriment or not & I look forward to finding an unspoilt niece when I get back.
    I trust that Ray [a reference to my mother's pregnancy with me] *continues well in health & I have no doubt that Mary has been commissioned to do lots of knitting this coming Winter.*

Considering his age, Wally is surprisingly interested in and knowledgeable about the family business:

    Unsettled appears to be the gown business condition, for each report I get contradicts its predecessor.
    Perhaps I will be so fortunate to learn from your next letter of the seasons really having started in full swing. When you mentioned having sold more of our own made-up stuff, I gaily pictured your having sold it to some retail shop but as it is, provided the cash is O.K. there is cause for congratulation.

*Is it not possible that another manufacturer would be interested
in our cheaper type of good work? Failing mutual satisfaction there,
might there not someone in the West End with whom we can
commence business?*

The final page of the letter was missing.

Oct 3 Friday
Pay – miserly $10.
55 mins Dual. Gentle 2 medium turns.
Infernal system of switches, levers & pumps
Received a copy of 41a P.T. [Physical Therapy] *graduation
booklet.*
*Meals are a combination of low economy, high speed, then one
length of arm.*

Oct 4 Saturday
*The review by Jack Dempsey, Wing Commander Hogan etc was
quite successful & 'B' won.*
Jack Dempsey spoke to us in the mess during lunch.
*Bus (104) to Montgomery town. First impression was that it
was extremely small.*
Went with Ginger through the stores leaving havoc behind us.

Jack Dempsey was also known as the 'Manassa Mauler'
because he was born in Manassa, Colorado. He held the world
heavyweight boxing title between 1919–1926. At the age of eight,
Dempsey took his first job picking crops on a farm nearby in
Steamboat Springs, Colorado.[63]

Jack Dempsey in his white suit

Oct 6 Monday
Have developed a phobia for skeleting [an irrational fear of bones].
Assed about on the radio of a B.T. [a type of aircraft] & found out how it works.
'The Way of all Flesh' stolen from my drawer.

The semi-autobiographical novel *The Way of All Flesh* by Samuel Butler attacked hypocrisy during the Victorian era.

Oct 7 Tuesday
Am disgusted with the fact that one is not permitted to sleep during ground school.
Am looking forward to some post now.
Meals have become more a matter of a strategy than of speed.
I wish the Russians would knock 'Jerry' out. [Jerry was the nickname given to Germans during the Second World War.]

Oct 8 Wednesday
Had long chat with Don & Chris & tried to impress them with the demerits of PG Wodehouse.

P.G. Wodehouse, author and humourist, moved to France in 1934 for tax purposes, and was interned by the Germans for about a year. He broadcast comedic talks over German radio to the United States before they entered the war; they were deemed controversial, and he never returned to England for fear of prosecution.[64]

Wally's 'long chat' most likely revolved around these broadcasts and P.G.'s relationship with the Germans.

Awoke feeling extremely fit.
Don & I were late for formation.
One-hour Dual flight.
Grand swim in pool.
Bags of procedure lecture in flying line.
Must acquire flying technique of stress planes.

If the stress state of a material particle is such that only non-zero stress components act in one plane, the particle is in plane stress [65] [I trust the reader finds this is clearer than mud].

Oct 9 Thursday

[Another letter to his family, this one was more interesting and quite amusing.]

F/C Wolman M.L.
Flying Cadet Detachment
Block 215
Class 42-B
Gunter Field
Alabama U.S.A.
My Dear Family

I hope you all fasted well [he referred to the festival of Yom Kippur] *& are enjoying the best of fortune & health.*

Of late I have read of increased German activity over the British Isles & I hope they have not been bothering you.

Today marks the eighth day that I am at Gunter Field. Not unnaturally, I have had no post arrive for me since I got here, but I look forward to a record mail some day this week.

Well, for lack of other subjects, I shall tell you all about my new abode.

Gunter Field is a camp holding some 400 aviation cadets; a great number of enlisted men (volunteers) & an equally great number of draftees [draftees were conscripts].

According to the 'cadet rules & regulations', we cadets may not condescend to speak to the latter two groups. Obviously, these 'rules & regulations' are disregarded as are the many other dozens of whims and fancies of some old potbellied general. Yes, we have managed to whip the American Air Corps system into an extremely feasible system & I'm afraid I have little to grumble with or at.

Last Saturday we took part in a military review given by the British aviation cadets, and one of the group who took the salute was Jack Dempsey. I thought he was badly in need of a shave, which was rather accentuated due to the fact that he wore a white suit. This review took place in the morning and in the lunch meal, he came into the mess & related one or two anecdotes.

In the afternoon of this same day, I went into Montgomery. Strangely enough & although that town is by no means big, I felt extremely out of place in the 'Metropolis' as I had become used to the easy going intimate & friendly wide-open spaces.

However, after visiting a number of local stores & somewhat disorganising the smooth running of most of them, I went to the flicks & saw a rather miserable effort of a film.

Like every other Southern town, Montgomery has a huge negro population & also, like every other town, it has infamous colour prejudice.

A case in point was an article in the newspaper which stated that a special guard was given to a negro who had 'accidentally' had a motor 'accident' with a car containing four white folk delivering fatal injuries to each of them & being seriously injured as a result himself.

The guard was placed to prevent a possible lynching.

Thursday – I have had to leave this letter for 24 hours.

To resume I believe Montgomery can become exceedingly interesting if one can find a patron with a car, especially if she is pretty (the patron not the car).

At the flying line, one has to learn to fly all over again & today for the first time I soloed in this B.T.13A.

Have I told you that the heat here has reached an all-time record high? In England today, it must be getting cold & dark early whereas out here the sun sets at about 6pm & sometimes the heat drops below 65 degrees.

Last week a hurricane passed near Carlstrom Field & from the lads there I learn that at 3am the planes had to be shifted inland to prevent possible damage. From the same source, I learnt that the junior class that we left behind when we came away, had been confined the weekend after we had left, due to the panties which we hung up the flag mast. Some people have no sense of humour.

I am looking forward of your all being well, Ray especially & I hope Charlie is in fine mettle.

Give my love to Shirley & accept it yourselves.
Write soon,
Ta Wally

Oct 9 Thursday
Have somehow acquired 'ring worm'. I am at this moment awaiting treatment.
Soloed in 345 [a type of aircraft] *today & surprised myself in doing so.*

Oct 10 Friday
Flew solo & Dual today & I believe I pleased Mr C all in all.
Started 'Kipps' [*The Story of a Simple Soul* by H G Wells, first published in 1905, and reputedly Wells's favourite work.]

Oct 11 Saturday
LT White took almost everyone's name for the most ridiculous of reasons.
Film, Dinner, Whitely, Roller Skating, Midnight Film.
Am ever & again desirous of female companionship.

Oh dear, again I am feeling so sorry for my 20-year-old uncle.

Bed 3 o/clock, after travelling with a drunken whore all the way back. [I doubt this was the type of company he sought.]

Oct 16 Thursday
Film on Sex Hygiene in hangar, which I thought good enough to put me off my oats ['oats' was slang for having sex].

Oct 17 Friday
My first game of Rugby (push & run & run). Picked ball off the ground [American football originated from the British game of rugby].

Strong wind & poor flying exhibition.
Soloed from Shorter [85 miles North of Maxwell airfield].

Oct 19 Sunday
In bed late, after breakfast I was disillusioned to find only grapes.
Mr Jim Macy proved a host indeed for we strolled with him through the Oak Park & then after promising to invite us to dinner, he took us to Huntingdon Girls College, where we were greeted by a bevy of pretty girls of whom I preferred Mary Walker and City Beat to the rest.

Oct 20 Monday
Collected my first star today after a pretty poor trip.
Passed all 3 Morse tests.

Oct 21 Tuesday
Sick parade.
90-degree stage. One-sided conversation with stage examiner.
Wrote to City Beat. [Wally frequently used nicknames for girls that he met – 'City Beat' was one of these girls. I do not know her real name.]
Bloody annoyed at not having received any letter from home since I arrived.

Oct 22 Wednesday
Sick parade.

Am certain I will fail engines exam for again I slept during lesson.

Did not post that letter to 'City Beat' but through Sue Read, rang her, Margaret Sue Jones, & made a date & asked her for one for Ginger.

Oct 23 Thursday
Margaret did not ring me.

Wally continued in his struggle to find a girlfriend. How frustrating when he was so ready to sacrifice his life for his country, but seemingly unable to sow his oats.

Surprised myself by staying awake & almost enjoying ground school.

[Ground school taught aircraft operation procedures and other essential knowledge to become a safe pilot.]

Lots of chaps received letters from home via Arcadia, not I.
'Lord Haw-Haw' on radio.

American-born fascist William Joyce, aka Lord Haw-Haw, was an anti-Semite and a member of Mosley's British Union of Fascists. Fleeing to Germany just before the outbreak of war, he took a job broadcasting Nazi propaganda during wartime. In 1945, he was tried, found guilty and hanged; he was the last person in the UK to be executed for treason.[66]

I finished 'The Little French Girl' by Anne Douglas Sedgwick.

This refers to the story of a French girl sent to England in quest of a suitable marriage. It describes her struggle to become enmeshed in the social standards between the two different countries.[67] It was not really appropriate for Wally, who struggled to form his own romantic liaisons.

Trouble in France due to assassination of two Germans.

Karl Hotz, the German commander of Nantes, was murdered by the French Resistance. The Germans soon retaliated: they shot 27 hostages outside the town of Châteaubriant, and another 21 elsewhere.[68]

Oct 24 Friday

Margaret, bless her, embarrassed me somewhat by ringing me this morning via admin office with sick parade & cadets present. She has arranged 'date' for Ginger.

Had 20-hour check with Whitmore, & as I couldn't hear him, we got bloody annoyed at each other.

Wally and his friends took a trip to Crampton Bowl, a ground purpose-built for baseball and American football; nowadays it is used primarily for the latter.

Photograph of an American football game

Met Marg & Betsy at Liggett's & Marg let Ginger drive her car to the bowl.
What a driver! Ball game extremely interesting. Bands, majorettes, popcorn. Coca Cola, cushions.
Drove for a coffee in a most haphazard fashion.
Camp 12:15.

Oct 25 Saturday
Sick Parade. No drill.

Played an extremely tough game of Rugby & badly scraped my leg & twisted my neck.

Why on earth was he playing a tough game of rugby while on sick parade?

Jay met us at Liggett's & we drove to his house.
Small yet extremely fine dinner & seated with his very old parents we sang to Cliff & Jay's accompaniment.

Advertisement for Liggett's drug store, mentioned by Wally

Oct 26 Sunday
Invitation to tea from Mrs Merton who can trace her family tree from Alfred the Great via the French Court & the Cameroons.
Met extremely charming girls there – Francis, Mary, Marcy.
Mrs M tried so hard to give us a typical English tea. Swing & Chopin & Wagner.
Took this fine lady for a stroll 'Constitutional' & felt honoured.
[And which fine lady was that?]

Oct 27 Monday
Sick Parade.
Sent Charles a friendship card & sent 3 A.A.C. Cards [instruction cards] *to Sydney & Charlie.*
President Roosevelt makes an aggressive speech following the torpedo attack on an American cruiser.

Speaking on 'Navy and Total Defence Day', Roosevelt said:
"We have wished to avoid shooting. But the shooting has started...
and history has recorded who fired the first shot. In the long run,
however, all that matters is who fired the last shot." [69]

"USS Kearny" (DD-432), a United States Navy warship was
torpedoed by a German U-boat in October 1941; she survived the
attack and later served in North Africa and the Mediterranean.

*Am in a dilemma as to whether or not Margaret is the girl for
me.*

I was bemused – finally, after much angst, he has a girlfriend,
but now he is confused as to whether she is the right girl for him!

Was his dilemma shared with anyone apart from his diary [and
me?].

Oct 28 Tuesday
*Feel pretty low as I haven't received a letter from home
since arrival.*

Wally was lonely. He was 4,000 miles away from family and
friends; telephone calls were expensive, and a lack of mail
exacerbated the isolation. Hence there are so many references to lack
of communication.

Nov 5 Wednesday
Rang Margaret but she was out.

Nov 6 Thursday
Again, she was out.

Nov 7 Friday
[This day was his birthday.]
*& So, I spent my birthday alone, in town, where I went to the
flicks.*
No Cards.
Sent birthday card to Shirley.

Nov 8 Saturday

Accepted blind date & met Ellen's sister Hilda.
A pleasant evening ended with us all seeing a film ('Hold Back the Dawn').[70]

Hold Back the Dawn was nominated for an Academy Award for Best Picture. It was a romantic drama starring Charles Boyer, Olivia de Havilland and Paulette Goddard.

Nov 10 Monday
Margaret invited me out to Huntingdon to see 'Much Ado about Nothing' which proved most amusing. Especially 'AAH', & the excess hair.

Nov 11 Tuesday
Parade through Dexter Avenue with rifles & bayonets. Sorry that 'Montgomerians' did not respect the silence.

Nov 14 Wednesday
Had decided to visit Synagogue but found I was scheduled for night flying.
Finished at 10:30, but stayed out till 12:00 in order to miss S.M.I.

Nov 15 Thursday
Ground school.
Did not miss S.M.I. as it was held late in the morning.
Took a number of snaps [photographs] *in the afternoon & went skating in the evening when I danced for the first time.*
Introduced Liggett's to the delights of Milk & Dash.

Nov 16 Sunday
Terribly annoyed that none of us woke for breakfast.
Saw film in Town. 'It Started with Eve' starring Charles Laughton [a musical comedy that was also nominated for an Oscar].

Jay called whilst I was out.

Nov 19 Wednesday

Could not get to Laurel but made trip to Jackson – Evergreen Gunter.
3.25 hours of interest. Lost my map on the way.
Went skating & saw Jay there. Would have been grand but for the fact that it was so crowded.

Nov 20 Thursday
Wrote number of letters.
THANKSGIVING.

Thanksgiving has since been moved to the fourth Thursday of November.

Grand dinner with Turkey, Cigars, Gigs, choc & beer, & with admin officers at top table – Grand Sing-Song.
Jay proposes trip to Pensacola (Florida).

Nov 21 Friday
Instruments – poor performance.
Ground Control to Con Hogan 'if you can hear me, waggle your hip'.
C. Hogan to Ground Control, 'if you can hear me, waggle your tower'.
Went to Clayton St Synagogue where an unorthodox service was held & 'The Keys of the Kingdom', a 1941 book by AJ Cronin, was discussed by Rabbi Blackshmuler (surprising because the story revolves around a Christian priest).

Wally's parents' home was maintained according to Orthodox Jewish principals – strictly kosher food, separate cutlery for 'milk and meat' dishes, and respectful of the religious festivals – yet Wally rarely mentions his faith; was this because he was so far from home, in distance and his way of life?

Nov 29 Saturday
Enlisted men of 2nd LT killed in crash.
About 18 kites cracked up in lesser number of days.

['Kite' described an aircraft, and probably referred to their training aircraft.]

Dec 1 Monday
Lieutenant Grine gave me some kind yet not inspiring advice – 'Hard Work'.

Dec 2 Tuesday
Completed my flying today.
Jay came out to see us & brought some pecans from his mother.
He was disappointed.
[By the pecans?]

After five months of hard training, Wally gets to enjoy a week's leave with his buddy Bill; they decide to travel to New York as tourists, and so Wally carefully records the journey in his diary:

Dec 3 Wednesday
Got my pass & together with Bill set out on a 4:00pm long haul.
Our first lift advised us to wait, and go with a friend of his in the morning.
Undeterred we got lift to Columbus.
From here we got a short lift nearby (14 miles) Honky Tonk.
[I have no idea what or where Honky Tonk might be.]
Here we waited some considerable time but eventually got a lift in a truck to Atlanta at 25 mph.
We got there at 12 o clock.

Dec 4 Thursday
'Wiggly Piggly' [Piggly Wiggly, a store in the South] *distributing van took us by devious ways, quickly to crossroad 40 miles from Athens.*
Cap got us to a lift to Athens.
Left my cap in car.
Made Toccoa but only got short hops from travelling salesman to Spartanburg. Here we were promised a lift to New York if we wait for a truck & so waited. Alas none showed up and so we

tried to get on the road again but failing to get a lift we slept the night in a truckers' home which did us a good deal of good.

Wally's journey from Montgomery to New York City

Dec 5 Friday
The day started fortunately for us & lifts were many & long.
One good lift took us at a whacking great pace to High Point &
here we met luck indeed, for we found a student from Selma
[Alabama] who was going to Washington. Sharing the cost of
gas with him we made Washington at 8pm.
Virginia & West Virginia are beautiful states with fine pines.
Despite our efforts we found no wealthy spouses in Washington
[Haha!].

Dec 6 Saturday

Woke fairly early & found Bill's cousin Vernon about to arrive.
A fine chap, Bill & I left them together. I went to the sights,
Lincoln memorial, then Washington Monument, the Capitol [the
Senate] & was duly impressed.

The Lincoln Memorial and the Washington Monument
[Photos by Izzy Holtz]

The Jefferson Memorial and the Capitol building, Washington, DC

At 12:30 we caught train for N.Y. Arrived N.Y. 4pm.
I will get a stiff neck.
[Peering up at those skyscrapers could give anyone a stiff neck!]
Vernon wants to take us to Radio City, we skated on the beautiful rink in Rockefeller Centre.
Pennsylvania Hotel our residence.
After dinner went out to find Walter, we waited for them at the Cafe Russe then we met them at No 1 Fifth Avenue.
Saw 'Keep Em Flying' at 2pm which I did enjoy. [He was referring to a comedy film starring Abbott & Costello.]

Pearl Harbour

Described by Roosevelt as "One day which will live in infamy", 7 December 1941 began innocuously enough, as Wally enjoyed a fine lunch with his friends.[71]

Dec 7 Sunday
Went to 96th Street but no luck, Post Office was closed.
Took a fine lunch & Walter left.

His flippant entries paid no respect to this pivotal day in world events; maybe he was even disrespectful when ignoring the devastating surprise aerial attack on the US Navy at Pearl Harbour.

I was astounded that this important piece of history – a day when 400 Japanese Navy planes sank four US battleships and numerous other craft, damaged aircraft, and caused the death of 2,400 US military personal – got no mention in his diary.[72]

The live commentary of the attack was almost certainly heard in every bar in New York City, as NBC relayed the broadcast across America:

"Hello, NBC. Hello, NBC. This is KTU in Honolulu, Hawaii. I am speaking from the roof of the Advertiser Publishing Company Building. We have witnessed this morning in the distant view a brief full battle of Pearl Harbour and the severe bombing of Pearl Harbour by enemy planes, undoubtedly

Japanese. The city of Honolulu has also been attacked and considerable damage done.

"This battle has been going on for nearly three hours. One of the bombs dropped within fifty feet of KTU tower. It is no joke. It is a real war...." [73]

His next entry reads:

We went pubbing & eventually made our way to Radio City where we saw an excellent film & stage show 'The Rockettes'.
At this hour Vernon left & Bill & I did the rounds met some drunks & then some limeys!
Left Bill in some cheap cafe drinking whisky on 23rd St.

The Japanese attack and its implication on their wartime role must have been discussed with his mates.

Dec 8 Monday
Went to the Post Office to try to find Mrs A's address but failed to.
Went out with Bill & midst the panic of Times Square, we were photographed facing gazing heavenward.
Met one Ray a U.S.P. CAF.
Drank a considerable amount of gut rot & in a poor state, went ice skating where I conked at all the girls, I think.
Bill didn't keep his appointment & after finding him happy in J.D.'S I went to see a film.

The banner headline in Monday's *New York Times* spoke volumes of the attack:

JAPAN DECLARES WAR ON U.S. AND BRITAIN;
MAKES SUDDEN ATTACK ON HAWAII

Japan followed their raid on Pearl Harbour with an attack the next day on Malaya, forcing Britain to declare war nine hours before the United States did the same.

Events that must have been a talking point around the city, did nothing to prompt a mention by Wally.

Dec 9 Tuesday
Met S. Klein & chatted with him in hotel lobby.

Surely the attack and Britain and US's entry into the war was discussed? Whatever took place, Wally continued his vacation as if nothing worthwhile had happened, and went shopping.

Went shopping this morning down Fifth Avenue.
Got fashion books & candy.
Empire State Building with Bill & after being duly impressed, went round a store where we met an Englishman.
With Vernon & Bill, then I went around to Hickory House where Joe Marcello provided excellent music & where we met the lesser stars of orchestra land.
Fortune teller forecast 2 merits and no scrumpy for me.
[Poor Wally cannot even get some positive news about his love life from a fortune teller.]

They now commenced the return journey to base, described by Wally:

Dec 10 Wednesday
Bill went on the roof looking for cats at 5:00am.
At 9:30am caught train for Montgomery.
Vernon had breakfast with us & I found myself sorry to end my acquaintanceship with so fine a fellow.
Met Anderson at Washington which did a little to relieve the monotony of the trip.
"Prince of Wales" & "Repulse" sunk.

Japan's response to Britain's declaration of war was a failed attack on Singapore. Returning early on this morning, the Japanese sank two British ships, the battleship *HMS Prince of Wales* and the cruiser *HMS Repulse.*[74]

Dec 11 Thursday
Morry's brother killed in air accident.

Izzy, my father's brother, was killed on 30 October, but Wally had just learnt the news.

Continuing a boring train journey, we arrived at camp at 12:10 [after a 27-hour journey].
Very many letters await including one from Harry. Also included many, many invitations.

Dec 12 Friday
Russians have scored a major victory on the East Front.

By early December, the Wehrmacht had realised it lacked the strength to capture Moscow, so it suspended its attack on Russia, providing the opportunity for the Russians to launch a counterattack.[75]

Hitler announced on this day that the Jewish race was to be annihilated.[76]

Have written consistently since arriving back, & still I have many letters to write.
Mr Marcus rang me up & invited me there. I accepted.
Had dinner with Mr M & later in the evening went round to the Marks's.
Fine folk, they gave me Scotch & Kimmel [a type of rye bread].
Was driven back.

Dec 13 Saturday
Did most of my packing.
Two Bullshit inspections.
Went to see poor film 'Sundown'.

It comes as no surprise to hear Wally's description of *Sundown* as a poor film, for despite receiving three Oscar nominations, the film was a failure at the box office.[77]

Had grand evening skating, am determined to find a regular partner.
Was complimented on my dancing.

Dec 14 Sunday

Had drink at the Rappaports', & I am interested in Bubbles.
The R's appear to be fine people.
On to the Trumpers & while she appears to be a cow, he isn't
bad. Poor class of a rich Jew.

Dec 15 Monday

Woke late & missed breakfast.
Packed.
Asked Lieutenant Phillips for my letter & he shook me by the
hand goodbye.
Trucks to Maxwell which should be alright.
Food – not bad.

Dec 17 Wednesday

Problem of the week appears to be, shall I or shall I not ring up
Bubbles R.
Smelly Feet???
[A most strange nickname for a girl!]

Dec 18 Thursday

Flew D.5. [most likely a DC5 aircraft] *for the first time. A fine*
ship I will like it, I think.
Received letter from Mrs Bloomfield, sentimental over Toronto.
[So, what on earth had happened there with Mrs Bloomfield?]
7.E.T [trainees] *came in with us to make it six to a room.*
Popped round to see the Makowskys & was invited round for
Friday dinner.

Dec 19 Friday

Flew today but didn't Solo – shame.
Am almost finished 'Green is my Valley' Llewellyn.

How Green Was my Valley, a 1939 novel by Richard Llewellyn,
won the US National Book Award for people's favourite novel in
1940.[78]

Good sleep in the ground shool.

Had an extremely fine old-fashioned Jewish dinner with Mr &
Mrs Makowsky. She is a fine woman
Apple pie made bed for me. [Another youthful prank.]
Bags of fighting in room.

Dec 20 Saturday
7 Day week schedule. Flying line.
Will take Hilda out tonight.
Ground school till four & I caused a rumpus by making the
class stay 5 minutes extra.

Dec 21 Sunday
The first Sunday I have ever flown. Flew as in a hang-over.

Dec 24 Wednesday
Link.

The flight simulator, named after its inventor and American
aviation pioneer Ed Link, was designed in 1929 in response to a
high number of plane crashes. The Link enabled pilots to learn the
technique of flying with the aid of instruments, which was
particularly necessary when they were flying in poor weather.[79]

A most miserable Xmas eve.

Dec 25 Thursday
Went out at 10:00am, mooched around town, tried to go skating
but it was closed & so I went to a film.
It was raining quite a lot & so once more I had a poor day.
Poured.
The boys again came in at about 2:00am.

Dec 26 Friday
Have a blind date for tonight.
Flew in the morning, instruments.
On inter phone – 'Look out you silly cunt'
Went to town & Minnie took us to her place where we had tea,
& later we went round to Marjorie's place where I met Sarah
who is unfortunately young, although tall & pretty.

Played games etc.
Mary's father – semi pissed, had great fun with all the lads.

Dec 27 Saturday
Went to town & rang the women, Minnie, Sarah, Marjory,
Miriam & Elizabeth.
Minnie ran round for a bit & when the girls eventually showed
up, we went to see 'Keep Em Flying' (the 3rd time).
[Abbot and Costello starred in the 1941 slapstick comedy *Keep*
'Em Flying.]

Dec 28 Sunday
Flew instruments with Don, & whilst I was under the hood, we
got lost.
Don asked me whether I would like to fly a little beam, but I
refused & stayed under the hood.

"Flying the beam"[80] described the use of radio transmissions
from radio stations to enable the navigator to fix his position. A
steady tone told the pilot that he was on course, and a Morse-code
dot/dash sound would signal they had drifted off course to one side
or the other.

Flew formation in the afternoon with Don & Thomas.
Thoroughly enjoyed it.
Had 5 hours up today & am bloody tired.

It was obviously great fun to fly and write about a rat race, but
there was also real depth to his other scribblings. I could so easily
have glossed over many of these scribblings, and momentarily forget
that these entries reflected Wally's deepest private thoughts,
particularly those about his family's financial difficulties and girls.

There was no-one who was emotionally close enough in
America who cared about him or his problems, and with whom he
could discuss them, but I can identify with my uncle's feelings,
especially when I am alone for long periods.

Dec 29 Monday
Had a really grand rat race today & Don & I flew a fair formation.
Had some S.H. Calisthenics.
Received letter from home.

Concerned both over the difficult straits my family find themselves in, & the way they appear to be worried over me.

The outlook for the Wolman family remained bleak – they were worried about Wally flying planes; they were fearful for their family in Poland with horrendous stories of Nazi murdering Jews; and they experienced constant terror from the constant bombing of London that threatened their family – and the end of the war was nowhere in sight.

Chapter 8

WALLY, 1942

Introduction

Without access to a 1942 diary, this chapter was created using relevant entries found elsewhere.

Wally would shortly complete his six-month training course in America, then return to England to enter the real war. The closest he had got to any action so far was standing on guard duty at RAF bases in England.

Feb 7 Sunday
Graduated 'WINGS'.
Awarded Pilots Distinction Badge.

Feb 10 Wednesday
Started back for England.
[He waited in Moncton, Canada, for his ship to return to England.]

Feb 15 Sunday
Fall of Singapore.

The superior training and equipment of the Japanese enabled their troops to advance 1,000km in less than 10 weeks and then, within seven days, General Yamashita bluffed the British into handing over their "impregnable fortress" when he demanded an unconditional surrender, despite being numerically inferior. Churchill described the loss as the "worst disaster" in British military history.[81]

Mar 12 Thursday
Set sail for England.

Mar 23 Monday
ARRIVED BACK IN ENGLAND.

Mar 24 Tuesday
On this day, Wally transferred to No 54 Group at Flying Training Command, Charborough Hall in Bournemouth, Hampshire. Then later, he moved to RAF Leconfield in Yorkshire on 19 May.

Wally's first letter after he returned

All correspondence posted from military bases was censored to stop the leak of classified information. Envelopes were unstuck; letters, postcards and parcels were examined, opened and read; and those parts that were perceived to be sensitive were selectively obliterated or redacted. Once marked accordingly, they were sent on to their destination.

Evidence that this first letter was examined is obvious from the tear mark at the top edge of the front page, which is where the address would have been.

Neatly scribed on sheets of wide-ruled lined paper, it was sent from either Bournemouth Training Command or Leconfield.

The letter below shows his concern and maturity in business matters for someone of his age.

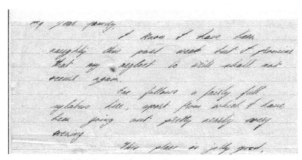

Note the rough tear along the top edge

My Dear Family

I know I have been naughty this past week, but I promise that my neglect to write shall not occur again.

One follows a fairly full syllabus here, apart from which I have been going out pretty nearly every evening.

This place is jolly good, all things taken into consideration, when I tell you that, in ten days I have had three eggs, you will get an indication.

I don't do very much flying here really, for I have yet to solo on the ship we use here, still I feel pretty confident.

Perhaps by now Lieber has got the 'gen' on 'the racket.' If she has, you know I am very interested.

About that dress for Harry's aunt, I leave the matter in your very capable hands. Harry's aunt wants a dress, if you can do so profitably, do so, otherwise I shouldn't be too concerned about it.

I trust my nephew is coming along sturdily.

You seem to have your hands full & more at the workshop. Let the manufacturers do the worrying, you just carry on like normal human beings by which I mean I hope you are not working outside of normal hours.

Before the books are next brought up to date, I should like to offer some advice. Perhaps I shall be able to get some leave in a month's time at which time I will advise you.

Now to be extremely practical, will you please forward me all my RAF shirts, socks & collars, and all my light underwear plus a

*towel, & my pyjama, &, most important, lots of handkerchiefs,
please. Thanks.*

*Possibly I shall send some of my things home for laundering
should the laundry situation not prove satisfactory, in which case I
shall beg your assistance.*

*Don't be too concerned about me, you ought to know I like
myself too much to do anything silly.*

*Give my best wishes to all,
Love to all, Wally.*

Second letter

Dated 21 May, each page is imprinted with the official motto of the
RAF, *Per Ardua Ad Astra* ("Through Adversity to the Stars"). This
letter was not censored, and the address was surprisingly left intact.

*21 May 1942
Sgt Wolman. M.L. 1382185
Sergeants Mess No 15.
A.F.U. LECONFIELD
YORKS*

*My Dear Family,
I have in a measure settled down here at Leconfield & today for the
first time in more than three months, I started flying once more.*

*The camp itself is a really good one of a pre-war type, therefore
it has many comforts.*

*The Sergeant's mess is a really grand affair & the food we are
served with is jolly good.*

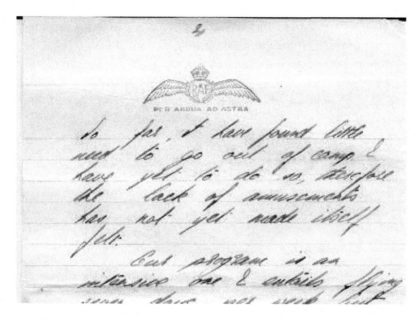

Little, pretty 'WAAFS' serve at the tables & all is well & I like
this place.

Fortunately, or otherwise, the nearest town of any size (Hull) is
about 12 miles away, while Beverly, a populated area, is but three
miles distance.

So far, I have found little need to go out of the camp & have yet
to do so, therefore the lack of amusements has not yet made itself
felt.

Our programme is an intensive one & entails flying seven days
per week, but we can go out every night after duty (6 o'clock
approx.) & one also gets 24 hours off duty once a week.

For the next few weeks, I can safely say I shan't get home
weekends, but it is possible that I shall get some leave in about a
months' time.

Whoever said that the RAF wastes petrol doesn't know his
facts; they are so careful here that everyone has been issued with
bikes with which to reach the dispersal points quickly.

Now you know that before coming here, cycling was not one of
my accomplishments & so I had to acquire the art very rapidly. With

Don's help I have, to some extent, mastered this weird & wonderful machine & in a crowd, will pass as a cyclist.

It is queer flying in this country, there is so very much cloud about.

Ceiling today was 800 feet & as I am used to an operational height of 6,000 feet you will readily see the vast difference. Still, it's great to be flying once again.

Seeing as this place is so very much out of the way, I am led to believe that the mail service is considerably slower than is usual, this must account for my not having heard from you today. I trust everyone is well & that Barry is doing fine.

Give my respects to all
Bags of love
Wally.

Sep 1 Tuesday

On this day, Wally was transferred to No 15 Group Coastal Command RAF Limavady County Derry in Northern Ireland, where he was to fly Wellington aircraft.

The success in battling U-boats and maritime units of the Luftwaffe was achieved with these support facilities.

Third letter

Wally and John Fox were RAF buddies. John was killed on 11 October, and although John's mother had never met Ethel, she wrote her a letter several days later sharing her grief. How on earth did John's parents deal with the sudden loss of a child when fighting for his country?

The letter below was censored with some words redacted.

15 October 1942
9 Farnan Road
London SW16
15-10-'42

Dear Madame

*I must apologise for not knowing your name as anything than
'Wally's Mother'.*

    *I have met your son on two occasions and was pleased that he
was a great friend of my son Johnnie.*

    *I know that John had heard from your son recently, but will you
kindly let him know that John Fox died in an aeroplane crash on
October 11th 1942. He was on an overland flight in* ▮ *& he and the
other four of his crew crashed a* ▮ *at* ▮ *in the morning. [These
marks indicate where words were censored.]*

    *This is sad news and if you do not feel like forwarding to your
son, we shall understand for they were great friends.*

Yours very sincerely
Margaret Fox

Nov 21 Saturday

The RAF records indicate that Wally's transfer to the 179th
Squadron at RAF Gibraltar Coastal Command coincided with the
second anniversary of his enlistment.

    The squadron, formed in September 1942, had just recently
moved to Gibraltar; its sole purpose was to patrol the approach to
the Mediterranean, looking for U-boats and enemy ships, again
flying Wellington aircraft.

Dec 17, Thursday

The Foreign Secretary, Anthony Eden, spoke to Parliament about
anti-Semitism in Europe.[82]

In his address, he said:

"The attention of the Governments of Belgium, Czechoslovakia,
Greece, Luxembourg, the Netherlands, Norway, Poland, the United
States of America, and the United Kingdom of Great Britain and

Northern Ireland...has been drawn to numerous reports from Europe that the German authorities...are now carrying into effect Hitler's oft repeated intention to exterminate the Jewish people in Europe.

"Jews are being transported in conditions of appalling horror and brutality to Eastern Europe.

"In Poland, which has been made the principal Nazi slaughterhouse, the ghettoes established by the German invaders are being systematically emptied of all Jews except a few highly skilled workers required for war industries.

"None of those taken away are ever heard of again.

"The able-bodied are slowly worked to death in labour camps. The infirm are left to die of exposure and starvation or are deliberately massacred in mass executions."

Chapter 9

WALLY'S 1943 DIARY

Introduction

Wally's 1943 diary was in better condition than his frayed 1941 pocket diary. As in his first diary, Wally started by describing his day-to-day activities.

Cover and a few pages from Wally's 1943 diary

Jan 1 Friday
The old year went out in bad grace, but '43 has opened with blue skies & bright sunshine.

Jan 2 Saturday
Fooled around the flight deck in the day & in the evening went to local cinema.
Received first letter from home dated 28th Decem-ber.
Borrowed £1 from Don.

Jan 3 Sunday
With all, but John, went on "RENOWN" for visit in afternoon.

The *HMS Renown*[83] was the lead ship in her class of battleships. After the First World War, she was extensively re-fitted as a "Royal yacht", with a squash court and a cinema, to carry Edward Prince of Wales on his tours of Canada, Australia and New Zealand.

In 1939, the *Renown* participated in the hunt for the battleships *Admiral Graf Spree* and the *Bismarck* in 1941. She transported Winston Churchill to conferences held with Allied leaders during the war, and was eventually sold for scrap in 1948.

Jan 4 Monday
Scheduled to take off at 09:00 but did not get off till 12:00 due to engine trouble & receiver bother.

Wally piloted the Wellington 'C' aircraft with five other sergeants – Wood, Smith, Leadley, Ridge and White.

Anti-submarine sweep, sighted but couldn't attack U-boat.
Took off at 11:57 to hunt submarines, flying on an anti-submarine sweep.
At 16:00 a periscope feather was sighted below their aircraft but at height of 500ft there was nothing to be seen of the wake. Landed at 19:45 in darkness.
Controversy now exists as to whether I got down in time but I am confident I did.

Jan 9 Saturday
Anti-submarine sweep West – Same crew.
On Wellington D flown on anti-submarine patrol sweeping West. Same crew.
Departure 07:52 landing 17:40.

Note from Operation Records Book: At 08:56, an oil streak about 1 mile long was investigated. Six motor vessels were sighted through the sortie & at 10:57 the aircraft homed into a Liberator aircraft.

The B24 Bomber, known as "the Liberator", was loaned to the UK as part of the Lend Lease support programme. It was also used for anti-submarine warfare.

Jan 10 Sunday
Did some construction work in the furniture line.
Went over submarine Dolphin (Ursula class) in afternoon.
Went to see film 'The Day will Dawn'.
[*The Day Will Dawn* was a 1942 war film starring Ralph Richardson and Deborah Kerr.]

Jan 12 Tuesday
Semi-gale continues.
Went for 3-mile road run with Don & came back sweating, went for a shower.
Popped down to line D checked on progress of 'D'.
In the afternoon Wing Commander Coombe told us of our impending fate. I face developments with trepidation.

Jan 13 Wednesday
Stand-off.
Bullshitted in best blue. [Wally's "best blue" outfit was most likely his RAF uniform.]
Went to see 'Xmas Party' in evening & as a result had a furious debate on morality.

Jan 14 Thursday
W/C Coombe informed us of one pending, splitting up.
Brassed!!!

Jan 15 Friday
Anti-Submarine Sweep. North West.
Poor navigation. Poor weather. Binding trip.

Note from Operation Records Book: *An unidentified aircraft was seen heading towards Gibraltar and a coaster, a Spanish M/V [motor vessel], 2 trawlers, 2 further Spanish M/V & a small conveyor & 2 more coasters were seen. Departure 07:54 Landing 19:28.*

Jan 16 Saturday
Put in application for a commission.
Went to very good R.A.F. v Black Watch. We lost 5-1.

Jan 17 Sunday
Letters from Home.
Took Dagul up.
Did some practice bombing
Went to see 'Uncensored' with Don.

Set in the era before the Nazi occupation of Belgium, the 1942 film *Uncensored*[84] starred Eric Portman as a Brussels nightclub owner and André Delange, who also published and secretly distributed an anti-Nazi newspaper, *La Libre Belgique*.

Jan 18 Monday
Rationing of bread.

Jan 19 Tuesday
Bought number of lemons & bananas for home.
Tried to get into 'Naval' but no use.

Jan 20 Wednesday
Convoy Escort in Wellington J

Note from Operation Records Book: *Up at 05:50 Down at 15:57. That's 12 hours flying, looking out for enemy ships and particularly U-boats.*
Saw whale & had quite a thrill. [A little excitement doesn't hurt when searching for enemy submarines.]

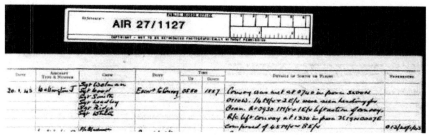

Extract from the Operations Record Book

The names of aircrew were listed in the Operation Record Book with details of their sorties and flights. Wally's name, being the first, indicates he was the main pilot on this flight. The centre columns provide the time of the aircraft's departure and return.

Jan 21 Thursday

A single dash indicates a missing aircraft. It's always a shock to see this stroke in the landing column, for it clearly indicates a tragedy.

The words in the right-hand column tell the story:

The aircraft took off on a sweep to the east with instructions to land at Tafaraoui [Algeria] but failed to do so. No signals or messages were received from the crew. The body of Sergeant Beale was washed ashore on the North African Coast some weeks later.

Entering data into these reports was traumatic. The author had to acknowledge that colleagues had lost their lives and pass the tragic news on to the next of kin.

Jan 22 Friday
Letter from home.
Went to Colonial Secretary & handed in application for Visa.

Jan 23 Saturday
TRIPOLI OURS

By the time this engagement between Britain and the Axis countries had started, General Rommel (aka the 'Desert Fox') was already on the run. Dashing for Buerat, Libya, he abandoned Tripoli after his defeat at El Alamein in November, thereby allowing British troops to enter the capital unopposed.[85]

Jan 24 Sunday
Went West for escort, but wireless transmitter went unserviceable & we turned back 5:30.

Note from Operation Records Book: *Saw a merchant vessel, destroyer and 2 Spanish motor vehicles. At 15:06 the wireless transmitter failed, so returned to Base.*

Jan 25 Monday
Find myself playing cards too much.
Drew a couple of tennis racquets from stores to play
Dick & Eric.

Jan 27 Wednesday
Nick & Young's crews unserviceable so we did escort.
Burst wheel on landing due to ground sloping on overshoot.
Bloody poor show; bloody little wind.

Jan 28 Thursday
Talk of detachment so went down to line early.
Am not detached due to yesterday's landing.

Jan 29 Friday
Had egg for breakfast.
Was scheduled to fly in evening but aircraft wasn't 'S-safe'.
Beat Eric 3-0 in tennis.

Jan 30 Saturday
Aircraft still unserviceable & rose early for nought.
Distinct trouble with aircraft on Squadron.
Have arranged to visit Spain tomorrow.

Jan 31 Sunday
Crossed line after lunch. Ponces – snotty begging kiddies – dim
soldiers – attractive females – 100 Octane sentry boxes.
Fruit purchased – cognac & coffee – locust beans.
NO BULLFIGHT.

Feb 1 Monday
Squadron grounded.
Bathed & had fun on beach in afternoon.
Wrote home.
Taffy Davies presented us with 2 eggs each.

Feb 2 Tuesday
Almost broke.
No mail!
Lecture on first aid by Flight Lieutenant Sutton.

Feb 3 Wednesday
BROKE.
Rostov threatened.
German 6th Army no more.

Stalingrad, an industrial centre, stretched 30 miles along the banks of the river Volga in Southern Russia. Hitler's offensive had commenced in July 1942, but by February, the Wehrmacht's 6th Army was defeated, and their generals surrendered despite vehement opposition from Hitler. The Battle of Stalingrad was termed the bloodiest in the history of warfare, leaving roughly two million casualties.[86]

Hitler had earlier proclaimed that after Stalingrad was captured, all of its male residents were to be killed and the women and children deported because they were communists and therefore "especially dangerous".[87]

Feb 5 Friday
Went to lecture on so called debate on 'Is there a Jewish Question'? With Gordon.
Had interchange of views with G.R.

Wally includes memorable events of his journey with the RAF as he enjoys the warm climate when not flying.

Feb 7 Sunday
Lots of mail for me.
P.T. [Physical training] – Rugby – Bathing on beach.

Feb 8 Monday
Bags more mail for me.
P.T. – beach.

One bonus for Wally in being stationed in Gibraltar was his easy access to food luxuries such as bananas and honey, which were not available in Britain at the time, so his family were naturally delighted when he returned home with this taste of sunshine.

Feb 9 Tuesday
88 brought down in Spain.
[The German Junkers Ju 88, classed as a medium bomber, had been adapted as a fighter aircraft.]
Bought honey for home.
Furious pillow fight in hut.

Feb 10 Wednesday
Had filling put in.
Swish & crew went home & hut is left miserable at base.
Flew 1 hour.

Feb 11 Thursday
Started 'South Riding'.
[South Riding was a 1936 novel by Winifred Holtby that evoked the lives and characters of the fictional Yorkshire Ridings.[88]]
Went to see 'Pimpernel Smith'.

'Pimpernel' Smith was a 1941 film that told the story of an academic, Professor Horatio Smith, who purports to be an archaeologist, but in reality, he was a smuggler of enemies of the Nazi state out of Germany as England prepared for war.

The film inspired the real-life heroic actions of Raoul Wallenberg, who led a similar operation that saved thousands of Hungarian Jews. Raoul disappeared in January 1945 aged 34, presumed murdered.[89]

Feb 12 Friday
Beach – Grand!
Talk by Squadron Leader Hall am. Woman & Poetry.
Much of interest, but lots of tripe.

Feb 13 Saturday
Lecture on fire control.
P.T. & Rugby on beach.
Finest day yet.
Really hot. Wrote various cards to people.
Girl waiter was most respectful at supper!!!?

Feb 14 Sunday
Beach!
BBC 6,000 Jews killed in Poland daily. None left in Warsaw.

Although this news was not true, it was correct that the Nazis were murdering Jews, with around 250,000 Jews deported to Treblinka in 1942 and killed in the gas chambers.[90]

There was no reason for Wally to doubt the BBC, for he had no credible way to check the facts. The question remains whether this was true, or was merely BBC propaganda.

> *Supper at Winter Garden.*
> *Saw 6 couples dancing all men!*

I'm sure it was amusing to see men doing ballroom dancing together, but in wartime there was a shortage of ladies.

Feb 15 Monday
Went over at 17.50 to submarine 'REGENT' the old crock.

The *HMS Regent*, a Rainbow-class submarine (a submarine originally intended for long-range operations in the Far East), was launched in June 1930. Not being very old, she was mainly deployed in the Mediterranean during the Second World War.[91]

Patrolling the southern Adriatic in April 1943, she struck a mine and sank with the loss of the entire crew.

ROSTOV for the Russians.

The Germans first captured this valuable transport hub in late November 1941; Rostov was crucial because it provided easy access to Soviet oil fields at Maykop, Grozny and Baku in south Russia. However, within one week, the city was liberated.

In July 1942, the Wehrmacht recaptured Rostov and held it until the Red Army retook it at the beginning of February 1943.

Map showing the locations mentioned
Source: Nationsonline.org

Yanks taking a licking in Tunisia.

They were certainly 'licked' in the Battle of Kasserine Pass,[92] which took place high in the Atlas Mountains. General Rommel's Panzer Army Africa realised fairly quickly that they were fighting inexperienced and poorly led American troops.

Feb 16 Tuesday

Finished 'O Absalom'. [Note: This is a Biblical quote; the real title of Faulkner's book was *Absalom, Absalom!*]

Wally was very well read, and enjoyed the works of American writer William Faulkner. Faulkner was later awarded the Nobel Prize in Literature in 1949,[93] which he received one year later in 1950 due to some debate over its suitability for the prize.

The *Guinness Book of World Records 1983* listed one of Faulkner's sentences totalling 1,287 words as "the longest sentence in literature". In 2009, Faulkner's *Absalom, Absalom!* was judged to be the "best Southern novel of all time" – not bad for a piece of literature considered such a difficult read!

Set around the time of the American Civil War in Mississippi, the complex story of *Absalom, Absalom!* describes the life of a poor man, Thomas Sutpen, and the creation of his wealth, dynasty and private life, which encompassed marriage, divorce and prejudice.

No Mail!

For heaven's sake, where were his letters? Did his family not recognise his need to hear news, however mundane, and his loneliness from being tucked away in Gibraltar? Recalling cries of "we will write every day!" as he left home made him so angry that their promises were not kept.

Wally's diaries were probably the only place he could share his feelings and the misfortunes he experienced – the flying accidents, concerns about one accident too many – and his only respite was the mail he received. His way of escaping these frustrations was through books and cinema, films being a great interest.

Feb 17 Wednesday
Went to see 'Sergeant York'.

Sergeant York was a 1941 film starring Gary Cooper. The film tells the story of Alvin York, a poor young farmer living with his widowed mother, who spent his leisure time fighting and getting drunk, until, when he was struck by lightning, he was drawn to Christianity. York had been a conscientious objector in the First World War, but after his request for exemption was refused, he joined the infantry and soon realised that sometimes fighting is a necessary evil. He was awarded the US Medal of Honour, and became one of the most decorated heroes of the war.[94]

Gary Cooper won an Academy Award for his performance, and the film became the highest-grossing picture of 1941. It boosted the morale of every young serviceman, and even encouraged an increase in enlistments.

Americans still taking a licking.
I wonder whether it will catch up with me?

I was deeply upset by Wally's words as I read them for the first time. He must have been feeling very negative when he wrote this. I saw clearly now, too, that these brief entries of his were more than just loose, throwaway lines. They were the expressions of his deepest fears and emotions at any given moment, those personal thoughts that could only be shared with his diary, since there was no one else in whom he could confide at the time – just me, since I am likely the only person who ever read them.

While others might have easily dismissed the fears and feelings of a young and immature 20-year-old, it seemed to me as I read this that right at that moment, he just really needed was a shoulder to cry on.

Feb 18 Thursday
Analysis of Accidents.
Mine was the only (accident) 'B' from Squadron 179 for December.

Learnt that I had had my log book endorsed 'gross careless-ness'.

I wonder whether it will catch up with me?

Dingy practice in Catalan Bay – Good fun. [He certainly needed fun at that moment!]

Social life around the camp was generally limited to private gatherings, so they often drank too much alcohol when they were standing around in the mess, as he recorded on this occasion:

Feb 21 Sunday

Submarine crew came round aerodrome & eventually Sid Baylis, Cox, Simon, Stan & George, had evening with us in mess. Semi pissed.

Other times they might visit British ships in the harbour, such as the submarines:

Feb 23 Tuesday

Submarine at 9:45am.
Boys received us really well.
Great day.
2 Dives & 2 Shoots.

Feb 24 Wednesday
WASHINGTON'S BIRTHDAY.

Wally was mistaken – George Washington was born on 11 February 1731 when the Julian calendar was in use. His birthday is now celebrated officially on Presidents' Day, the third Monday of February.

Feb 25 Thursday
Went to Naval for 'You'll Never Get Rich'

Dancers Fred Astaire and Rita Hayworth starred in the military-themed musical comedy of 1941, *You'll Never Get Rich*.[95] Featuring music by Cole Porter, its title stems from an old army song that includes the lyrics, "you'll never get rich / by digging a ditch / you're in the army now". The film, which was very successful at the box office, turned Hayworth into a star and gave Astaire's career a much-needed boost after his split with Ginger Rogers.

Wally's flying ability was called into question when he once again pranged on landing:

March 1 Monday
Pranged on landing (3rd).
Very rough & bumpy weather.
Have decided to chuck in.

It was no surprise to read of his decision to stop flying, recorded with other private thoughts in his diary.

March 2 Tuesday
Saw Wilson, made my report & told him I'd like to chuck in my hand.
I am now acknowledged as 'Crasher Wally'.
Am sick at heart.

Wally hardly spoke about his religion until this entry about visiting a local synagogue:

March 5 Friday
Went to Sephardi service in very fine Gibraltar Synagogue.

It gave me such a warm feeling to read of his visit to the Friday-night service – it was so special for him because it rekindled memories of Friday-night dinners gathered around the dinner table with his family.

Sundown is the start of the Jewish Sabbath, and although Wally was an Ashkenazi Jew (the Ashkenazi Jews most recently came from East Europe), he easily overcame the differences with the Sephardi service. ('Sephardi' translates as 'Spain'; the Sephardic Jews originated from Sepharad[96] [an unknown location], and are now referred to as Spanish or Portuguese Jews.)

The congregation gives facet spontaneously. Followed the prayers quite easily.

Wally records that it was a very attentive congregation, with little of the chattering seen at many others.

March 7 Sunday
'The Beverage Plan' at the Society.
Resolution: Teach the public.

'Social Insurance and Allied Services', a government report drafted by Sir William Beveridge, became the blueprint for the modern British welfare state when it was published in December 1942[97].

From "Congressional Record – House"

Among his many references to war stories, Wally mentions that VP Wallace's remark made headline news:

March 8 Monday
Letters from home tell of bananas having arrived o.k. Vice President Wallace makes his amazing statement.

1943   CONG

was speaking in Moscow. I should like to have the gentleman's reaction to this statement by Vice President Wallace. I quote:

Without a close and trusting understanding between Russia and the United States there is grave probability—

Note the word "probability"; not "possibility"—

there is grave probability of Russia and Germany sooner or later making a common cause.

It seems to me that is an unfortunate and inflammatory remark to come from the Vice President of the United States at a time like this, in speaking about one of our allies in this war. This is the type of remark that brings about disunity and distrust among partners in this war. Vice President Wallace also said something about isolationism in this same speech. It seems to me that when the Vice President occupies himself broadcasting doubt-creating and disunity-breeding speeches about international double-crossing and about a probable alliance between Russia and Germany he is himself practicing very much more dangerous forms of isolationism than anything he preaches against in his speech. Anybody in wartime who seeks

Newspaper clipping reporting Vice President Wallace's choice of language

Wally was referring to Vice President Wallace's statement that "Without a close and trusting understanding between Russia and the United States, there is a grave probability of Russia and Germany sooner or later making a common cause."

The statement was highly controversial because he had used the word "probability" about an American ally, rather than "possibility". Ethel's frequent illness was another burden for Wally, with his being so far from home. This message was particularly troubling, and efforts were made to get him back to England.

March 17 Wednesday
Was told at flight by Adjutant that mum is dangerously ill.
Squadron Leader Wilson will try to arrange for me to go home in 'C' tomorrow.
'C' didn't come back from Agadir today.
No news from home.

March 18 Thursday
No news from home. 'C' back at 2.

March 19 Friday
Buying & packing.
No news from home.

March 20 Saturday
After 'C' had been air tested & found O.K. it was made known that majors will be taken at 360 & not 270.
Wrote & called home.

It was not at all easy for Wally to get home; the war was a priority for aircraft, and even when they flew, there was the hazard of German fighters. But serving in Gibraltar's warm climate at least provided the luxury of fresh fruit and fresh eggs.

March 21 Sunday
1 dozen eggs for Society. Mr James asked how old they were.

March 22 Monday
Gave Jack 8 eggs. 6 for Louis.

March 23 Tuesday
2nd anniversary of Raie's wedding. [Wally spelt my mother's name in two ways; sometimes it was Ray, sometimes Raie. He also misspelt my name as Barry instead of Barrie.]

March 24 Wednesday
Cable: 'Mum improving'.
[Finally, some good news!]

March 26 Friday
'That this house welcomes State Organised Youth Movements (Compulsory)', a good debate.

As an ardent member of the Brady Boys' Club in Whitechapel, Wally had a keen interest in this debate.

The Brady Boys' Club was the first Jewish boys' club in the UK; it was founded in 1896 by philanthropists Lady Charlotte Rothschild, Mrs Arthur Franklin and Mrs N S Joseph.

The wrens very stout.
About 200 were present. The motion defeated.
Had argument with Lieutenant Cliff as out after curfew.

March 27 Saturday
Len Mitchell returned with the news that Swish was swinging the lead.

I can just imagine the cheers of delight on hearing any suggestion the war had turned in favour of the Allies.

March 29 Monday
Cycling down Main Street, car overtook me & buckled my back wheel.
Bags of mail.
Mum improving.

In Gibraltar, Wally's life did not continue without incident, as he mentions that a speeding car had buckled his bike wheel. Despite flying accidents and other incidents that troubled him, his everyday life continued as normal.

The mere sight of mail, particularly "bags of mail" always brightened his day, especially when it brought good news about his mother's health.

April 2 Friday
3 letters from home.
Mum O.K.
Mock Parliament. Education Bill almost defeated. Not so good an evening.

Why on earth should anyone argue against Rab Butler's exciting and innovative changes?

Chosen as 'President of the Board of Education' in 1941, Rab Butler's determination to introduce drastic reforms included: "Compulsory school attendance until age 15; free school meals and milk; and most importantly – free schooling at secondary schools." [98]

The Bill was passed into law in 1944.

Rab Butler had previously served in several ministerial positions, and subsequently became Chancellor of the Exchequer, Home Secretary and Leader of the House of Commons in the postwar years. A strong supporter of appeasement, Butler had encouraged efforts to negotiate with Hitler and had opposed going to war over Poland [99]. Hitler considered him to be a person "likely to be sympathetic to peace talks".

April 10 Saturday
Southall asked me if I wanted the skipper-ship back & I said yes.
Did some circuits with Blackmore O.K.

April 12 Monday
Made up three parcels for home.
[Must have been local fruits.]
Bags of mail. Lovely one from Barbara.

May 1 Saturday
Came up to town & had lunch with Usher, Lieber & Shirley at Plutocrat's Cafe.
Arts Theatre with Charles & Glasses.

May 15 Saturday
Lieber's treat.
Had poor lunch at Shearns.
Box at Palace for 'Full Swing' with the Hulbeets.

May 16 Sunday
Went round to the Bloomfields again & once more had fine lunch there.
Met Charles, Beattie & Minnie & went to Piccadilly for tea dance, after which I saw Bea home & went home.

May 17 Monday
Went with Leah & Charles to see 'The Magic Flute'.

May 18 Tuesday
Nuisance Raiders have been active of recent nights.

Six weeks have now passed since Wally's "hand was chucked in" and his flying stopped in early March, but after a spell of laying on the beach, relaxing and swimming, his enthusiasm had returned.

He did not allow the war to interfere with his social life, especially when he was in England – from lunch in the London's West End to the theatre and afternoon tea dances, despite the "nuisance raiders" recorded in his diary.

May 19 Wednesday
Went round to see Esther & got 50 fags for it.
Caught 2:50pm. WAT [Waterloo Station].
Arrived back at Chivenor 9:30pm.

Now that he was back in England, Wally continued his training at Chivenor in Devon. Pilots had started to train at Chivenor, near Barnstable in Devon, from the beginning of the Second World War; from 1942, anti-submarine patrols were also based there.

May 20 Thursday
Kit Unserviceable.
Did some link.
Nick wrangled a 4-day pass, starting tomorrow.
Went to dance in Broughton & met Bunny. Said Ta Ta to Tatty.

May 22 Saturday
Received recall telegram [meaning he was recalled to Chivenor base].

Bobby [slang for Policeman] *asked for my I.C.* [identity card] *when I took a stroll.*

Even national servicemen were not immune to police checks, as Wally noted.

May 23 Sunday
Rang Bunny & persuaded her to see me but it would seem I have been given brush off.

May 24 Monday
Kite still unserviceable.
Went to local cinema & saw 'He was her Man'.

Maintenance work continued on his plane, so Wally searched for other interests to keep him busy while he waited – but evidently Bunny did not wish to be one of them!

Instead, he went to see *He Was Her Man* – a poorly edited 1934 American crime film starring James Cagney.

May 25 Tuesday
After a long abstinence I resume my diary entries.
Kite still unserviceable.
Barnstaple with the boys.
Film, couple of drinks & dance at Conservative club after chips in street.

In his quest to keep busy while his plane remained unserviceable, Wally went dancing:

May 27 Thursday
Came second with Joan in Waltz competition at Conservative club.

May 28 Friday
And to the cinema: *Broughton Cinema.*

May 29 Saturday
And out for dinner: *Bideford for fine dinner but little else seemed to be on.*

It was another 10 days before his plane returned to service, and he next flew on Sunday, 30 May:

May 30 Sunday
Loaded kite.
Motor Transport driver W.A.A.F. potential date!!!
Left Chivenor at 10:30.

May 31 Monday
Landed from Chivenor at 7:30.

June 2 Wednesday
New order has come in making tour of duty out here 3 years including 18 months in N.W. Africa.

June 3 Thursday
N.F.L.D.S. [Debating society.]
7:30 Public Opinion by Mr Mayhew.

Christopher Mayhew was a Labour MP between 1945 and 1974, when he left to join the Liberals. He received a life peerage in 1981 and was raised to the House of Lords as Baron Mayhew.[100]

Within a matter of days, Wally had engine trouble again:

June 4 Friday
Took off 6:15am but engine trouble brought us back at 10:40.

June 5 Saturday
Sent some bananas to Edna.

Bananas could only be found in Gibraltar or Spain, so Wally must have returned there.

Went to see the ENSA show with Beatrice Lilley, Vivien Leigh, Leslie Henson etc.

ENSA – short for 'Entertainments National Service Association' – was founded in 1939 by Basil Dean and Leslie Henson, who provided entertainment for British troops during the Second World War.[101]

June 16 Wednesday
Have again neglected diary!
Lord Trenchard on Rock [of Gibraltar].

The Right Honourable Viscount ('Lord') Trenchard, born in 1873, was a poor academic who had failed many exams and struggled to pass the minimum standard for commissioned service in the British army. After learning to fly in 1912, he rose through the ranks of the Royal Flying Corps, and was ultimately instrumental in establishing the RAF.[102]

He is now recognised as the 'Father of the Royal Air Force', and the 'Patron Saint of Air Power' by Americans. I think his story is a powerful lesson for anyone who struggles with examinations.

July 5 Monday
Jobs after the war.

It is rather curious that the postwar job market was debated as early as July 1943 at a time when no-one knew how long the war would continue, or even that the Allies would ultimately defeat the Axis powers.

But then, was the writing perhaps already on the wall in May when German U-boat submarines withdrew from the Atlantic due to heavy losses, or in June, when 250,000 German and Italian troops surrendered in North Africa?

Or was it pure hope that drove this discussion?

About 23 people present. Poor evening.
Tussle with P.D. Drinkwater.

Many blank pages followed, with no entries for the next three weeks.

July 30 Friday
Received 'Ten' from SS Middleton.

Letters had become a reminder of life away from the battlefield – not only did they ease the pain of isolation, but they also raised morale. Wally must have been over the moon to receive 10 letters. Post arrived, despite the tough logistics of delivery; mailbags filled valuable space in ships, and ships were susceptible to German U-Boat attacks.

July 31 Saturday
Varying jobs... my activities have been such as to lead me to drop my diary.

A further 24 consecutive days passed without another entry, so there is nothing to learn about his life or loves.

Sep 11 Saturday
Transferred from Gibraltar to RAF Haverfordwest in Pembrokeshire Wales.

Sep 30 Thursday
Jewish Year, 5704, begins.
Slap in the face.

Had Wally upset another young lady?

Nov 7 Sunday
23rd Birthday.

[Note: This was Wally's birthday. Over the past three years of his life, he had gone from being a young kid to having to face the ravages of war. He was growing up fast on the way to manhood while being paid to kill people. He struggled to survive, and now he could only pray that the end of hostilities would come quickly, that he could resume a happier life among family and friends – and maybe even marry and create his own family.]

Final flight: Nov 19 Friday

On clear nights, an aircraft's position can be fixed with 'celestial navigation' – the ancient practice of using the sun, moon, stars and horizon, but since there was heavy cloud, the navigator plotted their flight path using radio transmissions.[103]

Lifting from a frosty airfield at 8:15pm, on their final training mission before moving to an operational squadron, Wally and his crew flew along a predetermined flight path. They continued on the same path even after the radio stopped working some five hours later, but once the fuel supply started to run low, Wally decided it was time to reduce their altitude and establish a visual position.

Now flying in low cloud with no clear visibility, their Wellington aircraft struck a rocky outcrop – 1,500 feet above sea level on the right-hand side of a hillside, close to the top of Moel y Croesau (Hill of Crosses) in Snowdonia, roughly six hours after they took off.[104]

Wally was killed instantly. Two other members of the five-man crew also died, but Sergeants Sinclair and Maskell survived after landing waist-deep in boggy ground.

View west across the moor towards the slopes of
Moel y Croesau in Snowdonia National Park, Wales
(Copyright Eric Jones)

Remnants of the plane wreckage were discovered as recently as 2001.

The telegram

Wally's mother Ethel and teenage sister Mary cared for the household, so when the doorbell rang and a telegraph boy gave them the telegram, they were alone.

The words of the telegram said:

Deeply we regret to inform you that your son Sergeant Maurice Lewis Wolman lost his life as result of an aircraft accident...

Seeing this flimsy piece of paper made it so real, as if it had just happened. I was simply heartbroken. My tears flowed as I reeled from the shock, feeling my family's deep despair, visualising their sobbing, hearing their screams of "No! No it cannot be true!"

I could sense the deep devastation of my loved ones on learning that their 23-year-old special boy was dead, that his smiling face would never again shine through the front door. It was unbearable.

It had felt as though every word in his diaries – all his emotions, his struggles with girls, his upset at flying mishaps, his worries about the family business – were shared privately with me through page after page of his scribbles.

Bad news leaves us in a state of despair, our whole world falls apart almost as if we're driven into the ground. We fear the very worst, and cannot get it out of our mind or our gut. The family had to endure the sadness for the rest of their lives, which was reflected in the words my mother spoke to my daughter in 2015: "Such a lovely man. But let's not talk about sad things."

The box

The brown cardboard box delivered by the RAF was the final evidence of the tragedy. Indelibly marked with the words 'Packing Material', his personal effects bought the stark realisation the tragedy was carved in stone.

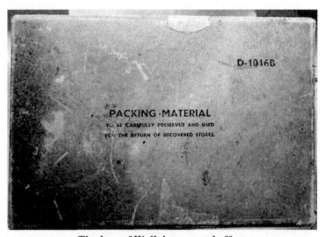

The box of Wally's personal effects

I had discovered the box 75 years after Wally's death. It was *Beshert* – 'meant to be', as translated from Yiddish, for it appeared just as I was writing our family history.

I cannot believe my mother purposely hid the box; most likely it was a matter of 'out of sight – out of mind' when she tucked it away in the back of her wardrobe. Lifting the lid, the first thing I saw was the leather wallet that contained his two wartime diaries, full of stories we had never known about – until now.

Brady Boys' Club

The obituary in the Brady Boys' Club Bulletin is self-explanatory: "Wally was one of the finest Club members Brady ever produced...

He was one of the most successful Club Captains we have ever seen."

BRADY BULLETIN
Incorporating VIEWPOINT

WAR ISSUE - NUMBER FORTY-ONE   DECEMBER, 1943

The Brady Member in the Post-War World

Sgt. Pilot Wally Wolman

It is with deep regret that on the eve of going to press we learn of the death of Wally Wolman whilst on active service as a Sergeant Pilot in Coastal Command. We understand that his death was due to a accident on Saturday night, November 20th. Firstly we wish to send our condolences to his family to whom he was the only, and a very loving son and brother. Their loss will be no more easy to bear for our thoughts, but nevertheless it may be of comfort to know that others are sharing their sorrow with them. Wally was one of the finest Club members Brady ever produced and will always be remembered as a kind, patient, thoughtful fellow, who when he couldn't help, refused to harm. In the period before the war he was one of the most successful Club Captains we have ever seen and his work at Brady was one of the factors which produced the grand spirit we connect with those days. He had many friends who for some time will be unable to appreciate that they will never see him again and to whom his sincerity and unselfishness will be an inspiration for the future.

Brady has lost one of its most interested supporters and someone who wanted more than anything else to become an active Manager after the war.

Wally's gravestone at the
Rainham Jewish Cemetery

The adaptation of a Thomas Ford poem, handwritten inside the *Cadet's Handbook* that Wally used at Carlstron Field, demonstrated that he was quite the romantic at heart:

There was a lady passing by

Was never face so pleased my mind

I did not see her passing by

But yet I love her till I die

Her gestures motions & her smile

Her wit, her voice my heart beguiles

Beguile my heart I know not why

But Cupid is winged & doth song I.

Commemoration, 1990

On the 45th anniversary of the end of the Second World War, the *Jewish Chronicle* newspaper published a commemoration of the fallen servicemen from both world wars. Their photograph of a pre-war Brady Boys' Club Gymnasium Group shows Wally pictured in the back row, fourth from the left.

Charles Spencer, his long-time friend, responded to the editor with the letter below.

Old pictures of pride an<

Noel Coward once pointed out the potency of cheap music; the same might be said of old photographs.

I was delighted and moved by the one showing a pre-war Brady athletic group (LONDON EXTRA, page 2, November 16).

Since no one would ever accuse me of athleticism it was with some surprise I recognised myself in the second row; but that pleasure was soon tinged by the realisation, in the words of your caption, that "many were killed in action."

In particular, I recognised my close friend at that time, "Wally" Wolman, who indeed, had been in my mind at this time of remembrance.

Many thanks for the memory, which like life, is a mixture of nostalgia, pride and sorrow.

CHARLES SPENCER
24a Ashworth Road,
London W9.

[The former chairman of the Brady Boys Club whose photograph appeared with the pre-war group, was Monty Richardson — Ed., LONDON EXTRA.]

Churchill's Dedication to Airmen, 4 June 1940:

UK Prime Minister Winston Churchill paid a solemn tribute to the fallen airmen in service of their country with these words: "May it not also be that the cause of civilisation itself will be defended by the skill and devotion of a few thousand airmen?

"There never has been, I suppose, in all the world, in all the history of war, such an opportunity for youth. The Knights of the Round Table, the Crusaders, all fall back into the past – not only distant but prosaic; these young men, going forth every morn to guard their native land and all that we stand for, holding in their hands these instruments of colossal and shattering power." [105]

Postscript: Synchronicity

I have noticed a strange trilogy of coincidences wrapped around the 20th of November: Wally enlisted on the 20th of November 1940, to commence training as a pilot/observer; he joined the 179th Squadron on the 21st of November 1942; and he was killed in active service on the 20th of November 1943.

Chapter 10

THE FRENCH CONNECTION

Introduction

I met my second cousin, Genevieve de Cointet, for the first time when she visited London in July 2014, accompanied by her husband Emmanuel. Her forthcoming visit had been foretold in an email from Ken Golish, which arrived in the early hours and explained that we had other relatives in France I had yet to meet.

Ken wrote:

There are relations in France that are related to you as well.
Georges Pasternak, my mother's first cousin, went to France before the war. His mother's mother was Chaya Sara Kirszenbaum, your grandmother's oldest sister.
He had three children and his only daughter is Genevieve (Pasternak) de Cointet. She would therefore be your second cousin, once removed.
I think she may be in London this week... you might want to contact her.

Parles-tu francais?
Je suis sur qu'elle aimerait entendre parler de toi.

Regards
Ken

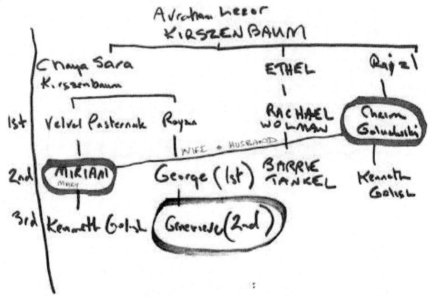

This image – provided by Ken Golish – shows
how Genevieve and I are related

Wednesday 9 July 2014

I arranged to meet Genevieve at 5:00pm at The Argyle Arms – an 18th century pub that was only a short stroll from Oxford Street tube. I was about to meet a complete stranger, whose sole connection with me came through the reproductive process of our great grandparents. I was curious: Would there be a recognisable physical bond? This was the second occasion in three years where I was to come face to face with such a relative.

Genevieve sat with her husband Emanuel at a small table in the first-floor lounge of The Argyle Arms. Her likeness resonated immediately: the rounded face, the hair shaping her head, the similarity between Genevieve and my grandmother Ethel, despite a distance of four generations – her great grandmother Chaya was Ethel's sister.

Ejzyk Pasternak, Genevieve's father, was my first cousin. She explained that Ejzyk changed his name to Georges.

After our formal introductions and a few sips of lager, Genevieve began to describe their family life in Strasbourg.

Me with Genevieve at The Argyle Arms

Ethel and Isaac

Ejzyk (Georges) Pasternak

Genevieve was born in France during the Second World War and was baptised at birth to hide her Jewish identity from the Nazis. Since the time of the first Crusade, Jews converted to Christianity hoping they would no longer be the target of violence that had been seen when thousands were killed in pogroms. It was different now because the Nazis wanted to destroy anyone with Jewish blood, so Genevieve's con-version at birth was meant to hide this. She had no further religious education.

Around 200,000 French Jews managed to survive the Holocaust by escaping to the so-called free zone in the southeastern part of the country, hiding in remote corners of the predominantly rural area.106

Secret rescue networks were established, including those by Catholic and Protestant clergy.

Monseigneur Jules-Gerard Saliege, the Archbishop of Toulouse, was an outspoken critic of the Nazis and Vichy's anti-Jewish policies. On 23 August 1942 priests in all churches in the archdiocese of Toulouse read out his public protest.

"…The Jews are real men and women. Foreigners are real men and women. They are part of the human species… they are our brothers like so many others. A Christian should not forget this."

Saliege was posthumously awarded the title "Righteous Among the Nations" honour by Yad Vashem in 1969.[107] [Yad Vashem is Israel's official memorial to the Holocaust.]

Genevieve spoke of the time in 1932 that her father studied in Paris, and her survival during the war years. I listened to her own story, and then sometime later she wrote to me describing it in more detail:

Genevieve's story, in her own words:

My father was born in 1911, in Chmielnik, Poland. He was rather silent about his life and family, so I am not sure I'll be of great help.

He'd arrived in France in 1932 with the idea of graduating as an engineer and afterwards intended returning to Poland to open his own business in the glass industry, assuming there was plenty of sand around his place.

He first worked in Paris for five years as a help to a butcher to pay for his studies and learn to speak French. Also, with some friends from Central Europe, he created a kind of student restaurant called 'La Cope', catering for foreign students.

There he met my mother and they got married on 27 December 1938. My mother helped him with his French during his studies and he got his diploma from the Institut National Polytechnique de Grenoble in 1939.

As for the dark period of the war, I do not know much. It was too painful for my parents to speak of.

It is obvious my father lived through the war hiding the fact he was a Jew. It was not the time to inform the children; they can always speak.

We were all baptised into the Catholic religion, though they were strong atheists on my mother's side. It was a kind of routine in the French hospitals run at that time by Catholic sisters, but further on we had no religious education whatsoever.

My brothers and I have built the family history from our parents' conversations. Most of their friends were Jews, and many were arrested and sent to camps.

My parents were haunted by these events and kept talking of them as if they had wanted to cancel them. That was their table conversation, but we, the children, remained silent. I remember how painful it was for me to listen to all that. I was six or seven. So, we understood my grandparents died like this, but we never have been told directly.

In fact, my father did know exactly. That was when he no longer had news from them, and that was all. He did not feel like talking.

My father did well in his job. He managed to buy a big flat in Grenoble for the six of us. My other grandmother lived with us.

And in the '60s he bought a huge summer house in rather a poor state, but we repaired it beautifully, doing most of the job ourselves. He ended his career in the export business at Schneider Electric Grenoble and had the opportunity to go back to Poland.

In 1987, as he was retired, he took the whole family (17 of us) on a private bus tour in Poland.

The summer house bought by Genevieve's parents

We went to Chmielnik, but his emotion was so strong that no questions were asked. He met a man there who could have been in school with him, and for the first time, he was told that all the Jews of the village were sent to Treblinka in October 1942.

Unfortunately, we do not speak Polish, so I think we missed many details.

Poland is a beautiful country, and we had a great time there. We toured the whole country.

It is only in 2009 that we learnt more, thanks to the internet. Emmanuel, my husband, did a good job researching. We had the chance to get in contact with Kenneth Golish. He also found the testimonies for the death of our grandparents on the Yad Vashem registers. So that was the end of all unspoken knowledge.

However, my father would easily tell us about his childhood in Poland. My father became French in 1939. He changed his name from Ejzyk (that was the Russian spelling, and he did not like it) into Georges in the late '50s. He wanted to be taken for a French man.

Although Genevieve and I did not meet again, we have connected in family Zoom calls with Ken Golish.

The terror that Genevieve's family suffered – being constantly fearful of the consequence of their Jewish heritage being discovered – is unimaginable, as is their joy when the war ended and they were finally able to live their lives in peace.

Later, I received an apt quote from my sister Margaret:

Each story is tragic in its way. Families decimated. Thankfully, some survived. We cannot begin to imagine the depths of sadness for that generation.

Chapter 11

TANKEL FAMILY: The beginning

Introduction

My maternal grandfather, Isaac Wolman, who was known by the affectionate Yiddish term *Zaida*, was the most delightfully humble man who was always remembered with deep affection.

Yoel Julius Michael Tankel, my paternal grandfather, known as 'Mike', was a different kettle of fish altogether. This debonair young Russian Jew landed in England in 1902, married my seven months' pregnant grandmother Sarah, built a successful construction business and earned a reputation as a philanderer.

Born in 1881, Mike was raised in Žagarė, an old Jewish community in Lithuania. At a guess, I'd assume they lived in the wealthier neighbourhood of 'New Žagarė', which was separated from the smaller 'Old Žagarė' by the Svete River and connected by a wooden bridge.[108]

Mike's emigration

At the time Mike and his siblings left to sail by ship to London and then on to America, many Jewish parents were feeling devastated as they watched their families slowly disintegrate as their children left home for foreign destinations, knowing the distances and separation made it unlikely they would ever meet again.

As the ship embarked from the Gulf of Riga, salty sea air filled Mike's lungs and the port faded into the far distance as the ship left on its six-day journey. He had only just recently turned 21. This first ocean voyage took him one thousand miles away from the pogroms and anti-Semitism that had motivated his migration.

When he arrived in London, he was questioned at the immigration desk through an interpreter. The answers in his native Russian tongue were mostly incomprehensible to English ears:

"Where were you born?"

"Žagarė" he replied.

"How is that word spelt?"

Similar question-and-answer sessions took place in every entry port the refugees fled to, with many words spoken in strange foreign accents that were difficult to comprehend, and resulted in the creation of new names and fictitious towns. Hence, Žagarė became 'Sagker' on his naturalisation report, despite no such place existing.

Starting a new life

Mike's relatives in London welcomed him, and their family friend, Mr Tannenbaum – a builder – offered him job.

Mike quickly grasped sufficient amounts of the language to be able to speak in broken English – English mixed with Yiddish enunciated with an East European accent – and within 12 months, his passable English was thought good enough to start his own business.

Three years later, in 1906, he established his own business under the name of 'J.M. Tankel – Master Builder & Decorator', with an office in Whitechapel. The company was incorporated in April 1934; later, Mike's two sons, Gerry and Alf, would take control of the business.

On beholding the photographic portrait of Mike taken in 1906, I was hypnotised – his striking features are so very different to those of the old man I remember. He was unquestion-ably handsome and had an eye for fashion, so it was obvious why the girls fell for him.

But while Mike's smartness, hard work and polished skills brought new business, he struggled to balance the books.

Julius Michael Tankel, aka Mike, circa 1906,
photographed by Oscar Baumgart, a leading
portrait specialist in London's East End

I don't know when or where he first met my grandmother Sarah, but being two youngsters living in close proximity, their social lives must have overlapped. Sarah was fatherless and a vulnerable 18-year-old when she fell pregnant early in 1906. They married in September and she gave birth to my father Morris in December.

His mother-in-law, Annie, funded him through his financial difficulties – construction can be a financially precarious business – paying the wage bills of his workers or pawning her jewellery to keep the business afloat, and occasionally concealing him whenever creditors knocked at the door.

Arrival of the Zeppelins

In May 1915, after Britain had already been at war for 10 months and as the First World War raged in Europe, giant Zeppelin airships filled with hydrogen gas floated across the English Channel[109]; despite their difficulty manoeuvring in high winds, they finally reached London and commenced dropping bombs over the north of the city. It was the first time London had been attacked by air, but it would not be the last.

Aircrews dropped bombs through trap doors to hit random targets. Buildings around Hackney, from Stoke Newington to Stepney and Leytonstone, were the first to be struck. Seven people were killed on this first incursion.

Despite the destruction they caused, these huge ships, twice the length of an airliner, were an incredible spectacle. Airship attacks continued until more traditional aircraft replaced them in the latter stages of war. Was the change to more traditional aircraft due to a shortage of cows? This is not a facetious remark – it is a hard, sad fact that to construct a single airship 600 feet long required the slaughter of 250,000 cows to extract the outer membrane of their intestine – the most reliable material for use in making the bags that held the hydrogen. The construction of a further 140 airships forced a ban on bratwurst sausage-making everywhere under German control to preserve the material – a most unpopular move.

I recall how this discovery stopped me in my tracks. I thought it was written in jest until it was verified by articles in *The Independent* newspaper and the Sky History channel.

By the time of this first air-raid attack on London, Mike's business had been established for nine years, and now that he had the capacity to do larger construction works, he won contracts to repair buildings damaged by the Zeppelins.

Military service

As soon as Britain declared war, volunteers from across the nation were invited to join the armed forces. But by late 1915, the government faced appalling casualty figures and a decline in voluntary recruiting. It therefore passed the first Military Service Act, thereby introducing conscription. From early March 1916, all single men between 18 and 41 years old were liable to be called up.[110]

As a second Act was passed in May 1916 that also included married men, I was intrigued to discover how Mike avoided being called up.

Naturalisation disclosures

The answer lay in the small print of a Special Report prepared by Special Branch and recorded on his naturalisation application form.

Classified as having a "C1-grade medical condition" by the National Service Medical Board in October 1917, meant that Mike was "able to stand service conditions, march five miles, shoot with glasses and to hear", thus proving he was fit for duty.

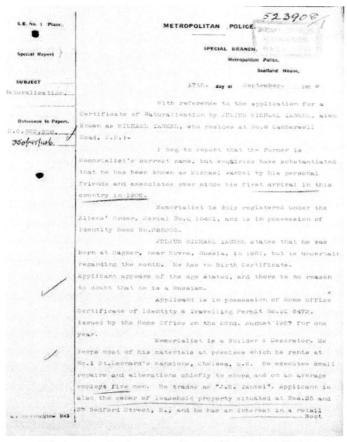

Mike's naturalisation report from the Metropolitan Police

The main reason for his exemption from service was noted in the final paragraph of page 3, which stated: "He worked as Superintendent of the Aerial General Supply Company from 1916 until the Armistice, and was granted exemption... due to his large technical knowledge of aeroplane construction, and regarded almost indispensable by management."

The words "large technical knowledge of aeroplane construction...indispensable by management" were unquestion-ably garbage. It was impossible for Mike to have had any "technical knowledge of aircraft construction". He did not have an engineering degree, he was a dreadful driver – his driving licence was obtained in the years before tests were mandatory – and the first plane manufactured in the UK only had its inaugural flight in 1912, just as Mike was busy building up his small construction business.

The synchronicity of his employment by Aerial, which allegedly started in 1916, coincided with the Act becoming law, which was suspicious in itself. Were his skills not so valuable during the first two years of the war?

I am convinced that bribery played its part in securing the necessary paperwork to avoid Military Service.

Philandering

The fact Mike was married to my grandmother Sarah did not deter him from extramarital affairs, as I discovered when I learnt of my aunt Yvonne.

Mike was 60 at the time he pursued the recently widowed Joan Harding, an affair that resulted in a pregnancy. Their child Yvonne was born in May 1942, six weeks after me; he and my father had both conceived around the same time.

Mike's second marriage to Minnie Kutz in 1947 did not last long; doubtless there were other women in his life.

His children, angered not just by his affairs and the baby, but primarily because of their mother's unhappiness, detached thems-elves from him. Sarah was adored but now lived alone.

Alf and Gerry, his two sons in the business, mostly ignored him even as they worked together in the same office, denying him access to see their children – his grandchildren.

Tankel relations

I had not heard Mike's name mentioned at our home until the family's attempt to reconcile my grandparents – sometime around 1949, when I would have been around seven.

The venue for the reconciliation was our home, and the reunion lunch was held one Sunday when Rose and Bella, my father's sisters, drove from London with Grandma Sarah.

Our home buzzed with excitement, especially for me – I was about to meet this mystery grandfather for the first time. I found a quiet corner of the room and waited, for I was extremely shy.

Eventually, the heavily built stranger arrived. Mike showed little sign of emotion, no more than a sheepish grin. He gave my hair a light tousle, and I was very surprised by his strange foreign accent, which was far more pronounced than that of my *Zaida*.

Any positive thoughts must have quickly dissipated when my grandparents sat at opposite ends of the table, but once everyone was seated around the carved wooden dining table, they enjoyed the lunch.

The occasion became the catalyst for Mike's move to Hove to be closer to my parents, for our home was one place where he felt welcomed.

I witnessed his building skills at first hand when my parents moved house. A partition, removed to create a larger dining area, necessitated the reworking of a cornice that had to match an existing perimeter. Mike, perilously balanced on the top rung of a stepladder, worked a perfectly formed cornice mitre while in his late 70s, despite not having touched a trowel for decades. The quality of his workmanship was impressive, surprising and inspiring.

Annie and Sarah Freedman

Yaakov Frydman (Freedman) married Annie Gro in their hometown of Zakroczym (from the ancient Polish word *zakrot*, which means river crossing), near the Vistula River in Poland, in the 1870s. My great grandparents were second cousins.

Yaakov continued his work as a boot-maker in the town until a combination of financial restraints and the Warsaw pogrom of 1882 instigated his move to seek a better, safer life in London. Annie joined him in 1885 and their daughter Sarah – my grandmother – was born in London in February 1888.

Two other children died – Solly from a ruptured appendix when he was 18, and his three-year-old brother Nathan from an unknown illness.

London turned out not to be the panacea he sought, so in 1888 he sailed to New York. Within two years, he sent Annie the money for the family's tickets, but they never went because Yaakov was trapped in the smoke and fumes of a fire that spread through his New York tenement building. He died from pneumonia a few days later.

*Annie Freedman holding Nathan with Sarah
(seated), and Myer and Solly at the back*

Devasted, widowed and with little money, Annie rented a market stall in London, competing with male traders to support her two children. In her old age, she sold knick-knacks, garlic, spices and matches from a tray that hung around her neck as she wandered around the crowded market streets of London.

Yaakov's death was one of those real 'sliding doors' moments. Had he not died, Annie would have moved to Brooklyn, Sarah would not have met Mike and I would not be writing this story.

Annie Freedman in the market

Allan (aka Rami), Mike's son

Weekend visits to my new-found grandfather, who was now living in Hove, soon became a routine event. Nothing much out of the ordinary occurred, until suddenly it did.

There was a young boy playing on the lawn, who said, "Have you come to see Dad?"

"Pardon?" I was confused and remained confused when he repeated the question.

"Dad. Are you here to visit Dad?"

It then transpired that this boy was Allan, Mike's son from his second marriage. Like so much else in our family life, no one had deemed it necessary to tell us of Mike's other family.

Allan changed his name several years later to Rami, and eventually moved to Australia. In 2009, he responded to the email I sent telling him of his newly found half-sister Yvonne with some poignant words:

The sadness is the secrets our family kept, so much about them we don't know. It's hard to judge people, but why the secrets.? I suppose the war years were very different to nowadays.

I remember a photograph Dad kept on a desk in his Holland Road house, a picture of a young man dressed in an RAF uniform. I asked a couple of times who's in the photo, but he never told me. When he moved to Flag Court, the photo didn't reappear.'

For my Bar Mitzvah present, Dad gave me £50 [it was 1962] to buy anything I wanted. I returned home with a beautiful Grundig tape recorder, thanked him for the present and showed him the machine. He took one look and became very angry. He threw it against the wall and smashed it to pieces. I'd never seen him like that before and I was scared. He then took another £50 from his pocket and told me to buy something else and make sure it had nothing to do with Germany. I asked why and he said, 'They killed my son.'

We never spoke of this again and I realised later that the picture of the man in uniform had been his son.'

When you and Jenny got married, I assumed Dad and I would go to your wedding. I told Dad I'd have to get permission from the headmaster to return home for the weekend. I was excited because for the first time I'd meet the whole family. I wanted to be part of this family. Dad told me that I couldn't go to your wedding. He said

*it was something in the family that he couldn't tell me about. I
remember feeling so small, as if I didn't exist.'*

*I was very hurt. Over the years I've often thought about the
funny side of the family, and tried to forget about the coldness and
the hurtful ways they could treat people in their own family.'*

Rami and my nephew Matthew in 2009 with his caravan

Rami was found dead in his caravan in 2011. He died from
asphyxiation, and sadly never got to meet his sister Yvonne.

Mike's End

Mike moved into my parents' home early in 1965 after his health
deteriorated. He was confined to bed and was cared for by a nurse
until he died, aged 84, in March 1965. The once-sprightly Mike had
become very depressed towards the end of his life. He had no
friends, and his divorce had scarred the relationship with his
children, although his grandchildren regularly visited.

His reconnection to my father Morris was a major reversal from
the hostile relationship 40 years earlier, to such a caring one at the
end. Despite their past history, they had finally bonded.

Both Mike and my grandfather *Zaida* passed away in March 1965, within five days of each other.

Both grandfathers sat together at my wedding in October 1964: left,
Zaida (Isaac), 80, smiling, and right, Mike, 83, once so full of joie
de vivre, now sad.

Chapter 12

MY FATHER, MORRIS TANKEL

Introduction

Morris, known to his friends as Morry, was an enigma, probably from the moment my grandmother first gave birth in December 1906.

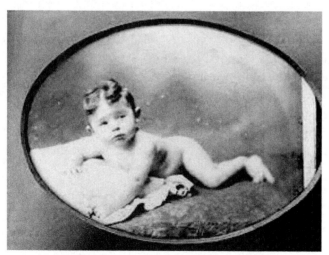

My father Morris (Morry) Tankel as an infant

"Enigma: A person described as a bit of a mystery. You never know what that person really thinks, or what his or her motives for doing something are, not easily understood especially because he or she has a confusing mixture of qualities that seem to be in opposition to one another." — *Merriam-Webster Dictionary.*

I know very little about my father's early years, just that he worked as an apprentice painter in his father's building business, and that he was knowledgeable about shoes and had lived in Australia – but only recently have I learned the truth behind his shoe story.

Illegitimate?

My eyes shifted around the desk as if the scattered papers would yield the words that could best express my feelings at the discovery that my father was actually illegitimate.

Shock, horror and amusement filled the gap. The certificate stated that my grandparents had married in August 1908, two years after my father's birth. Mike's age is recorded as 22 on their wedding certificate – yet another untruth, since he was born in 1881 and was actually 27 at the time.

It seems that my 17-year-old grandmother could not resist the charms of this dashing Lithuanian and soon fell pregnant. I can only imagine the embarrassment when she told her mother: "What have you done? Are you crazy? We have no money and no father to help you. Do you really think this good-for-nothing will look after you and the child? That damned Russian."

Sarah refused to have an abortion, which infuriated her mother even more: "I warned you, he is a good-for-nothing."

My father's illegitimacy suggested many scenarios. Was Morry truly born out of wedlock? Was Mike his father, or was our grandfather someone different, meaning that we may not really be from the Tankel family?

It was of course remotely possible that Mike had adopted Sarah's baby, but that was not in keeping with his style. So, a big question remained: If we are not Tankels, then who are we?

DNA

Since all the protagonists were dead, my original idea to exhume a relative and check their DNA was shelved after my two sisters objected, so we turned to modern technology.

Using the Family Tree DNA (FTDNA) website familytree dna.com was certainly an attractive and economic solution, however this particular online research had shown zilch.

Despite this negative result, I still believed a connection must exist somewhere, since so many of our family had immigrated from Latvia and Lithuania.

The company's headquarters is located in Houston, Texas. The technician who answered my phone call explained that my test result will only connect to those people testing on the FTDNA platform.

This must be an anomaly in the business of DNA testing, for it limited the scope for matches. However, my new tech friend advised me that two DNAs from different platforms can be com-pared if both are listed on GEDmatch.com (or similar) websites, as these integrate data from other DNA facilities around the globe as and when contributors actively apply. So, I actively applied.

The results appeared three days later. Ken Golish, my second cousin, topped the list. The next name to appear was a website – www.ariella.com.au.

Ariella's website told me she was a master tailor living in Melbourne, Australia; a mysterious connection that raised further questions. Was she an unknown offspring (another surprise?) of my father, seeing that he'd lived in Australia for 10 years from 1928, or was she a relative of my cousin Yardena, Rami's daughter?

Eventually, I discovered she was Yardena's sister. Their father was Allan (Rami), Mike's son from his second marriage. Now, at last we knew that Mike was indeed our grandfather.

A note in Mike's naturalisation report revealed that the marriage certificate he provided verified his wedding date as 12th September 1906. This contradicted information from the Beth Din (the rabbinical court of Judaism), and since there is no hard evidence, perhaps it was a forgery. But at least it inferred that my father was not illegitimate after all – he was just *nearly* illegitimate!

Dancing

When the 'Charleston' craze hit dance halls in 1923, ballroom dancing was the single most popular pastime, and I'd guess floors were packed on a Saturday night.[111] [The Charleston is thought to have emerged in Charleston, South Carolina – its origins being the 'Juba' danced by enslaved African Americans and first performed by the Whitman Sisters in their Harlem stage act in 1913. It was later included in two Broadway shows, the all-black *Liza* in 1922 and the mainstream *Runnin' Wild* in 1923.]

With his natural rhythm and confidence, Morris soon learned the moves and became an active participant.

Australia

The more I wrote – the more I examined my family history – the more I recognised familiar traits from my childhood, traits that must have lay behind my father's behaviour and originated from his growing up.

Morry was a distant father. His presence was mentally overpowering, and his daily moods were a constant concern to us. Despite being physically present, he was a parent who rarely conversed with us. I constantly worried he would criticise everything I did, which I think is what lay behind my lack of self-confidence and inability to easily communicate with others.

I can see that my father's unconscious approach to being a parent originated from Mike. Perhaps he also inherited it, despite revolting against his father's discipline and fighting for his independence. The rows between the two of them became relentless, for both were strong willed and charismatic, and their personalities often clashed.

This strained relationship made it difficult for them to work together, so Morry left the building company to manage a shoe shop in the Camberwell Road that Mike funded. However, the rows continued, finally reaching the point where my grandmother Sarah could stand it no longer. It was then decided my father would go to Australia.

I imagine the scene in their home during yet another disagreement. Sarah held no prisoners when she said: "Morry, stop bickering. Just leave home, you can book a passage on a ship and go visit my brother in Australia."

Sarah's brother Myer had emigrated to Australia in 1921, so Melbourne seemed the perfect place to send Morry as it would provide the ideal opportunity for her eldest child, now 22, to make his own mark in the world, although she must have doubted that she would ever see him again.

Morry in Melbourne

The *SS Moreton Bay*[112] was a screw steamer built to carry 542 passengers in tourist class. She sailed in late September 1928, and after passing through the Suez Canal stopped at Port Said, Port Aden and Colombo. Finally, she crossed the Indian Ocean, berthing in Fremantle, Perth, on 1 November. Morry disembarked in Melbourne three days later at the end of this 10,000-mile journey, an experience that established his love of cruising.

Vintage postcard of the SS Moreton Bay, ca. 1921

ABERDEEN menu

Australia needed more people to expand its population and predominantly encouraged British immigrants by offering financial assistance for fares. Although immigrants were generally expected to move into a rural area, Morris settled in Melbourne with his uncle Meyer at 483 Rae Street in Fitzroy North. The expertise he gained from managing the shoe shop in London provided the perfect reference to gain employment with a large shoe company in the city.

Melbourne proved to be the ideal place for this fun-loving young man. The 'Palais de Danse' in St Kilda[113], an enormous dance venue that bustled with 3,000 patrons on a Saturday night, quickly become his regular night out.

St Kilda was renowned for its magical atmosphere, and this seaside resort provided the perfect opportunity for Morry to meet people and make new friends.

Ces [Sarah] Taitelbaum soon became his girlfriend, and they married in November 1931. However, after he had an affair with

Lila Rodda, as I had discovered through the result of my son's DNA test, they divorced in 1938 and he returned to London.

Mike and Sarah sent this picture postcard of my father
Morry and Sarah (Ces) when they got married

Sarah's divorce affidavit states that my father's addiction to gambling was the primary cause of divorce, but I believe this was fabricated by her gambling-loving family to help her get the divorce.

Chaim Freedman, Myer's grandson, shared his knowledge of the divorce: "Morry became involved with the Taits, his wife's family. Known as card gamblers, they were distant cousins of his grandmother. I was told the Taits got him into debt from gambling, and this led to his divorce from Ces in 1938 when he fled back to England. [As we discovered later on, this was not correct.]

Rami (Allan), Morry's half-brother, had lived in Melbourne since the mid-1970s, and he learnt this version from an old bookmaker friend of my father's: "It was he [Ces's father] who got into trouble with gambling debts, but Morry took the blame as he was disappearing from Melbourne for London."

Whatever my views of Morry as a parent (my thoughts are expressed elsewhere), I do not believe he reneged on a gambling wager or debt. But, as we discovered many years later, this affair marked the time when another side to his personality began evolving.

Back in London: When Morris met Rachel

Returning to London, Morry was listed in this census as working in the family business, but that was short-lived as he entered the world of bookmaking soon after.

Tankel Household (10 People)
 25 Alkham Road , Hackney, London, England

	FIRST NAME(S)	LAST NAME(S)	DOB	SEX	OCCUPATION	MARITAL STATUS
	Julius M	Tankel	20 Feb 1881	Male	Building Contractor Co Director	Married
	Sarah	Tankel (Freed)	01 Feb 1886	Female	Unpaid Domestic Duties	Married
	Maurice	Tankel	13 Dec 1906	Male	Builder Assistance Clerk	Divorced
	Alfred	Tankel	15 Aug 1914	Male	Building Contractor Co Director	Single
	Sorry, this record is officially closed. Check if you can open a closed record.					
	Rose	Silverstone (Scholar,Tankel)	08 Apr 1921	Female	Dress Cutter	Single
	Sorry, this record is officially closed. Check if you can open a closed record.					
	Sidney	Carroll	30 Oct 1910	Male	Grocery Provision Shopkeeper	Married
	Bella	Carroll	11 Sep 1908	Female	Unpaid Domestic Duties	Married
	Rebecca	Plummer	02 Sep 1886	Female	Housemaid	Single

Census dated 1939

At that time, London boomed with dance halls, and Morry naturally danced at them all – the Café de Paris, the Astoria Dance Hall in Charing Cross Road and the Paramount in Tottenham Court Road.

From the moment they first met on a dance floor in 1939, my parents ardently tripped the light fantastic, jitterbugging to the music of Joe Loss and gliding across the floor to Geraldo's Orchestra.

They won several dance competitions and prizes during this time, acquiring a wealth of trophy cups. Cheekily, they often posed as beginners to enter competitions in small ballrooms, and easily beat their peers to scoop cash prizes. Eventually they were found out and asked not to return. I admire their chutzpah, though – we always thought our parents were too honest to do something like that, but clearly not!

Their wedding was booked for the 23rd of March 1941, but it could not proceed without Morry providing the vital evidence of his divorce documents that were filed away in Australia, so the date hung very much in the balance.

A copy of his divorce certificate arrived four days before the wedding, certified by Prothonotary Walter Kelly in Melbourne and dated 19 March. It remains a mystery how it came to be delivered in time, especially during wartime. But it did, for I hold the copy.

My parents, Morris and Rachel, from their wedding

Morris Tankel, 'Turf Accountant'

The euphemism used at the time to describe my father's work was 'Turf Accountant' or 'Commission Agent'; that actually meant serving as a 'middleman' between professional gamblers and bookmakers. It involved placing bets on behalf of the professional gamblers with small bookmaking firms.

Large bookmakers either cut the odds when substantial wagers were placed or refused to take bets because of the gamblers' success in betting. My father's role was to place these bets in smaller sums with a discreet number of small bookmakers, and in return they paid him commission based on the value of the bet. Through this work, however, he was able to earn a good living.

For his job, my father used a spare bedroom on the first floor of our family home, which was converted into an office. A work surface was fitted beneath the sill board of the west-facing window, which extended along the entire length of a wall. It was hardly visible beneath the day's racing papers, which were carefully unfolded to show every single race of the day. Betting slips and pens were strategically placed on the desktop to access and record the wagers, and six black Bakelite telephones were spread within arm's length.

In those days, every phone had a different telephone number, so callers had to keep redialling if one phone was engaged. Saturday afternoons were particularly frantic, as several race meetings were held simultaneously, and it was always a big panic when the starting time (the 'off') of races clashed.

Even worse was the pandemonium if all six phones rang at the same time – that's when the cavalry (my mother) was called in to help. My mother cared for our household and was only called on to assist him as and when he got very busy. If she was busy working elsewhere in the house, his screams of *'Raie! Raie!'* would resonate down the street whenever he beckoned her. Sometimes they might have both been holding two or three phones at the same time, trying to take and/or place wagers in frenzied moments before the race started.

The 'blower' sound system, commonly used in betting shops, fed the live audio and transmitted the latest racecourse information – from up-to-date betting odds and race commentaries to the final results from every racecourse. The humourless descriptions and bland information were relayed with no sense of drama or emotion.

Every bet was made on credit. If bookmakers or gamblers did not pay their debts, then my father was obliged to honour the bet at his own cost. A gambling debt is unenforceable by law, so the only recourse was to report the debtor to Tattersalls, the betting governing body. Those who defaulted on their bets got banned from racecourses and bookmakers' betting licences were revoked until the debt was repaid.

The atmosphere in my father's office was unpleasant and unhealthy, something we later thought must have contributed to his early death. I remember the hot afternoon sun pouring in through the windows, the cigarette smoke wafting out of dirty ashtrays, and the sound of his loud voice yelling in anger, particularly when he'd had a bad day from following his 'good information' and losing – it all added up to a very stressful environment.

The 'memorable wager'

Gambling hard-luck stories are ten a penny, but my father's misfortune was to be able to tell the best of them.

A reliable client (Mr X) told Morry of "strong" information he had received about two horses – 'Prelone' was to win the Cesarewitch and 'Loppylugs' was to win the Cambridgeshire. Both races were to be run in the following month of October (this was in 1956).

Mr X wanted to take the huge odds of 100/1 that were being offered by bookmakers William Hill. The high prices were available because at this stage, most of those horses that had been entered would not run. William Hill responded that Prelone was still available at 100/1, but the odds on Loppylugs had shortened to 25/1.

Mr X then declined to bet at the reduced odds, but Morry decided to place his own wager of £10 each way on both horses – that's £750 in today's money.

William Hill was a more personal business than today's giant public bookmaking company. Nowadays, the anonymous voices we hear are probably from a call centre located anywhere in the world.

At that time, Morry frequently spoke to the same clerk, just as he did on this occasion. Sometimes she asked him, "Mr Tankel, would you like to bet the double?" This time, she didn't ask. He didn't place it, and boy, was he sorry!

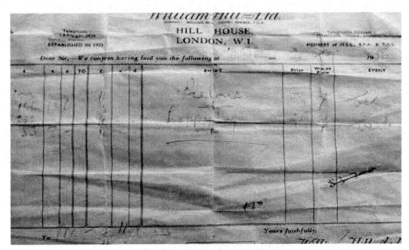

The famous betting voucher

Prelone duly won The Cesarewitch at 20/1, and two weeks later, Loppylugs won his fourth victory of the season at 14/1, when beating the top weight by half a length in The Cambridgeshire race. My father's return was £1,482 (£31,000 in today's money). The additional return for a £5 each-way double would have been £16,420, equivalent to £400,000 in 2022. He was gutted, hence the voucher was framed and hung as a permanent reminder.

Cooking, decorating and bridge

Work and ballroom dancing were not my father's only interests – he was also a keen cook, decorator and bridge player.

It was rumoured that he became the main chef in our household because he disliked my mother's cooking, and so we got treated to a variety of different well-cooked recipes. His favourites were a traditional Jewish stew called *cholent*, calves'-foot jelly (yuck!), salt beef and cheesecake, and the small cheesecake buns he made were spectacular. Sadly, of course, we don't have the damned recipes.

As a competent bridge player, my father won many cups in tournaments. He had been an enthusiastic decorator since working for his father, and his favourite form of relaxation was redecorating our home, hence the house always looked immaculate.

A common theme that ran throughout my memories of him was the constant cigarette dangling from his mouth whenever he played bridge, painted or cooked. Some even commented that the cigarette ash enhanced the flavours in his food.

Theatrical friends

In 1944, my parents decided to move to Brighton to escape the London bombing, and so shortly after my sister Margaret was born, they rented a flat in Russell Square, Brighton.

As I said earlier, my father Morris was an enigma. Among his many quirks, he had a penchant for creating strong friendships with leading artists in the world of variety theatre. I could never fathom which aspects of his personality attracted so many magnificent entertainers to form such warm bonds with him, for those same attributes of warmth and an outgoing, friendly nature were not apparent within his own family, as he rarely communicated with his children.

My father felt very much at home in the Hippodrome theatre in Brighton. The variety theatre, which was built in 1902[114], attracted many famous actors and comedians to its stage – Harry Houdini, Lillie Langtry, Gracie Fields, Laurel and Hardy, and even Sammy Davis Jr all appeared. Laurence Olivier made his stage debut here, allegedly falling over in his first entrance.

Founded in the fifth century after the Saxon invasion, Brighton started life as a quiet fishing village,[115] but by the beginning of the 20th century it had become a fashionable seaside resort with a population of 120,000, many of them of either a genuine or dubious 'artistic' bent. That colourful vibe has continued to this day, with the city being a renowned 'gay pride' centre in England.

Max Miller

Among my father's many theatrical friends was the legendary Max Miller.

Max was a popular comedian in the 1930s, so beloved by theatre audiences for the risqué jokes and innuendoes in his songs that his natural nickname was 'The Cheeky Chappie'[116]. Easily recognisable in trademark flower-patterned suits and plus-fours, by 1943, he was the highest-paid variety star in England, frequently earning over £1,000 (£48,000) in a single week.

A master of the double entendre, Max was known for his brash behaviour and clever wit, which earned him invitations to perform at three Royal Variety shows. Much of his material was considered too 'blue' for broadcasting. His song, 'Let's Have a Ride on Your Bicycle' was banned by the BBC, but it became so popular the ban was eventually lifted.

I have no idea why my dad and Max became friends, for they were such completely different personalities, and yet their friendship continued to grow and develop long after they first met in the Hippodrome theatre bar.

Max gifted this photograph to
my parents

Max became a frequent visitor to our home, sometimes accompanied by his wife Kath. Although he was extremely funny on stage, Max was quiet and reserved in private surroundings.

I fondly remember his attendance at my Bar Mitzvah party, which was a roaring success. He achieved hero status when he sat at our upright piano and engaged in a sing-along with our family and friends, especially when he sang his signature tune, 'Mary from the Dairy'. The lyrics went like this:

I fell in love with Mary from the dairy

But Mary wouldn't fall in love with me.

Down by an old mill stream

We both sat down to dream

Little did she know that I was thinking up a scheme.

*Comedian Max Miller in his trademark
flower-patterned suit*

'Monsewer' Eddie Gray

Another famous theatrical friend of my father's was Eddie Gray, who went by the comic stage name 'Monsewer Eddie Gray'[117]. This masterful comedian – a renowned former member of the 'Crazy Gang' [a group of seven comics who also achieved huge popularity and were especially loved by King George VI; they were invited to give private performances for the Royal Family, and appeared on the Bill at several Royal Variety Shows] – was considered by many of his contemporaries to be the best comic in Britain.

His off-the-cuff jokes often showed total brilliance – like the time he stood by a post box shouting into the slot, "Hang on, we're getting help!"[118] And then there was the occasion I'd spotted him wearing an odd pair of socks to our home, one red and one green. When I asked him why, he retorted, "Yes, I've got another pair just like this at home."

Metal-rimmed glasses and a handle-bar moustache adorned his face during a successful career that spanned several appearances at Royal Command Performances. His trademark stage chat was to speak in 'fractured French': "Je got 'ere un packet de cards, cinquante deux in numero. I cuttee in deux, with vang-seess ici and vang-seess there-si." The multi-talented Eddie was apprenticed to a juggling troupe when he was just nine years old, and already considered to be *a* 'juggler extraordinaire'.

'Monsewer' Eddie Gray

His huge sense of humour was apparent at one Sunday lunch in our home, where he joined two other comedians, Roy Hudd and Joe Church, and Max Miller's widow Kath. They all sat around the table telling jokes relentlessly for hours, with Eddie consistently the funniest. It was a very memorable lunch.

I don't recall how long my father and Eddie had known each other, but I was aware they had become close friends, and that Eddie and his wife regularly dined at our home.

It was on one such occasion in May 1969 that my sister Margaret stayed at the house. She had just received a proposal of marriage from her South African boyfriend, inviting her to spend her life living with him in Johannesburg.

As Eddie was celebrating the news, he joked about the fact she didn't have an engagement ring and invited the family to watch his performance at the Brighton Hippodrome next evening. Midway through the act, he stopped the performance and shouted out to Margaret, sitting in a box with the family – "Margaret, show us your ring!" knowing full well she didn't have one. The audience roared with laughter.

Four months later, in mid-September, Eddie suddenly died. My father was devastated and became seriously ill four weeks after that. We suspected the shock of Eddie's death may have contributed, but who knows? The stress of his job, his smoking and his daily alcohol consumption were also no doubt contributors to his illness.

Sunday, 7 September 1969

Jenny and I married in 1964 and lived in an end-of-terrace house in a small close in Harrow Weald, in North London. Our daughter Lara was born in 1967 and our son Joel was born two years later in 1969.

The date for my son Joel's circumcision was chosen to allow my parents to attend since they usually worked on Saturdays. Morry was given the honour of holding the baby for the ceremony – the final time that his hands were steady enough to participate in such a delicate ritual.

Sunday, 5 October 1969

"We're coming to see the children." This was the ultimate surprise, for suddenly after five years of marriage, my parents had decided to drive 60 miles from Brighton to have lunch with us as they had a sudden urge to see their grandchildren.

In my subconscious, I knew something was amiss as my nimble-fingered father fumbled to open the camera, but it never occurred he had a brain tumour.

That afternoon the Prix de l'Arc de Triomph – an important horse race run on the first Sunday of October at Longchamps in Paris – was televised. It was a memorable event because never before had I watched a horse race with my father, despite it being his business.

Unknown to me, my parents had had two minor motor accidents on the drive to London, and a few more on their return home; it was a nerve-wracking experience for my mother as she could not drive, and had to rely on my father for the entire 60-mile journey.

When she telephoned a few days later, I learned of their minor scrapes as he drove both there and back, and that my father had handed cash over each time to compensate the other drivers. She then asked me to drive down to Hove to help prepare for my sister's wedding since my father was incapacitated.

Margaret's wedding took place on 19 October, and the next morning my father underwent surgery to remove a malignant brain tumour.

Thursday, 23 April 1970

My father died at home in the early hours and was buried the following day before Shabbat in accordance with Jewish custom. He was only 63 and my mother, just 52, cared for him throughout the final three months of his life.

Unashamedly, I admit I felt no sense of loss. Not then, nor at his funeral. I have no recollection of ever loving him nor of feeling his love, nor do I recall a single happy memory. I just felt a sense of relief, a sense of release. How sad that his legacy is my anger at his lack of parenting. It was the strangest experience to feel the dissipation of that domineering personality who had been a controlling figure for 28 years of my life.

My sister Sarah is 16 years younger. She feels the same way, but she did add that he was entertaining and fun to be with, and sometimes he took her to the local Chinese restaurant (not something he did with me).

My sister Margaret tells a different story about her difficulties in connecting with him, and the anger she feels for being sent to secretarial school because he didn't consider her worthy of further education.

Alone for the first time since she married him at the tender age of 22, my mother Rachel faced an uncertain future, so in 1972, she sold the family home and returned to London to live closer to us and to her sisters.

Chapter 13

FAMILY SECRETS: 2

Introduction

Hand-written envelopes don't often drop through my letter box, so I was bemused, but this particular letter was more than being amused: it was an electrifying shock that disclosed the secret of my grandfather's child, born out of wedlock when he was 60, whose name is Yvonne.

Yvonne is our new aunt

Up until that sunny August morning, nothing of consequence had happened for a while, but that was before the post arrived.

Admiring the neat hand-written address on the face of the envelope, I slid the paperknife beneath the flap trying to guess who sent it, thinking that if it was not from a friend, it was most likely a postal scam.

I was then quite surprised to read:

2nd August 2009
Malcolm Drive
Duston
Northampton

Dear Mr Tankel

I am writing to you in the hope that you can help me.

There it was, the perfect opening gambit to a confidence trick, introducing a hard-luck story. Then the words flowed on as if streaming from a Catherine Cookson novel.

I am trying to build up my family tree and have discovered that Mr Julius Michael Tankel (died in Hove in 1965) was my mother's father.

I was dumbstruck. Your mother's father? My grandfather is your mother's father?

She was born in 1942 in New Bradwell, Bucks. I believe that he had a son called Morris and that you may be related to Morris.

This had suddenly become very serious, for Morris was indeed my father.

I hope that this letter has not upset you in any way as that is not my intention.
*   If you are related to any of the aforementioned, I would be most grateful if you would be so kind as to contact me, as I am anxious to find any information or even just a photograph of Julius Tankel.*

Thank you in anticipation.

Kind Regards
Jane Harding
P.S. Can you please contact me even if you are not related to Julius Tankel, so I can omit you from my search.

The shock plundered my breakfast as I spilt my Nespresso coffee over the porridge. I had to reconcile the fact that my 60-year-old grandfather, Julius Michael, had gotten a 27-year-old woman,

Joan Marjorie, pregnant. Joan's deceased husband was named as the father to avoid suspicion from gossiping neighbours.

Why on earth had this been swept beneath the carpet for 70 years? Even government documents are made public within 20 years, so clearly, we were deemed unworthy to be told.

My mother acknowledged that she knew, so why the hell had she never shared even the crumbs with her children, who were now all in their mid-60s told?

I wrote back immediately to ask for evidence of the birth certificate, and received the following reply.

Dear Barrie

The information you requested regarding the birth certificate is a lot more complicated, and is somewhat difficult to put in a letter as my mother's birth was a result of an affair between my grandmother and Julius Michael Tankel (which I believe Sarah Tankel [his wife] was aware of).

As you can appreciate, in those times this was a very delicate situation, and Julius Tankel could not be named on the birth certificate. My mother is more than happy to speak with you and discuss all the information that was given to her [by her mother] with regard to this.

Regards Jane

I telephoned as arranged and listened to her softly spoken voice as Yvonne told me of her mother's liaison with my grandfather, their financial hardship and that Mike did nothing to help.

She had tried to dissuade her daughter from making contact and perhaps disrupting our lives, but her persistence meant Yvonne's dream to discover her pedigree would also finally come to fruition, albeit seven decades later.

Jane achieved what she had wanted since a child – a photograph of Mike to pin to the wall and watch over her. Her perseverance had paid off when she traced me through the internet.

This knowledge could so easily have upset any of us. My sister Margaret initially wanted no part of the episode, and equally, my cousin Michele put it out of her mind, refusing to discuss the subject openly with her mother, Rose. She thought it too upsetting for an 85-year-old, which I fully understood. Maybe they even chose to doubt the facts. I felt differently, for this is part of my pedigree.

Therefore, I decided to write to her again:

8th August 2009

Dear Jane

I had an interesting conversation with your mother last night [Jane had provided her mother's telephone number and arranged for me to call her in the evening of Friday 7 August, so I could learn firsthand the story of my grandfather's affair], *and am pleased to enclose these photographs.*

Mike, aged around 25

**Photo from my wedding, six
months before he died**

Please send me a photograph of you and your mother. It will be interesting to see the family resemblance.

I told your mother that Mike (as he was known) had remarried and had had more children, but that marriage ended in tears as well! My father took his son Allan under his wing until he went to Israel. They all now live in Australia.

Most of my father's siblings have passed away and there is now just one sister and one brother.
Best wishes
Barrie

She replied within a few *days:*

115 Malcolm Drive
Northampton
NN5 5HJ

Dear Barrie
Thank you for the photographs. I am sure you would agree 67 years is a long wait to see a picture of your father, but with your help we got there in the end.

I can see a resemblance. I think it's in the eyes.
I have enclosed two photographs, one of me, and one of my mother that was taken in December 2007.

I would like to say how grateful I am to you for acknowledging my letters and being so kind and understanding when you called last week. Taking into consideration the circumstances we were unsure of how or even whether we should approach you, as we did not have any idea of what reaction we could have.

We could not have asked for a better outcome.

Kind regards,
Jane

Daughter – Jane Harding   Mother – Yvonne Harding

*Rose (née Tankel) my father's
sister and Yvonne's half-sister*

Yvonne, age 12   Michele, my cousin – Rose's daughter

The resemblance between Yvonne and the Tankel family is striking – those laughing eyes and smile left little doubt in my mind that Yvonne was Mike's daughter, and our half-aunt.

Regretfully, a few years passed before I tried to reconnect with her, but it was to no avail. I thought that perhaps they had emigrated, since few people change their mobile numbers, but then in late June 2019, while I was holidaying in Majorca with Margaret, an email arrived from Yvonne:

Dear Barrie.
I hope you are keeping well.

Such a long time since we were in contact, I think it was about 10/11 years ago.
  I've recently downsized my home and realised much to my distress I've mislaid the photographs of my father you sent me. If it's at all possible, would you be able to send me copies? I would very much appreciate this.

I'm now living in Collingtree Park, Northampton.

Best wishes,
Yvonne Walding

One week later, I greeted Yvonne at Euston Station and we shared a taxi to a small restaurant in Fitzroy, where we went to meet my sister Sarah.

Yvonne first shared the sad story that her daughter Jane had died shortly after they returned from a holiday in Majorca, coincidentally the place I was staying when I received her email. She told us how much Jane would have loved to sit at this table.

Then she told us her own story, and soon afterwards sent me this note explaining her story in writing.

Yvonne's story, in her own words
At the time of my birth, my 27-year-old widowed mother was living with her three children at her parents' home, a typical three-up,

*two-down property. She worked a few hours a day and when she met
your grandfather, they started the affair. She was his secretary.*

*Discovering she was pregnant must have been an absolute
nightmare with three other children, her father and blind mother to
look after, and little money. Disgusted by the affair, her mother
provided no support.*

*In 1942, most births took place at home, but since Grandma
refused to allow me to be born at home, she stayed with her sister in
the next village.*

*Mike obviously told his wife Sarah because they visited and
offered to adopt me. Grandma wanted to accept (because with me
not being there, the shame would go), but my mother refused,
causing some argument, but thankfully my grandfather said NO, so
we remained in their home.*

*After school one day, when I was then six years old, my sister
asked Mum if I was adopted. She said children at school didn't
believe I was their sister, since we didn't look alike.*

*We were told we didn't have the same father and made to
promise not to speak of this to anyone.*

*Not a day passed when I didn't think of him. What did he look
like? Did I look like him? Did he ever think of me? So many
thoughts went through my young head.*

*My mother was a wonderful woman, very strong, and when I
look back, my love for her grows. I cannot remember her having
pleasure in life – it was all work and looking after us children and
her parents. Money was very short and we often had to hide when
the rent man came.*

*Mum's wedding ring was in the pawn shop more times than on
her finger, but this helped to put food on the table. Eventually we
were evicted.*

*At this time, although she was unwell, we moved to a flat which
she scrubbed alone until it was spotless, and only then would we be
allowed to enter.*

*Many times, she must have asked herself 'Is this it, is this my
life?' but her loving arms were always there to comfort us if we were
hurt or unwell. She was just amazing.*

Luck was on her side when she successfully applied for a live-in housekeeper job working for an elderly gentleman, and that prompted our move to Northampton.

At that time, there was just one sister and myself living at home. My brother was in the Navy and my eldest sister went away to work as a nanny.

Eventually, she married the gentleman, but he was everything Mum wasn't. He had no gentleness or generosity of spirit, and I'm sure he was relieved when we left home. After he died in 1983, Mum's life became easier and she had a good happy 20 years until she died at the age of 93.

She carried the shame of this illicit affair throughout her life. She said the guilt was hers, but she would not have wanted life without me.

Since meeting Barrie and Sarah, I have learnt a great deal about my father. Sadly, I never had the chance to meet him and to ask the questions that remained in my head from childhood, but I know he was the one to miss out for not knowing me, and being able to enjoy the love and joy we might have brought each other.

Sarah and I retain connect with Yvonne, who occasionally joins the Zoom calls with our new half-sister Annette [her half niece!], she has joined us for dinner, and on Jewish festivals we explain the significance of each event because 50% of her bloodline is Ashkenazi Jew. She appreciates this connection despite knowing little about the Jewish religion.

Chapter 14

FUTURE GENERATIONS

Introduction

With our ancestors long past gone, the future belongs to their – and our – descendants.

In my case, we're a small family, three sisters and their offspring. The story of my recently discovered sister Annette is told in Chapter 1, and now it is time to tell a little about my two English sisters, Margaret and Sarah, and their offspring, as well as my own children and our cousins – the next generation of Tankels.

Margaret

Margaret was always 'MAT' to me, as I called her by her three initials. Correspondence between us started and ended with 'Dear MAT… love BAT'. To my grandchildren, I was always the 'BATman'!

When she was five years old, my sister Margaret was sent to St Martha's Convent Boarding School in the ancient village of Rottingdean, around five miles away from our home in Hove, after she stubbornly refused to eat. The idea that was conjured up was that strict discipline from the nuns would produce a magic cure. I have no idea what would have followed if that didn't work.

Instead of investigating the root cause, this seemingly drastic step was taken, when possibly it was something at home that had unsettled her, or perhaps she simply didn't enjoy eating. Nowadays, a quick search of the internet or an appointment with a children's nutrition expert would be the first call for advice, but in the late 1940s, no such help was available, and so my parents relied on our family doctor to provide the right answer.

Hence, when she arrived on the doorstep of St Martha's, Margaret was lonely and confused. She slept in a small cubicle, and resided in an environment that would have been alien for any child – especially one that was raised in a Jewish home.

After she returned home one weekend with a large cross hanging around her neck, her convent schooling was immediately terminated. My mother Rachel, who had been brought up in an Orthodox Jewish home, insisted she went to a new girls' school – Wistons.

Later, Margaret was sent to secretarial college when she turned 15, which made her angry that she was not considered worthy of further college education. My father was ignorant in such matters; he had little confidence in his children. He believed Margaret should work as a shorthand typist until she got married and that I should train as a hairdresser!

Margaret's memories of our father are different to mine. She described him as loving and fun, but adds that he had an "out of control" temper, and that his unpredictable behaviour was often hard to live with. He liked to cook on a Sunday, and although her friends and the beach were calling her to join them, she had to remain at home and do the washing up. When she wanted to spend an evening with friends, she had to wait until he fell asleep on the settee before creeping out of the house. Everyone feared his temper, including our friends.

It is impossible to understand why he felt this urge to control and inhibit our growth as individuals. Maybe it was a fear we would repeat his mistakes, and as he had no idea or desire to educate us in the ways of the world, he tried to deny us the opportunity of learning for ourselves.

At this point I am reminded of the little advice he gave me as sex education. The first time my friend Vernon invited me to join him [I was aged 16] for an evening out with other friends, he called out to me, "Just be careful!" as I left the house.

When she moved to London, Margaret took a job as a personal assistant to Audrey Slaughter, the editor of *Honey*, a new magazine for teenagers.

After the six-day war in the Middle East, she spent a year in Israel working as a volunteer on a kibbutz. On returning to London, my impulsive sister decided to join our parents while they were holidaying in South Africa, and there she met the delightful Stan. Three weeks later he proposed, and they were married later that year.

Margaret and Stan have three children. Marc, the eldest, represented South Africa in the 1999 and 2007 Touch Rugby World Cups; he played in Sydney Australia, and then in Stellenbosch, South Africa. His sister Karen is an aspiring author who has published a cookery book and is now in the process of writing two children's books. Their youngest sibling, Daniel, is a keen long-distance competitive cyclist. He competed in the Cape Argus race in Cape Town – the world's biggest bike race.

Daniel later emigrated to Sydney, Australia, with his family in 2021 – another generation spreading their wings in a new country.

Margaret, Sarah and I celebrating our
mother's 90th birthday in New York

Few words can express our sorrow when Margaret died after a short illness on 1 June 2022 – we are simply devastated.

Sarah

Laat Lammetjie ['Late Lamb'] is a South African term that describes a child born many years after his/her siblings, an appropriate term to describe my sister Sarah, for I was 15 years old when my mother broke the news of a forthcoming baby.

Guillain-Barré syndrome is a rare and serious condition that affects the nervous system, and although most people fully recover, the resulting muscle weakness has confined Sarah to a wheelchair for the past 10 years. Nevertheless, this handicap has not deterred her from supporting her husband Ian in his soccer (football) tournaments, particularly in the international Jewish Maccabiah Games – the third-largest sporting event in the world – travelling with the team to Antwerp, Argentina, Israel and Mexico.

Sarah and Ian have twin sons, Mark and Matthew, who are also Spurs fans and soccer players. They have both won silver and gold medals for soccer in the Maccabiah Games.

My children, Lara and Joel

My obsessive drive to succeed no doubt emanated from my fervent desire to prove my worth to my father, and although not everything in life has worked out successfully, the fruits of my first marriage – my daughter Lara, the eldest, and my son Joel – have been reward enough.

I first met Jenny, their mother, as we both boarded a tube train at East Finchley station on her first day at my college – the Regent Street Polytechnic, [now known as the University of Westminster]. I wasn't even supposed to be there, for on Monday mornings I always took an early train from Brighton to Victoria station, so our meeting was serendipitous.

Lara's career with book publishers Dorling Kindersley (DK) resulted in the publication of several children's books bearing her name as author – my favourite being *Drive a Fire Engine*, which was inspired by her son's obsession with firefighters. Lara now lives in the Bronx with her American husband Doug and their three children.

It was a sad day for me when I learnt they were leaving London to reside in New York, but his career (as an intellectual property lawyer) drew him home after they had lived in London for nine years. An amazing husband, parent and son-in law, Doug has led his family to the peak of physical fitness.

My son Joel had emigrated to the US four years before Lara, where he joined a small travel agency until the pandemic hit businesses around the world.

Joel lives within half a mile of Lara in the Bronx with his wife Hillary, a school psychologist, and their son Levi. My six-year-old grandson is as equally athletic as his cousins.

Charlie, Doug and Lara's son, is my eldest grandson. He graduated from Brown University in 2018, where he majored in neuroscience. Charlie played in the Brown Ultimate Frisbee team for five years from 2013, and reached the US quarterfinals of the Nationals in his final year. He uses his neuroscience training and skills working at a hedge fund.

Charlie's sister Isabel (Izzy), my sole granddaughter, is a talented graphic designer – she has skilfully designed the cover of this book.

Isaac, the youngest sibling, is another talented sportsman. My favourite recollection of him is the video of him as this tiny 9-year-old dribbling the ball through the entire team of soccer opponents to score a magnificent Messi-style goal – that was very impressive.

My cousin Irving Scholar

Following a successful career in property development, in 1982 Irving Scholar, my first cousin on my father's side, moved to Monaco. Shortly afterwards he purchased a controlling share in Tottenham Hotspur (Spurs), the football club he had idolised since childhood.

Irving brought innovations to Spurs that have changed the face of top flight football (soccer). Spurs was the first Premier Club team, known as First Division in 1982, to list on the London Stock Exchange. He substantially increased the broadcasting fees TV companies pay to televise games and he also capitalised on the club's merchandising.

Business magnate Alan Sugar purchased Irving's shares in the club in 1991, shortly after Spurs won the FA Cup.

Cousins Stevie and Linda Marcus – Shirley's children

My cousin Stevie Marcus's gap year in Israel was so exhilarating for him that he sacrificed his business law studies, and instead made *Aliyah* [*Aliyah* describes the return of the Jewish people from their exile in the diaspora back to the land of Israel], settling in Kibbutz Alumin in the Negev Desert in southern Israel. Thirty-five years later, he now has a large family and recently became a grandparent.

Linda, Steven's sister, was TV presenter Jeremy Beadle's personal assistant. She is now married to Gary and they live in North

London near her parents and my first cousin Shirley and her husband Harold.

Someday, I hope this younger generation will be writing their own family histories.

Chapter 15

FINAL
REFLECTIONS

The weight, the research, the remembering, the tears and the writing slowly lifted from my shoulders as my fingers tapped the final letters of this memoir onto the keyboard.

I had experienced angst from the moment I visualised my 32-year-old grandmother Ethel leaning far out from her carriage window for that last glimpse of her mother, who was frantically waving a white handkerchief. The figure grew smaller and smaller until it slipped behind a cloud of steam that slalomed along the tracks as the train slowly pulled out of the Polish station. Tears soaked each cheek as both knew in their hearts that this was the last time they would ever see each other.

My hand rested on Wally's shoulders as I delved into his deepest private thoughts, knowing I was almost certainly the first person to read his diaries in the 77 years since he was killed.

I tracked Chaim along his lonely journey through Nazi Poland – I studiously read every word of his memoir – I felt his suffering as he acknowledged the pain of his family, and realised he would never see siblings, nieces or nephews again. I adapted his memoir, the first person to analyse it in any detail.

I questioned why he wrote the memoir. Was it cathartic to fight through his disturbed memories and exorcise demons? Did he suffer more nightmares as he wrote?

I have also wondered whether I unknowingly pursued an agenda to search and find my roots. I certainly discovered from my grandfather's genes that he had been led down a wasted emotional path, as shown in his cavalier approach to women.

As he was married and divorced twice, it seems remarkable that apart from my father and Allan, each of his children's marriages remained intact.

The same cannot be said of his 17 grandchildren; six remain with their first spouse, but seven of us have been divorced at least once, and four have never married. The question remains: Did his genes skip a generation?

The Tankel stories have helped me to realise that the coldness displayed by my father's family has impacted my own ability to relate to other people. Prompted to visit my father's grave recently, I stood glaring at his stone and screamed out loud. It was too late to awaken him from his stupid selfishness, to make him aware of his failure to nurture us. Fortunately, our mother held our emotions together.

This has been a long voyage of discovery, but it has helped me to know where I came from, why my father was as he was and why so many other things were as they were. Before I began writing this, I only stood at the bottom of a pit – an introverted, shy child, lacking in self-confidence and suffering from low self-esteem – until I finally tugged at the rope and dragged myself out and into the clearing mist. It has taken me far too long, but I now feel I have finally found my place in this world.

ACKNOWLEDGEMENTS

This book is based on true events, beginning with the moment my grandparents left their family behind in Russia at the end of the 19th century to make new lives in England. It would not have been possible to tell such powerful stories without first-hand tales and considerable help from many.

Most stories really did appear as if from nowhere: the letter from Jane Harding that dropped onto my doormat; the Facebook connection from Ken Golish; the discovery of Wally's diaries in my mother's apartment; the result of my son's DNA test that led to the discovery of my sister Annette; and my grandfather Mike's naturalisation papers, which were discovered through an internet search engine.

I owe thanks to each of my VIP contributors, whose amazing stories and conversations has helped create the narrative of our family: **Wally Wolman**, my mother's brother, whose diaries were returned by the RAF after his death; **Shirley Marcus**, my first cousin and the last remaining family member to have known Wally, and her recollections of growing up in Coulsdon; **Chaim Goluchowski**, my mother's first cousin, whose own memoir chronicling his sufferings and experiences of the Holocaust was so powerful and disturbing; **Ken Golish**, Chaim's son and my second cousin, for sharing his father's memoir and introducing me to my French second cousin Genevieve de Cointet; **Chaim Freedman**, my second cousin on my father's side, for documenting the Freedman family history that told of the tragedy of my great grandfather, Yaakov-Bendyt Frydman; **Genevieve de Cointet**, my second cousin on my mother's side, for sharing family story of life in France during the Second World War; **Irving Scholar**, my first cousin on my father's side, for his story of buying the Tottenham Hotspur

Football club; **Yvonne Walding**, my rediscovered aunt, whose mother was my grandfather's lover, for telling us of her life growing up with her single parent; and to **Annette Irvine**, my newly discovered sister, found in 2021 through a DNA match with my son Joel.

I am also grateful to the Royal Air Force (RAF) Headquarters Air Command for providing copy records of my uncle Wally's career and the circumstances of his death.

The National Archives, based in Kew in south-west London, contains "1,000 years of history from the Domesday Book to the present". Most importantly for me, it holds the service and operational records of the armed services. My visit proved most fruitful when I discovered details of Wally's flights and learnt of the dreaded 'dash' – the mark that identified lost aircraft and crew.

I also give thanks to the many others who have been hugely instrumental in guiding me through the process of creating a readable story: to my children, Lara and Joel; my sisters, Margaret and Sarah; to Bev; Diane and John; Emma; Erica; Fiona; Joy; Julia; Marian; Naomi; Robin; Sherry; Toby; Trevor and Wendy; and to my editor, Jane Cahane. The value of their help and feedback – both positive and negative – cannot be overstated. It has been a powerful aid in helping me to complete this book.

Finally, thanks to everyone at London Writer's Salon (LWS) for creating such a vibrant environment in which to write, and to the many LWS individuals who gave their time and provided advice – from the Critique Sessions to the 'Page to Stage' and Open Mic sessions – and also to my lovely friends in the Sacred Circle.

REFERENCES

1. Poem – Maya Angelou, American poet, memoirist and civil rights activist, from her book, *I Know Why the Caged Bird Sings*.

2. Neville Chamberlain at Palace – https://www.theguardian.com/world/from-the-archive-blog/2018/sep/21/munich-chamberlain-hitler-appeasement-1938

3. Dunkirk – https://www.english-heritage.org.uk/visit/inspire-me/dunkirk-1940-the-making-of-the-miracle/

4. Enemy Aliens – https://blog.nationalarchives.gov.uk/collar-lot-britains-policy-internment-second-world-war/

5. Battle of Britain – https://www.iwm.org.uk/history/8-things-you-need-to-know-about-the-battle-of-britain
   Blitz – https://www.bbc.co.uk/teach/the-blitz-eight-months-of-terror/z7dyxyc

6. V1 bombs – https://www.iwm.org.uk/history/the-terrifying-german-revenge-weapons-of-the-second-world-war

7. Dr Bina Nir, 'Transgenerational Transmission of Holocaust Trauma and Its Expressions in Literature' – https://www.mdpi.com/2313-5778/2/4/49

8. Poem – Lemn Sissay MBE, poet and chancellor of the University of Manchester, from his autobiography, *My Name is Why*, Canongate Books Ltd, 2019.

9. Kibbutz – https://www.jewishagency.org/what-exactly-is-a-kibbutz/

10. German military definitions – https://www.translationdirectory.com/glossaries/glossary261.php

11. Volksdeutsche – https://www.yadvashem.org/odot_pdf/Microsoft%20Word%20-%206345.pdf

12. Star of David – https://www.holocaustcenter.org/visit/library-archive/holocaust-badges/

13. Synagogue – https://jewishlodz.iu.edu/items/show/1929

14. Treblinka – https://www.holocaust.cz/en/history/concentration-camps-and-ghettos/treblinka-3/

15. Nuremberg – https://nuremberg.law.harvard.edu/

16. Grodno – https://www.jewishgen.org/yizkor/grodno/grodno.html

17. Kielce – https://www.jewishvirtuallibrary.org/kielce-poland-virtual-jewish-history-tour

18. Duvet – 'The Secret History Of: The Duvet', by Kate Watson-Smyth, (*The Independent*, 27 August 2010).

19. Handywomen – https://academic.oup.com/shm/article/25/2/380/1735509

20. Cable Street – http://www.stgitehistory.org.uk/media/cablestreet.html

21. Sir Oswald Mosley – https://www.britannica.com/biography/Oswald-Mosley

22. Newspaper support for Nazis – https://www.independent.co.uk/news/media/revealed-the-fascist-past-of-the-daily-mirror-77871.html

23. Mosley wedding – https://jaquo.com/mitford-marriages/

24. Franco and Nazis – https://www.facinghistory.org/holocaust-and-human-behavior/chapter-7/intervention-spain

25. Bank station – https://www.londonremembers.com/subjects/bank-station-bomb

26. Waddington air base – https://www.bcar.org.uk/waddington-history

27. Wannsee – https://www.dw.com/en/wannsee-conference-nazi-germany-formalized-final-solution/a-37197330

28. Tobruk taken – https://blog.nationalarchives.gov.uk/the-battles-of-tobruk-1941-42-part-one/

29. Jews House – http://www.jtrails.org.uk/trails/lincoln/places-of-interest#pc461

30. Anti-Semitic Roof Tiles – https://www.visitlincoln.com/things-to-do/interest/anti-semitic-roof-tile

31. Benghazi capture – https://military-history.fandom.com/wiki/Western_Desert_Campaign

32. Bulgaria invaded – https://military-history.fandom.com/wiki/Military_history_of_Bulgaria_during_World_War_II

33. National Day of Prayer – https://www.historyextra.com/period/modern/praying-britain-national-day-prayer-history-when-deliverance/

34. Berlin bombed – https://www.forces-war-records.co.uk/world-war-two-timeline-of-events-1941#March1941

35. Yugoslavia – https://www.reddit.com/r/europe/comments/87jhnm/belgrade_27_march_1941_the_day_when_the_people_of/

36. Mavis Batey – https://www.theguardian.com/world/2013/nov/20/mavis-batey

37. Admiral Cunningham – https://placeandsee.com/wiki/battle-of-cape-matapan-peloponnisos

38. St Paul's – https://ww2days.com/londons-st-pauls-survives-overnight-hit-5.html

39. Jan Smuts – https://ww2db.com/person_bio.php?person_id=703

40. Habbaniya – https://military-history.fandom.com/wiki/RAF_Habbaniya

41. Rudolf Hess – https://www.smithsonianmag.com/history/will-we-ever-know-why-nazi-leader-rudolf-hess-flew-scotland-middle-world-war-ii-180959040/

42. "I have nothing to offer…" – https://winstonchurchill.org/resources/speeches/1940-the-finest-hour/blood-toil-tears-sweat/

43. Crete Invasion – https://winstonchurchill.org/resources/speeches/1940-the-finest-hour/blood-toil-tears-sweat/

44. Lido Purley – https://museumofcroydon.com/blogs/w8lri3v6ww0aq30bh3u1ibuduyrff3

45. Kimpton – https://kimptonpc.org.uk/

46. Red Army – https://www.iwm.org.uk/history/operation-barbarossa-and-germanys-failure-in-the-soviet-union

47. Crisis over Japan – https://www.history.com/this-day-in-history/united-states-freezes-japanese-assets

48. 'Gone with the Wind' – https://www.cnbc.com/2019/07/22/top-10-films-at-the-box-office-when-adjusted-for-inflation.html

49. Turpentine – https://floridatrailblazer.com/category/turpentine-history/

50. Biplane – https://www.flyingbulls.at/en/fleet/pt-17-stearman

51. Lend-Lease Act – https://history.house.gov/Historical-Highlights/1901-1950/The-Lend-Lease-Act-of-1941/

52. Medicine Balls – https://physicalculturestudy.com/2020/01/29/the-long-history-of-the-medicine-ball/

53. Calisthenics – https://www.menshealth.com/uk/building-muscle/a759641/complete-guide-to-calisthenics-everything-you-need-to-know/

54. Volleyball – https://ncva.com/info/general-info/history-of-volleyball/

55. Tailor Exercise – https://fairviewmnhs.org/Patient-Education/Articles/English/t/a/i/l/o/Tailor_Sit_Trunk_Turn_for_Back_Pain_During_Pregnancy_85678-0000-----

56. 'Tommy' – https://www.wearethemighty.com/mighty-history/how-british-troops-got-the-nickname-tommies/

57. 'Lazy Eights' – https://www.flightliteracy.com/lazy-eight/

58. Pierre Laval – https://ww2db.com/person_bio.php?person_id=257

59. Fireside Chats – https://www.history.com/this-day-in-history/fdr-gives-first-fireside-chat

60. Chandelle – https://www.pilotmall.com/blogs/news/the-chandelle-maneuver-what-it-is-and-why-you-should-learn-to-fly-it

61. Kissengen Springs – https://www.hmdb.org/m.asp?m=67655

62. Vultee BT-13 – https://airandspace.si.edu/collection-objects/vultee-bt-13a-valiant/nasm_A19600288000

63. Jack Dempsey – https://www.biography.com/athlete/jack-dempsey

64. PG Wodehouse – https://www.bbc.com/culture/article/20200602-the-man-who-wrote-the-most-perfect-sentences-ever-written

65. Plane Stress – https://www.collinsdictionary.com/dictionary/english/plane-stress

66. Lord Haw-Haw – https://www.historic-uk.com/HistoryUK/Historyof Britain/Lord-Haw-Haw-William-Joyce/

67. The Little French Girl – https://www.goodreads.com/book/show/6435424-the-little-french-girl

68. Karl Hotz – https://www.executedtoday.com/tag/karl-hotz/

69. President Roosevelt speech on SS Kearny – http://ibiblio.org/pha/policy/1941/411027a.html

70. Hold Back the Dawn – https://www.imdb.com/title/tt0033722/

71. Roosevelt speech on Pearl Harbour – https://www.ushistory.org/documents/infamy.htm

72. Pearl Harbour attack – https://www.history.com/topics/world-war-ii/pearl-harbor

73. KTU Live Broadcast of Pearl Harbour attack – http://historymatters.gmu.edu/d/5167

74. HMS Repulse – https://www.renownrepulse.com/hms-renown.html

75. German attack suspended – https://www.iwm.org.uk/history/operation-barbarossa-and-germanys-failure-in-the-soviet-union

76. Annihilation of Jews – https://www.sciencespo.fr/mass-violence-war-massacre-resistance/en/document/holocaust.html

77. Film 'Sundown' – https://www.theaceblackblog.com/2017/01/movie-review-sundown-1941.html

78. 'How Green Was my Valley' – https://owlcation.com/humanities/How-Green-Was-My-Valley-A-Memorable-Novel-Set-in-Wales

79. Link Simulator – https://www.nasflmuseum.com/link-trainer.html

80. Flying the Beams – https://flyingthebeams.com/

81. Singapore – https://fulcrum.sg/fall-of-singapore-80-years-on-lessons-transcend-time-and-place/

82. Anthony Eden speech on anti-Semitism – https://api.parliament.uk/historic-hansard/commons/1942/dec/17/united-nations-declaration

83. HMS Renown – https://naval-encyclopedia.com/ww2/uk/renown-class-battlecruisers.php

84. 'Uncensored' Film – https://www.derekwinnert.com/tag/uncensored/

85. Tripoli – https://www.forces-war-records.co.uk/blog/2018/01/11/75th-anniversary-on-this-day-1943-into-tripoli-montgomery-marched-in-triumph

86. Stalingrad – https://warontherocks.com/2017/08/the-motherland-calls-the-battle-of-stalingrad-75-years-later/

87. Hitler states all men to be killed – https://www.history.com/topics/world-war-ii/battle-of-stalingrad

88. 'South Riding' a book – https://www.fadedpage.com/showbook.php?pid=20120805

89. 'Pimpernel' Smith a film – https://tvtropes.org/pmwiki/pmwiki.php/Film/PimpernelSmith

90. Treblinka – https://www.britannica.com/place/Treblinka

91. HMS Regent – https://military-history.fandom.com/wiki/HMS_Regent

92. Kasserine Pass – https://www.history.com/this-day-in-history/battle-of-the-kasserine-pass

93. 'Absalom, Absalom' a book – https://www.encyclopedia.com/arts/educational-magazines/absalom-absalom

94. 'Sergeant York' a film – https://www.imdb.com/title/tt0034167/

95. 'You'll Never Get Rich' a film – https://www.imdb.com/title/tt0034409/

96. Sepharad – https://ixtheo.de/Record/1563039591

97. Beveridge Plan – https://www.parliament.uk/about/living-heritage/transformingsociety/livinglearning/coll-9-health1/coll-9-health/

98. Education Act – https://www.bbc.co.uk/schoolreport/25751787

99. RAB Butler – https://www.thefamouspeople.com/profiles/rab-butler-6263.php

100. Christopher Mayhew – https://www.independent.co.uk/news/people/obituary-lord-mayhew-1282313.html

101. ENSA – https://military-history.fandom.com/wiki/Entertainments_National_Service_Association

102. Lord Trenchard – https://military-history.fandom.com/wiki/Hugh_Trenchard,_1st_Viscount_Trenchard

103. Celestial Navigation – https://timeandnavigation.si.edu/navigating-at-sea/navigating-without-a-clock/celestial-navigation

104. Hill of Crosses – https://www.aditnow.co.uk/documents/Prince-Edward-Gold-Mine/moel-y-croesau-bomber.pdf

105. Churchill Speech – https://winstonchurchill.org/resources/speeches/1940-the-finest-hour/we-shall-fight-on-the-beaches/

106. How 200,000 Jews survived in France– https://www.france24.com/en/europe/20220127-how-three-quarters-of-french-jews-survived-the-holocaust-despite-the-vichy-regime

107. Monseigneur Saliege – https://www.yadvashem.org/righteous/stories/saliege.html

108. Žagarė – https://kehilalinks.jewishgen.org/zagare/others.html

109. Zeppelin Airships – https://www.independent.co.uk/news/world/europe/q-how-many-cows-does-it-take-to-build-a-zeppelin-a-250-000-8782723.html

110. Conscription – https://www.parliament.uk/about/living-heritage/transformingsociety/private-lives/yourcountry/overview/conscription/#:~:text=In%20January%201916%20the%20Military,certain%20classes%20of%20industrial%20worker.

111. 'Charleston Dance' – https://www.ccpl.org/charleston-time-machine/tracing-roots-charleston-dance

112. SS Moreton Bay – https://www.poheritage.com/Upload/Mimsy/Media/factsheet/93825MORETON-BAY-1921pdf.pdf

113. Palais de Danse – https://cv.vic.gov.au/stories/built-environment/the-palais-theatre-melbournes-home-of-live-music/palais-de-danse-1913-1920/

114. Hippodrome Theatre – https://www.theargus.co.uk/news/8624311.home-of-the-stars/

115. Brighton History – https://localhistories.org/a-history-of-brighton/

116. Max Miller – https://www.maxmiller.org/

117. 'Monsewer' Eddie Gray – http://www.mmhistory.org.uk/cce/2005/Margaret/Web%20Pages/NEBs%20Interview_Monsewer_eddie_gray.htm

118. https://www.theguardian.com/media/2004/jul/20/television.artsfeatures

119. Guillain-Barre – https://www.nhs.uk/conditions/guillain-barre-syndrome/

I have also used the following online resources in my research:
        Chabad.org
        Ancestry.com
        Cablestreet.uk

GEDmatch.com
History.co.uk
Historynet.com
Jewfaq.org
MyJewishlearning.com
The Weiner Holocaust Library.org

AUTHOR BIO: And now something about me

Growing up within 200 metres of the beach and the sea in Brighton and Hove was the perfect place to spend my childhood.

I qualified as a Chartered Quantity Surveyor after studying at the Regent Street Polytechnic, and created my highly respected Quantity Surveying and Project Management practice in 1970.

Retirement came prematurely, in 2002, after I was diagnosed with mesothelioma. Mesothelioma is a killer cancer that grows from a single fibre of asbestos breathed 20 years previously; those fibres are slow killers. I did not question the diagnosis, for I had worked on dozens of building sites filled with asbestos fibres, so it was perfectly possible I had contracted the disease.

The surgeon was 99% certain about the diagnosis and told me "It is incurable". I cannot articulate the distress a death sentence causes, but thankfully he was mistaken.

The lymphoma was identified by an 'Interventional Radiologist' at John Hopkins hospital in Baltimore as the cause of my pleural thickening, and a course of chemotherapy saved my life.

After a period of recovery, I practiced as a project management consultant for the next 15 years. I was honoured to be selected as Chair of the Project Management Faculty Board, a new division within the Royal Institution of Chartered Surveyors (RICS); I then became Chair of the Advisory Board for the PM Diploma Course at the College of Estate Management. Later on, I served as trustee of North London's Kiln Theatre (formerly the Tricycle Theatre) for seven years, before retiring from the Board in 2021.

THE UNTOLD is my first book. My grandchildren inspired me to write this history when they raised questions about their ancestry for school projects.

The investigation made me think: If I do not record our family history then how will my great-grandchildren learn about their ancestors?

So I began, and that moment turned to be *Beshert* – the Yiddish word for "meant to be" – for soon, a trail of family secrets appeared: the story of my grandfather's illegitimate daughter; a secret memoir of my mother's first cousin's life in concentration camps; and then her brother's diaries from his time as a pilot during the Second World War.

Finally, in January 2021 an older sister was discovered, she lives in Australia. Not one of these stories was known when I started along my writing journey – and now they are available for future generations. It has been a privilege to share our history with others.

Along this writing journey, I was instrumental in persuading various celebrities to contribute poems to the charity book *Pound a Poem*, to be included alongside poems written by schoolchildren in aid of the charity Rays of Sunshine (https://raysofsunshine. org.uk/).

The podcast series 'Fantasy Holidays in a Time of Covid' was created together with Joy Cox and other fellow writers from the

London Writers Salon (https://londonwriterssalon.com/), and currently has 44 episodes.

I also contributed the chapter 'A Kiss is Just a Kiss' to *Writing in Community*, an anthology of writing from the first year of the London Writers Salon, which was published in November 2021.

Printed in Great Britain
by Amazon

84380593R00183